D1570802

YALE LAW LIBRARY SERIES IN
LEGAL HISTORY AND REFERENCE

THE
COLORADO
DOCTRINE

WATER RIGHTS, CORPORATIONS,

AND DISTRIBUTIVE JUSTICE

ON THE AMERICAN FRONTIER

David Schorr

Yale

UNIVERSITY PRESS

New Haven & London

Published with assistance from the foundation established in memory of
Amasa Stone Mather of the Class of 1907, Yale College.

Yale University Press books may be purchased in
quantity for educational, business, or promotional use.
For information, please e-mail sales.press@yale.edu
(U.S. office) or sales@yaleup.co.uk (U.K. office).

Set in MT Baskerville and MT Bulmer types by IDS Infotech, Ltd.
Printed in the United States of America.

Library of Congress Cataloging-in-Publication Data

Schorr, David, 1971–
The Colorado doctrine: water rights, corporations, and distributive justice on the American
frontier / David Schorr.
p. cm. — (Yale Law Library series in legal history and reference)
Includes bibliographical references and index.
ISBN 978-0-300-13447-6 (cloth: alk. paper) 1. Water rights—West (U.S.) – History.
2. Water rights—Colorado—History. I. Title.
KF646.S36 2012
346.78804´691—dc23

2012009929

A catalogue record for this book is available from the British Library.

This paper meets the requirements of
ANSI/NISO Z39.48–1992 (Permanence of Paper).

10 9 8 7 6 5 4 3 2 1

To my parents,

Julianne Bohm and Jacob Schorr

The country was without law, but each individual brought with him the principles of equity and justice which were a part of his education. It was soon found that the water of the streams was inadequate to supply all the land. They found a new climate, new conditions calling for new laws applicable to the conditions . . . In time . . . a series of rules or laws were adopted . . . embodying principles of equity and justice. They were recognized and obeyed, the settlers recognizing, as before stated, a fact which later corporations and settlers have not yet apparently recognized, or, if recognized, have disregarded, that the supply of water in the streams was not sufficient for all the land. Instead of parceling it out generally and making it practically valueless to any, . . . they adopted the only rule founded in equity that could be rightfully adopted in the premises, viz., that of prior appropriation, such appropriation to be controlled and limited. Such prior appropriation was so much as could be beneficially used upon the land for which the appropriation was made.

—*Armstrong v. Larimer County Ditch Co.*, 27
P. 235, 237 (Colo. Ct. App. 1891)

CONTENTS

CONTENTS

PREFACE

The subject of this book—the early history of the prior appropriation doctrine of western water law—stands at the intersection of several academic fields. The doctrine is, first, a major concern of water law scholarship, and it is also prominent in property law in general. In particular, the more theoretically oriented among property law scholars, especially those with an economic bent, have displayed intense interest in the doctrine, which has served as an icon of private property in natural resources.

The development of the appropriation doctrine is clearly also a historical topic, falling in the realms of several historical subdisciplines, including legal history, western history, and environmental history. Western water law has played a prominent role in both environmental history and western history. In the former it has been viewed as an example *par excellence* of exploitation of the environment through private property, though coming on the cusp of the transition to the "Conservation era," characterized by state management. In the latter, its connection to the aridity of the American West, European-American settlement, and capitalist exploitation—all central themes of the regional historiography—has guaranteed it pride of place.

The conventional view of the appropriation doctrine has also fit nicely into the dominant legal-history narratives of Gilded Age America, with its subsidies for capitalist development.

Prior appropriation is of ongoing interest to those involved in environmental and natural-resource policy debates, as the region and the world struggle with questions of justly and efficiently allocating scarce water (and other resources) to various users and uses, private rights versus societal control, corporate takeovers of water systems, and more.

The concerns of this book, then—born of a personal concern for the environment, an intellectual interest in property theory, and an unsuccessfully repressed attraction to historical research—are the concerns of several fields of inquiry, each with its own assumptions, agendas, and approaches. In particular, resolving the tension between the normative, prescriptive imperatives of both environmental law and policy and property theory, on the one hand, and the historian's professional ethos of narrating and interpreting without passing judgment, on the other, has proved challenging. Moreover, the methodology (historical and positive) and the overarching concerns (policy-oriented and normative) exist to a great extent on totally separate planes; what did or did not happen in the past bears no necessary relationship to normative questions such as what justice requires or how best to manage a resource.

That being said, writing on the law has a long tradition of mixing the historical and the prescriptive—legal discourse, both academic and practice oriented, tends to invest the historical with normative significance. Many environmental historians, too, have owned up (with not a little discomfort) to the presentist and policy-focused orientation of their field. More fundamentally, an interdisciplinary work such as this is not free of its rewards. In this case, in particular, I have felt at every stage the advantages conferred by being able to read the historical sources with a sensitivity to the intricacies and insights of property law and theory, as well as the immense profit in being able to challenge the abstractions of property theory with the reality of property as revealed in the manuscripts, newspaper articles, and government reports written more than a century ago. In the end, I hope the reader will agree that these benefits outweigh the difficulties described above, and will excuse any discordant notes that nonetheless resulted from working at the juncture of several fields.

ACKNOWLEDGMENTS

A book project that has gone on for too long has the happy side-effect of increasing the number of people involved in bringing it to its successful conclusion. The downside is that lapses of memory have no doubt led to my forgetting some of those who extended me their help along the way; to them I extend my apologies.

This book, my first, is a welcome opportunity to thank those who planted the early seeds of my attraction to historical research. Joseph Leblanc at the Hebrew Academy of Greater Washington fed my love of history and pushed me to overcome writing anxieties. Fabulous teachers at Columbia and Yale—Amy Aronson, Kenneth Jackson, Simon Schama, John Mack Faragher, Mary Habeck, Ivan Marcus, and the late James Shenton and Robin Winks, as well as John Keegan, encouraged me in my dreams of reading and writing history for a living. Alon Tal's talks at the Yale Hillel inspired my hasty but happy decision to go to law school in Israel, and Justice Eliahu Mazza's willingness to take a risk on a new immigrant as a law clerk gave me otherwise unobtainable insight into how judicial decision-making works, as well as one of the most stimulating experiences of my life.

Alon Harel encouraged my initial interest in water law and distributive justice in his seminar on distributive justice at the Hebrew University Faculty of Law, and has continued to provide encouragement in the years since. Carol Rose's writing on water law was the inspiration for my interest in this subject, and she has provided valuable insight and guidance as my research has progressed. Andrea McDowell encouraged me to delve into the laws of the Colorado mining districts. Robert Ellickson, Guido Calabresi, and Lisa Heinzerling provided welcome guidance on my path into academia; Lisa was also kind enough to allow me to participate in her workshop at Georgetown Law while I was living in the D.C. area. Special thanks are due to Henry Smith, whose enthusiasm for the thesis, guidance as my doctoral adviser, and help in getting the book published were all critical for my project, and to Justice Gregory Hobbs for his enthusiasm and facilitation of my research.

At various stages of my writing and research, I was provided with valuable input by Gregory Alexander, Hanoch Dagan, Christoph Engel, Dan Ernst, Mason Gaffney, Ron Harris, Gregory Hicks, Arvid Nelson, Donald Pisani, Ariel Porat, Glen Robinson, Joseph Sax, Katrina Wyman, anonymous reviewers for Yale University Press and the Israel Science Foundation, and the editors of *Ecology Law Quarterly*, where earlier versions of Chapters 2–4 were published. Participants in the Western Water Workshop in Gunnison, Colorado; a workshop on commons theory at the Max Planck Institute for the Study of Collective Goods in Bonn; the International Water History Association conference in Tampere, Finland; the IVR in Cracow; and workshops at the law schools of Tel Aviv and Georgetown Universities also provided helpful feedback. Hagit Brinker, Gadi Ben-Dror, and Hadar Yuhas all did fine work as research assistants on this project as well as others. The support and skill of Michael O'Malley and Bill Frucht, my editors at Yale University Press, were crucial in pushing this project along, and I am grateful to Joyce Ippolito for her sensitive and careful copyediting.

The research for this book was made possible by the assistance of a large number of institutions and individuals dedicated to preserving knowledge and helping others access it: librarians, archivists, and staff at the Colorado State Archives, the Denver Public Library, the Colorado Historical Society, the library of the Colorado Supreme Court, the Carnegie Branch of the

Boulder Public Library, the Fort Collins Local History Archive, the archives of the University of Colorado at Boulder and Colorado State University, the Bancroft and Doe Libraries at Berkeley, the Law Library at Georgetown, the Beinecke Rare Book and Manuscript Library at Yale, the Library of Congress, and the libraries of Tel Aviv University all provided crucial assistance. The wonderful libraries of Yale and the long arm of its interlibrary loan department were extremely helpful in obtaining material in the first year of my research. I am particularly grateful to the McKeldin Library of the University of Maryland at College Park; its gratis service to a student of another institution proved critical to my being able to complete my dissertation while living in Maryland, exemplifying a standard of service by a public institution of higher education that unfortunately cannot be taken for granted. All told, the resources provided by these institutions, the helpfulness of their staffs, and the collaboration of many more in shuttling books around the world and making historical records available on the Internet are cause for optimism about the state of our civilization. Thanks are also due to Mayorga Coffee in Silver Spring, Maryland; Cafe Hillel in downtown Jerusalem; and Coffee Shop in the Rechavia neighborhood in Jerusalem, which provided not only liquid stimulation but also the space and atmosphere that I needed to progress in my writing.

I have also been extremely fortunate in finding my academic home in the Faculty of Law at Tel Aviv University, a great center of legal history and scholarship in general. My gratitude for the warm attention and care shown me by Ariel Porat and Hanoch Dagan is exceeded only by my respect and admiration for their leadership of the institution. Ron Harris and Assaf Likhovski have become friends and mentors, helping me along at every stage of this project and others. My friends and colleagues in the academic, administrative, and library staffs have created the kind of supportive atmosphere that makes TAU an ideal place to work. The writing of this book was also made possible by generous funding I received at TAU from the Cegla Center for the Interdisciplinary Study of the Law, the Law and Environment Program, the David Berg Institute for Law and History, the Vice-President's Fund for Encouragement of Research, and the Porter School of Environmental Studies.

Finally, I offer warm thanks to my wonderful family—to my children for their patience and understanding for my preoccupation with

Colorado and my computer; to my wife, Tunie, for her love, confidence, and absorbing of the family burdens neglected by me while working; and to my loving parents, whose unflinching support and overwhelming generosity at every stage of this long project, including surrendering their home for years to hordes of noisy children, made it all possible. I have dedicated this book to them—an insufficient but heartfelt gesture of my gratitude and love.

CHAPTER 1

INTRODUCTION

We conclude, then, that the common law doctrine giving the riparian
owner a right to the flow of water in its natural channel upon and over
his lands, even though he makes no beneficial use thereof, is inapplicable
to Colorado. Imperative necessity, unknown to the countries which gave
it birth, compels the recognition of another doctrine in conflict therewith.
And we hold that, in the absence of express statutes to the contrary, the
first appropriator of water from a natural stream for a beneficial purpose
has, with the qualifications contained in the constitution, a prior right
thereto, to the extent of such appropriation.[1]

With these words the Colorado Supreme Court made history. *Coffin v.
Left Hand Ditch Co.*, the court's seminal 1882 decision, has become one of
the most prominent cases in American property law.

Prior to the mid-nineteenth-century gold and silver rushes into the
American West, the property law of surface waters throughout
the United States was the "riparian rights" doctrine, inherited from
the English common law. In this legal regime, all landowners along a
stream had rights to use the water flowing by or through their land. The
quantities and manner of use were variable, depending on the uses and

demands of other riparians; each had the right to demand that others limit themselves to "reasonable" uses. What was reasonable was decided on a case-by-case basis by courts.[2]

Symbolizing to this day the rejection of the common law of property in surface waters in the most arid portions of the western United States, the *Coffin* opinion abrogated entirely the system of riparian rights inherited from the common law, and so laid out what became known as the Colorado Doctrine of "pure appropriation" for property in water. Under the appropriation doctrine, water rights are created (appropriated) not by landownership, but by diverting water from the stream and putting it to use. Conflicts between users are resolved by the criterion of temporal priority; a user whose right is "senior" to another's has the right to demand that the holder of the "junior" right cease his diversion if it is not leaving enough water in the stream for the senior user to satisfy his own right.[3] *Coffin* was widely influential in the adoption of the appropriation doctrine by other western jurisdictions in the years that followed, and it has remained a leading case in practically all modern discussions of water law.[4]

For all its salience, though, *Coffin*, along with the appropriation doctrine for which it has come to stand, is today widely misunderstood, largely due to ignorance of the social and legal context in which it arose. Both decision and doctrine have become associated with a set of values—the preference for private over common property, the privatization of the public domain, the facilitation of markets in natural resources—that have little to do with the ideology behind the decision or how contemporaries saw it. Analysis of the available historical evidence makes it quite clear not only that *the doctrine of appropriation as developed in nineteenth-century Colorado was viewed at the time as striking a blow at private property in order to advance distributive justice,* but also that *it had that very effect as its central goal.*

While the primary purpose of this book is to challenge the received wisdom regarding the ideology of western water law, relying primarily on an examination of contemporary sources, the significance of the argument goes beyond revision of the historical record for its own sake. Historians and theoreticians of property rights have tended to agree that the primary concern driving the rejection of riparian doctrine in favor of appropriation in the western United States was economic growth, part of that nineteenth-century "release of individual creative energy" by American law, to use Willard Hurst's phrase,[5] or the common law's characteristic tendency toward efficiency, as some economic analysts of the law would have it.[6] The claims advanced in this book, stressing considerations of widespread distribution of property as the primary motivating factor in the adoption of appropriation law, challenge these consensus views regarding property law and American legal history in general. In doing so, they raise the question as to whether considerations of distributive justice have been given their due in study of these fields. Given the value American legal culture places on arguments from past practice and precedent, they also challenge current paradigms of natural-resource law.

Property Rights and Prior Appropriation

Why does society create rights of private property, particularly in natural resources? A major issue in property theory, environmental policy, and environmental history concerns the ever-shifting relationships between various property regimes—with common and private property typically the main characters in the drama. For centuries, philosophers, economists, lawyers, and others have struggled to explain, on the descriptive level, why these various forms exist, as well as how and why the governance of particular resources moves between the types. On the normative level, they have often sought to justify (or condemn) particular forms of property and the transitions between them. While the famous negative accounts (tragedies) as well as their lesser-known positive ones (comedies) are based on a utilitarian narrative of efficiency concerns, this book will suggest that the issue be viewed in distributive terms—as a "morality play."[7]

In recent decades, with the ascendance of efficiency or wealth-maximization approaches to law, a dominant school of thought has stressed the advantages of private property over common property. Writers on the subject have emphasized, on the one hand, the gains in social welfare made possible by private property, with the clearly delineated rights and powers, certainty, and transferability made possible by its exclusivity;[8] and, on the other hand, the inefficiencies inherent in common property—at its open-access extreme a veritable tragedy.[9]

3

Descriptively, in an approach identified with economist Harold Demsetz, the focus on allocative efficiency has led scholars to portray the progression from common to private property as guided by a sort of continual cost-benefit analysis, the tipping point of privatization being reached when the increasing value of a resource renders the advantages of its privatization greater than the administrative costs of establishing and maintaining a private-property regime.[10] Prescriptively, it has led many to advocate increasing privatization of resources as a way of increasing aggregate welfare.[11]

More recently, the literature has seen a more complicated view of the private/commons relationship, as economics-oriented scholars have shown that the transition to private property may be driven less by efficiency than by interest-group manipulation of the law to redistribute resources in their favor.[12] Others have pointed out not only that common ownership need not rule out effective management,[13] but that in many contexts it may actually be more efficient than private property—in Rose's felicitous formulation, a "comedy of the commons."[14] At the same time, a developing literature on the "anticommons" has made the case that "too much" private property, in the form of overly fragmented entitlements to resources, may lead to its own tragedy, as resources so burdened suffer from underutilization and underdevelopment.[15]

What has generally been left out of all these analyses, however, is an appreciation of the role that considerations of distributive justice may have to play—in both positive and normative terms—in the selection, development, and evolution of property regimes. The classic welfarist law-and-economics approach typically tags distributive issues as "merely" so; the question of fair distribution, in this view, is irrelevant to the optimal allocation of rights, and best relegated to a tax-and-transfer mechanism outside of private law.[16] While public-choice analysis attributes importance to "distributional" factors in the creation of property rights, these are of the decidedly pernicious sort, as powerful interest groups bend the law to enrich themselves at the expense of societal welfare.[17] Critical legal history, too, has tended to see the development of property rights as a story of redistribution in favor of the rich and powerful.[18] Despite what seems to be a basic intuition that distributional fairness should play a role in the allotment of property rights, this angle is largely absent from contemporary writing on property theory.[19]

This book explores this third approach to the development of property rights, arguing for the explanatory power of distributive justice in understanding the origins and evolution of the prior appropriation doctrine of water law in the western United States. This episode in legal history may seem a surprising one to illustrate the role of distributive justice in property rights; for not only is the history of prior appropriation a well-worn topic in the historical, property theory, and natural resources law literature, but the consensus view of that history would seem to make any distributive-justice basis for the doctrine unlikely.[20]

The outline of the standard story is well known, having achieved mythical status in the property theory and natural resources law literature.[21] The first whites to arrive in most of the territories of the Pacific and Rocky Mountain West in any sort of numbers were prospectors and miners of precious metals, a generally coarse bunch, interested in getting rich quick and lacking concern for the niceties of legal doctrine or communal values. The regnant principle in the gold diggings in regard to property in mining claims was "first in time, first in right," an expression of the frontier ethics of individualism, initiative, and exploitation.[22] When it came to resolving disputes over water use, the miners, finding the eastern law of riparian rights unsuited to the exigencies of their environment, applied the rules they had created for mining claims to surface water claims, and created a new system of property rights based on the priority of appropriation of the water. Applying the miners' rules to water rights provided security of title to those displaying the entrepreneurial initiative necessary to make the earliest claims on the water, thereby facilitating economic expansion. This new doctrine, with its exclusive private-property rights, stood in bold contrast to the common-property regime of correlative rights under the English and eastern U.S. riparian doctrine. Nonetheless, it was particularly suited to the arid climate of the new western territories and states, and so the miners' rule of prior appropriation became the guiding principle of water-rights law in the western United States, symbolized most clearly in the Colorado court's complete rejection of riparianism in *Coffin*.[23]

Despite this broad agreement on the circumstances surrounding prior appropriation's creation, lawyers and scholars have sharply disagreed over the meaning of this mythical episode in legal history, again roughly dividing into "optimistic" and "pessimistic" camps. To some, the rule of prior appropriation represents the possibility and promise of efficiency in natural resources law, with the extension of this model to other resources devoutly wished. On this view, the certainty and transferability associated with the creation of private-property rights benefit society by enhancing efficiency, particularly in comparison with the common-property-like riparian rights doctrine.[24] For this group, Demsetzian efficiency provides the key to understanding the creation of the prior appropriation doctrine in the West: the high value of water induced by its scarcity in this region, argues an influential article, outweighed the definition and enforcement costs associated with the creation of private-property rights in water and thus made the prior appropriation doctrine possible.[25] Criticisms of the western law from this quarter tend to focus on certain efficiency-impairing aspects of the law, depicting such elements of western water law as public ownership of waters, the requirement of beneficial use, and the rules of forfeiture and abandonment as foreign impurities that have seeped into the law.[26]

In contrast, other scholars, particularly those with an environmentalist bent, see in prior appropriation a symbol of everything that is wrong about private-property regimes in natural resources: environmental degradation, inequality, unsustainability, giveaways of public property, corporate control of the environment. Like their opponents, this group also views the doctrine as a creature of the individualistic frontier, but for them the abandonment of the riparian doctrine's equitable sharing in favor of exclusive rights by appropriation was a tragedy, with the greater good of the community being sacrificed to greed.[27]

Eric Freyfogle, for instance, spins a tale of a certain Boone in Aridia, in which Boone, the first settler to arrive at the only river in an arid country, claims the whole river for himself, forcing all subsequent settlers to pay him for the privilege of watering their lands; Freyfogle argues that Boone's priority in time is unimportant in terms of natural justice.[28] "Water law certainly promoted economic growth," writes historian Donald Pisani, "but the requirement that law achieve some measure of justice in allocating a scarce resource was not met."[29] Scholars from this quarter tend to stress not only the welfare-enhancing qualities of common property in water (particularly in encouraging sustainable use), but also its moral advantages.[30]

6

While advocates on either side of the debate over private property and natural resources thus sharply dispute the *meaning* of the myth of prior appropriation, they tend to agree with the consensus of most historians of western water law about at least two important features of the story: first, that the law of prior appropriation originated in the practices of the miners in the Sierra Nevada Mountains and their successors in the Rockies, and second, that the primary concern of the appropriation doctrine was wealth creation, accomplished through the efficiency advantages of private-property rights in water.[31]

However, this consensus view, which stresses the wealth-maximizing focus of prior appropriation, seems unlikely, as it fails to explain—other than as foreign implants in the pure capture doctrine—the many aspects of the law generally agreed to be inefficient, such as the beneficial use requirement and forfeiture for non-use.[32] It also falls short in accounting for such features of western law as the constitutional or statutory declarations of public or state ownership of waters found in all appropriation states.[33]

It is, moreover, contradicted by the historical evidence. The sources to be examined in this book are of four types. First, the unofficial codes of Colorado's mining districts in the early years of white settlement in the area are usually identified as the source of the state's doctrine of prior appropriation. Contrary to the standard view, these rules generally expressed a concern for broad and equitable distribution of resources, and included the roots of those supposedly eastern imports the contamination by which some have bemoaned.[34] The miners' ideology and analogs to their rules are clearly discernible in Colorado's official water law, as found in the next group of sources, the water-law statutes of Colorado's legislature and the relevant sections of the state's 1876 constitution. These, too, exhibit a concern with equitable distribution of water and limiting the power of corporations, a value not usually thought to be part of the prior appropriation milieu. Third, the decisions of Colorado's supreme court in its first decades advanced a like commitment to equal access and the prevention of concentrated control over water. Throughout, the ideological assumptions behind the law created by Colorado's pioneers are illustrated by the fourth group of sources—contemporary primary sources and published works.

In the following chapters, these historical sources will be explored, with the aim of building a new picture of the creation and early evolution of the appropriation doctrine. Chapter 2 presents a new account of Colorado's mining district laws, generally considered to be the font of the state's appropriation doctrine, and explores the ideological background of, and precedents for, both the miners' codes and the appropriation doctrine. It argues that the Colorado rules advanced certain ideals of distributive justice, as part of a broader nineteenth-century agrarian reform movement in American law and politics. Chapter 3 analyzes the genesis of the appropriation doctrine itself, as laid down in territorial statutes, the Colorado state constitution, and early judicial decisions, with *Coffin v. Left Hand Ditch* as their climax. Chapters 4 and 5 carry this analysis forward into the two decades following *Coffin*, focusing on the legal doctrines used to curb the power of corporations and speculators and reserve the state's water for bona fide users. Chapter 4 focuses on Colorado's draconian regulation of water corporations, highlighting the historical distinction between private property and corporate property that motivated the law. Chapter 5 discusses the beneficial-use rule of appropriation law and the difficulties it created for efficient allocation of the resource, arguing that the type of property regime created by the law (an anticommons), typically viewed as a disastrous result, was the anticipated and desired outcome, for reasons of distributive justice. Finally, Chapter 6 examines some theoretical issues raised by the historical study, and concludes with thoughts on practical implications of the view of the appropriation doctrine advanced in the book.

CHAPTER 2

THE SOURCES OF THE COLORADO
APPROPRIATION DOCTRINE

As noted in the first chapter, the history of rules for water rights in the mining districts of the American West is not a new topic, and there would seem to be little left to add. (The uses to which miners put water are illustrated in Figs. 1 and 2.) Yet the analysis presented in this chapter leads to conclusions that diverge significantly from the conventional story. These new insights were made possible, first of all, by throwing as wide a net as possible, in an attempt to gather all surviving records of Colorado miners' laws, as well as contemporaries' relevant commentaries. To the best of my knowledge, the survey of Colorado mining district laws made as part of the work on this book is the most comprehensive carried out to date, including all extant published and unpublished sources, covering 91 distinct mining codes (10 of them never before mentioned in print sources) from 78 districts, as well as numerous amendments to codes. Next, the interpretation advanced here is based on a close reading not only of the sections dealing explicitly with the question of priority in appropriative rights, but of the entirety of the codes, including sections dealing with other aspects of water law, such as rights of way for ditches, as well as provisions seemingly unrelated to the history of the appropriation doctrine, such as those covering service of legal process in the mines.

Figure 1. Placer Mines at Cripple Creek, Colorado, late nineteenth century. Courtesy Denver Public Library, Western History Collection, X-61292.

Depicting ditches and sluice boxes used by Colorado gold miners.

Finally, my approach is based on a reading of the historical sources with an eye both to property theory and to the larger historical context in which these legal texts were produced.

Prior Appropriation in Colorado's Mining Districts

First examined is the role of priority in the miners' rules. Though scholars have seen this element of the law as most strongly associated with the themes of individualism and private property, a careful reading of the mining rules shows that it was part of a larger scheme of limiting the extent of mining claims. Next, the use requirement, sometimes derided as an inefficient and exotic graft on the pure-property western system of water law, is shown to have been an integral part of the larger scheme of limiting property rights from the inception of the system.

Figure 2. Waterfalls at Montgomery, C.T. Photograph by George D. Wakely, 1864. Courtesy History Colorado (Original Photographs Collection, Scan #20004792).
The water power is being used to turn a water wheel and "arrastre," a machine used to grind ores and release their precious metals.

Finally, viewing the miners' laws in the light of doctrinal elements already present in the eastern system of riparian rights reveals that the real break with riparian rights was not in the transition from absolute sharing to a system of priority, but in the breaking of the rule that water be used on the land of riparian owners, a requirement that would have given riparian owners real monopoly power in the arid West.

A Matter of Priorities

On May 6, 1859, John Gregory made the first major discovery of gold in the mountains of what was to become Colorado. The members of his party were able to work on the claim undisturbed until about the twenty-third of the month, but word of the strike quickly spread, and by the first of June it was estimated that there were 5,000 people in the Gregory Diggings camp northwest of Denver (Fig. 3).[1]

GREGORY GOLD DIGGINGS, COLORADO, MAY, 1859. Page 181.

Figure 3. Gregory Diggings, from Albert D. Richardson, Beyond the Mississippi: From the Great River to the Great Ocean (Hartford: American Publishing Co., 1867). Courtesy Denver Public Library, Western History Collection, X-11447.
Note the early use of water in sluice boxes.

The June 8, 1859, regulations of the Gregory Diggings, consisting of only ten sections, were one of the earliest examples of miners' laws from the lands later to be incorporated in the Colorado Territory. It was the first such surviving code to mention water rights, and it influenced many of the later miners' codes adopted in the territory.[2] The Diggings regulations were cited in historian Robert Dunbar's standard account of the miners' rules regarding prior appropriation:

> Sometimes [the laws] indicated that priority of claim gave the better right; more often they omitted reference to priority, leaving that to the unwritten law of the gulches. Some of the Colorado miners, however, were explicit in their declarations of prior rights in water. When the organizers of the Downeyville Mining District met on July 29, 1859, to write their code, they included an article that read: "In all gulches or ravines where water may be scarce the oldest claimants shall have preference [*sic*] and priority of right to water." Two months later, on September 26, 1859, the miners who formed the Illinois Mining District gave those using water on their claims "priority of right." Similarly in Gregory Gulch the rules provided that in case of scarcity of water, "priority of claim" would prevail.[3]

Dunbar's statement regarding the Gregory district's rules apparently is a reference to Section 8 of its regulations, which reads:

> Eighth—resolved that in all cases priority of claims, when honestly carried out, shall be respected.[4]

This provision, which appeared (often with slight modifications) in many later codes, indeed seems to award legal force to priority of appropriation (for all mining claims, not just water).[5] However, the meaning of the section in this case could not have been that water rights were to be governed by the prior appropriation system, as can be seen from the very next section, which limited the amount of water a miner could divert, irrespective of priority:

> Ninth—resolved that when two parties wish to use water on the same stream or ravine, for quartz mining purposes, no person shall use more than one half of the water.[6]

Section 8 was thus clearly not intended to institute a system of prior appropriation for water claims. The language of a later, more developed code of the same Gregory Diggings may better indicate its true meaning:

In all cases when parties shall have complied with the law as far as possible priority of claim when honestly carried out shall be respected.[7]

The purpose of this provision was nothing more than stating the unremarkable principle that in a case of two bona fide claims to the same mining site, the earlier claimant should prevail. This is simply an instance of the equitable rule of *qui prior est tempore potior est jure* ("he who is first in time is first in right"), which applies to two claimants to the same entitlement. Such a rule is practically an inevitable adjunct to any system under which competing claims might arise.[8]

This highlights the point that the original Gregory code, like the codes of the other districts, did not have as its main concern the distribution of water. In fact, many codes made no mention at all of how water was to be allocated in the "diggings." Virtually every Colorado miners' code, however, *did* legislate limitations on the size and number of mining claims that might be staked by any one miner.[9] For example, the original Gregory code limited mountain claims to a patch of ground 100 feet long and 50 wide in which the miner could dig, and gulch claims to 100 feet along the length of the gulch for panning for surface gold, significantly smaller than the 600-foot claim size in the Spanish code that had previously applied in Colorado.[10] As in most jurisdictions, miners could hold only one claim of each type by "preemption" (that is, appropriation of an unowned claim), though a bonus claim was typically allowed for the discoverer of the lode, and there was generally no limit on the accumulation of claims by purchase.[11] A further limit on the concentration of claims was the general requirement that claims be worked; claims left unworked beyond a prescribed period (usually a matter of days) were forfeit and could be claimed by another.[12]

These limitations are important to understanding the rationale behind the various provisions regarding water in the mining district laws, a theme to be more fully developed later. For now it is important to note that they effectively limited the amount of wealth in the form of mining claims that any miner could legitimately acquire from the public "commons" to that amount that he could reasonably work. Beyond that level, accumulation of wealth by "appropriation" was not allowed.[13]

Returning to the direct treatment of water rights in the miners' laws, a remarkable characteristic of the seventy-odd codes that explicitly dealt with water rights is the seeming multiplicity of approaches to the subject. This diversity belies the standard account of the birth of a revolutionary western water law in the crucible of the mining camps. While some laws made some reference to priority, others (and sometimes even the same ones) declared that water should be divided proportionately among the users.[14] Still others, as well as some in the former groups, imposed strict limits on the amount of water that might be claimed, as will be discussed below. A necessary corollary to limiting the size of a water right was the restriction of each miner to one claim only by appropriation, a limitation made explicit in most codes and implicit in all.[15] While several codes seem to have remained within the common-law tradition of limiting the locus of use to riparian lands, whether by limiting the right to take water to those whose mining claims were adjacent to the stream, by giving priority to riparians, or by forbidding interference with the natural flow, many explicitly granted easements for ditches to non-riparians or to "bring water into the mines."[16]

Although at first blush a chaotic array of discordant and competing norms and values, these mining codes in fact express a single, overarching principle: not efficiency, as represented by some, but rather *broad distribution* of water rights. The distributive ethic is evident, first of all, in the rules establishing a certain, uniform size for water claims (along with the corollary limitation of one water claim per miner), discussed above. While a few codes defined the maximum claim amount in terms of flow or quantity of water, limits were most often by length along the stream (to be used for washing gold from the dirt or for powering quartz-crushing mills): "33 feet in length up and down the stream"; "300 ft on the creek or gulch"; "not exceeding in distance two hundred and fifty feet measured in a straight line and touching the centre of the stream at each end."[17] These rules were similar to those setting out the sizes of the various types of mining claims, discussed above. Other laws gave each claimant a certain measure of head, or fall, on the stream: "No [quartz or lumber] mill site claim . . . shall occupy more of the stream in length than will be sufficient to raise the water by a dam to the height of fourteen feet"; "a sufficient distance on such stream to secure a fall of thirty feet from the dam to the mill"; "a sufficient distance along any stream to give a head twenty feet and sufficient fall for a ditch to convey said water"; and even simply "sufficient head . . . to run a mill."[18]

Though not articulated in precise philosophical terms, the water rules of the Colorado mining districts had as their guiding principle *equality* (of opportunity, since only some claims would turn out to be valuable), modified by a guarantee of *sufficiency*. Briefly put, the sufficiency principle, a principle of distributive justice defended by moral philosophers such as Harry Frankfurt and Joseph Raz, states that justice requires that each person should have enough. It is the sufficiency principle that explains the role of priority in this legal system dedicated to distributive justice.[19]

While the miners' laws generally advanced an ideal of equality in claim sizes, they were also sensitive to the moral importance of sufficiency. Strict adherence to a rule of equality would have led to constantly decreasing claim sizes; with each newcomer to the mining camp, the claims would have had to be reapportioned. Beyond the prohibitive administrative costs of such a system, it would have been impractical (and unfair) for another reason: claim sizes would have decreased past the point where they were too small to be of any real value.[20] (It bears keeping in mind that the population of Gregory Gulch is said to have increased from two prospectors to four or five thousand in the month following Gregory's discovery on May 6, 1859, and to ten or fifteen thousand a month later.) The approach adopted in most of the codes, laying out standard claim sizes and limiting them to one per person, avoided this pitfall while preserving a relatively high level of equality. The claim size, measured in the square feet of placer diggings, length along a stream, or feet of head, represented the best judgment of the miners as to the amount of the resource that could be worked by one person. On the one hand, it was a minimum, ensuring that each miner received enough space or water for a workable claim. On the other hand, it was also a maximum, limiting the accumulation of wealth by any one person, and thereby maximizing the number of people that could stake claims in the district, or "divid[ing] wealth among a large number of people," as a nineteenth-century guide observed.[21]

The element of sufficiency is also thrown into relief by the different methods of calculating the claim size for water. Those codes allowing a certain length or area along the stream must have reflected an assumption that the chosen figure approximated a reasonable amount of water or water pressure for the use of a miner; yet rules of this type retained an element of arbitrariness that was absent from those directing a maximum claim size in terms of length "sufficient" to produce a given head. In the former, the mandated figure might miss the mark, leaving the claimant with more or less than was really necessary for his purposes; in the latter, the length of the claim would vary with the topography of the site, but would always represent the head sufficient to run a mill.

The equality principle is, of course, most obviously apparent in the rules calling for equal apportionment of the water in a stream. One instance is Section 9 of the original Gregory Diggings laws quoted above. The reference to "two parties" in that law probably reflects the reality that a miner, after using water, would return to the stream substantially the same quantity as he withdrew, so that the question of division would generally arise only among miners working on opposite banks. This seems to be the assumption in other codes as well, such as this one from the Nevada District:

> Resolved, That miners working lode claims shall be entitled to one half the water from the gulch . . .; but those so using it shall return it to the gulch by a ditch unless it be needed for use by parties below, in which case those last using it shall conduct it in a ditch as prescribed above.[22]

This rule tracks riparian law in ensuring every claim holder an equal right to use the water of the stream for mining activities. Other codes stipulated that if a miner were unable to return his diverted water immediately below his claim, he would be required to divide it equally with the miners whose claims were being bypassed by his ditch.[23] All these laws, apparently legislating for a situation in which water was used without substantial consumption, basically retained a rule that looked a lot like the eastern riparian rule of equality.[24]

In contrast, in circumstances where water would be consumed with use, a rule of strict equality would have been unworkable and unfair, as argued above. Indeed, we find that other codes, perhaps reflecting different mining practices, addressed this concern. In these the equal-sharing rule was subject to the caveat that in case of insufficient water for all, priority in time would give some a better right than others. Such a rule was Section 17 of the 1860 Gregory Diggings laws:

Be it further enacted, That if two or more parties wish to use water on the same stream or ravine for quartz mining purposes, no person shall be entitled to use more than his proportionate share of water, but in case there shall not be water sufficient for all, priority of claim shall determine the right to such water.[25]

Priority was not the primary rule of decision for water rights here or elsewhere; the codes did not allow the pioneer to claim as much water as he wanted, or could physically divert. The primary rule was that each party was entitled to a proportional share of the water. The element of priority acted as a supplementary principle, having legal effect only in cases where there was not enough water for all the parties wishing to use the water to realistically do so. This was essentially the point made by Justice Stephen Field, himself a former miner, in an oft-quoted passage on the California miners' codes: "And they were so framed as to secure to all comers, *within practicable limits,* absolute equality of right and privilege in working the mines."[26]

A schematic, hypothetical example will illustrate how the above rule would have worked: A stream has a flow of 60 cubic feet per second (c.f.s.) in an area where a flow of 15 c.f.s. is normally required to power a quartz mill. A and B are the first to arrive in the area and erect mills. Each of them has the right to insist that the other refrain from using more than 30 c.f.s. When C arrives and builds a mill, he can insist that A and B restrict their use to no more than 20 c.f.s.; even if one or both had been using more than that before he got there, they must reduce their use in order to accommodate him. D then arrives on the scene and demands his proportional share. A, B, and C must further reduce their use to 15 c.f.s. The egalitarian principle of proportional use is controlling, and the newcomer's right is no weaker than that of those first on the scene. When E appears, however, the rule of priority comes into play. He cannot demand that A, B, C, and D reduce their use below the 15 c.f.s. mark, the flow necessary to power a mill. Equality can reduce the property rights of the mill owners only to a threshold level of basic sufficiency.

Though not always made explicit, this notion of priority was seemingly at work as well in the more numerous codes in which water use was limited by length or head, discussed above. In these laws, the egalitarian impulse limited the amount that could be claimed by any person, while priority determined whose claims were valid when there were not enough to go around (as well as the identity of the owner of each specific, geographically delimited claim).

Some such miners' laws did, however, explicitly mention the secondary rule of priority. This is the normative context of Article 8 of the Downeyville district laws, cited by Dunbar in the selection quoted above: Article 5 of the code had already limited the size of a river claim (200 feet in length and from stream bank to the base of the adjacent mountain); priority was thus but a secondary rule of decision, effective only when the number of claimants exceeded the number of viable claims.[27] In fact, this is the context of all the priority preferences for water claims in Colorado's mining district laws: Every code with such a rule also explicitly limited the size of a water claim in one way or another.[28]

Priority as a tenet of water allocation appeared, then, in a small minority of the Colorado miners' laws, and then primarily in two contexts: (1) situations governed by a proportionate sharing rule, for cases when there would not have been sufficient water for any if all comers were allowed in with an equal share; and (2) codes in which limits were placed on claim size, for cases when there were not enough claims to go around. It also was an implicit, background principle in the other codes that placed limits on claim size. In all three cases its role was decidedly second-fiddle.

In contrast, the ideal of equality, though not taken to its logical extreme, dominated the water-rights regulations of the miners' laws, finding expression in some codes in equal-sharing rules for water, and in others in the limitation of claim sizes. The limits set on the amount of water that could be claimed encouraged equality both by limiting the size of the water right that any one person could acquire by appropriation, and by maximizing the number of people with rights in the resource. The egalitarian principle retreated only when necessary to ensure sufficiency of claim size.

The Use Requirement

A related aspect of the miners' laws (briefly mentioned earlier) was the requirement that mining claims be worked, a condition both of acquiring and of maintaining the right. This requirement bears discussion, as we find it resurfacing in Colorado water law proper. This condition applied to water claims as well, as a water claim was considered one of the types of claims (placer, gulch, and so on) that could be acquired by preemption and therefore was subject to the same work or use requirement. Some codes treated the work requirement for water claims explicitly but in general terms, as in the Montgomery District's rule that claims for mill sites and "water power" (see Fig. 2, p. 11) would not be valid "until the party or parties making said claims shall make reasonable demonstration towards the use & occupancy of the same."[29] Other codes, such as the November 1859 By-Laws for the Government of Central Mining District (see Fig. 4), went into more detail:

> All mill companies shall have 20 feet head on stream, large enough to run mills, and shall hold the same so long as they use said water power. If not used in fifteen days after taken, shall be forfeited, unless a statement is filed, under oath, with the recorder, that the party holds said water power while he goes to the States, or any other place, for proper machinery &c. When such statement has been filed, specifying the time that the party will be absent, said claim must be considered sacred until said statement expires.[30]

Here the water claim was valid only as long as used and, in a further instance of the sufficiency principle, an exception was made only for the proprietor who was taking active steps toward construction of his mill, and only for as long as necessary to procure the necessary equipment.

The suggestion made by some scholars that the beneficial-use requirement for water claims may have been justified in efficiency terms as a way of defining and publicizing rights without the need for complicated recordation is contradicted by the evidence. Most mining district codes made provision for the recording of claims, which seems to have been a simple procedure; in many, recordation was mandatory. Also, many explicitly required a minimum quantum of work, even with recordation, as a condition of a claim's validity. In these, at least, the work requirement evidently served a purpose beyond the publicity or notice function.[31]

The function of the work or use requirement was, rather, to prevent speculative appropriations; in other words, appropriations intended not for immediate use but for resale at a profit, especially by absentee owners.

LAWS AND REGULATIONS

OF THE

CENTRAL MINING DISTRICT.

Miners' Meeting.

At a meeting of the miners of this district, held on the 21st day of November, 1859, Capt. THOMAS DUNSTAN was called to the chair and JOHN H. R. DUNSTAN was chosen Secretary.

A motion was then made and carried, that a new district, to be known as "Central Mining District," be erected according to the limits prescribed in the following resolutions, to wit:

Resolved, That we, the people of Central Mining District, hereby enact and create a new district, to be known and called as hereinbefore stated — to be bounded as follows, to wit: on the north, by Jefferson and Deadwood diggings; on the east, by the summit of the Rocky Peaks; on the south, by Enterprise and Quartz Valley Districts; on the west, by the summit of the Snowy range.

The meeting then proceeded to the election of the following officers: CAPT.

have 20 feet head on stream, large enough to run mills, and shall hold the same so long as they use said water power. If not used in fifteen days after taken, shall be forfeited, unless a statement is filed, under oath, with the recorder, that the party holds said water power while he goes to the States, or any other place, for proper machinery &c. When such statement has been filed, specifying the time that the party will be absent, said claim must be considered sacred until said statement expires.

ART. 10. No water claim shall be sold unless improvements are on it to the amount of $100.

ART. 11. When Water Companies are engaged in bringing water into any portion of the mines, they shall have the right of way secured to them, and may pass over any claim, road, or other ditch; but shall so guard themselves in passing, as not to injure the party over whose ground they pass.

taken as true, and execution issued. If he appear and answer, the Justice (or President) shall summon a venire of nine persons, from which each party shall strike off one until there remain three, who shall proceed to hear the evidence of the parties, with or without counsel, and try the case. Any juror may be challenged for cause shown either by his own evidence, or the evidence of others.

Should the party losing feel aggrieved by the decision, he may appeal to a jury of twelve men, by paying costs already accrued; which jury shall be selected by the Justice (or President) and their decision shall be final.

ART. 21. The Sheriff shall have power to serve notices and executions, and he shall have power to summon parties: put parties in posession of property, decided to be by law; summon jurors, and do such service as a Sheriff in any other place may do, and shall be entitled to receive double the legal fees provided by the

Moreover, it was not an arbitrary limitation, but expressed the contemporary "producer ethic," which found particular virtue in the labor of the individual, a theme discussed later in this chapter.[32] The anti-speculation goal was also at the root of the specific limitations on claim sizes, including for water rights, found in many of the miners' codes. In these codes, with their unambiguous, predetermined claim sizes, the legislated maximum claim dimensions limited appropriations to the amount a miner could reasonably work or use. The use requirement primarily played a role in reclaiming speculative claims from private ownership and returning them to the pool of unowned property, making them available for new, bona fide claimants. Logically, however, the element of use was itself a measure of legitimate right; if any unused portion of the claim automatically became *res nullius*, available anew for appropriation, then claim sizes were ipso facto limited to the amount that could be used. In the context of Colorado water law, both functions ultimately found expression in the doctrine of beneficial use, as will be discussed in greater detail in Chapter 5.

The Real Demise of Riparian Rights

To the extent that the traditional common-law riparian-rights doctrine reflected an ideal of equality, the laws enacted by the popular assemblies of the Colorado miners' districts were not truly revolutionary. While the mechanics of the water allocation system may have changed in many instances, with claim sizes and use requirements replacing the correlative rights derived from notions of reasonable use, the underlying principle of equality remained dominant.[33]

Even the dimension of sufficiency, reflected in the rules that allowed each appropriator to have the minimum amount of water necessary for mining or running a mill, was not as great a departure from riparian doctrine as might at first be thought. Though, generally speaking, the common law held that water in a stream was to be shared equitably, as common property, by all the owners of riparian land, there was an exception to this rule. As explained in the 1842 Illinois case of *Evans v. Merriweather*, when it came to domestic, or "natural," uses (drinking, household uses, and watering livestock), a riparian owner might take as much as needed from the stream, without regard to the wants of the other riparian owners below him, even exhausting the entire flow of the stream, if necessary. The court had also speculated on a possible extension of this principle to irrigation, under circumstances other than those prevailing in Illinois:

> The supply of man's artificial wants is not essential to his existence; it is not indispensable; he could live if water was not employed in irrigating lands, or in propelling his machinery. In countries differently situated from ours, [however,] with a hot and arid climate, water doubtless is absolutely indispensable to the cultivation of the soil, and in them, water for irrigation would be a natural want. Here it might increase the products of the soil, but it is by no means essential, and can not, therefore, be considered a natural want of man.[34]

The way was thus open under traditional riparian law to prevent the principle of equality from diluting the water right available to each owner beyond the point of usefulness. The miners' codes' adoption of the priority principle to prevent the excessive shrinking of rights was thus not a radical break with eastern riparian law, but a logical extension of the rationale of the "domestic-use exception." It was fairer, too. While the Illinois rule allowed the upstream owner in times of scarcity to empty the stream to satisfy his "natural wants," thereby attaching priority of right to a morally arbitrary criterion (position on the stream), the miners' rule adopted a more ethically satisfying test, recognizing the equity of work performed by granting priority to the first to begin using the water.

That being said, the laws of the mining districts did substantially diverge from the model of riparian rights in another dimension, one related to their rejection of *Evans*'s privileging of the upstream owner: the miners' laws began to reject as well the law's reservation of the privilege of acquiring water rights to only those lands situated adjacent to the body of water. Some codes, it is true, remained within the riparian tradition in this regard, either forbidding the use of water far from the gulch, or, while apparently allowing use on non-riparian lands, giving priority of right to the riparian owners.[35] (Some laws also established a residual rule that riparian law should apply in cases of lacunae in the code; in practice this would mean that riparian-law rules would govern the regulation of external effects caused by water use, as opposed to questions of the validity of the appropriation itself.)[36] The overwhelming majority, however, not only gave no preference in water rights to those holding mining claims on the stream's banks, but went one step further. Riparian owners, even in the absence of a rule forbidding non-riparian use, might have succeeded in monopolizing the water in a stream by refusing stream access to non-riparians. To avoid this outcome, many miners' laws granted non-riparian miners easements "for bringing water into the mines" in ditches across other claims, usually on condition that they not cause damage to the servient claim. Many codes also made specific provision for rights of way over mining claims for companies or individuals supplying water to the mines (see Fig. 4, Art. 11).[37]

Here, then, was the true departure of the miners' codes from the law of riparian rights. Owners of riparian land would not be members of an exclusive club, privileged vis-à-vis all others in owning rights to the water. Nor would they be able to exercise effective control over the waters (and lands) adjoining their plot by denying outsiders a right of way to carry the water to their lands, or by charging for the privilege. This abolition of the exclusive privileges of the riparian club dovetailed with the widening of the circle of potential appropriators by limiting claim sizes. The opportunity to own a water right in a stream was now open to all who could use it, regardless of where they had managed to stake their mining claim.

The Principles of the Miners' Laws Restated

The common themes of the Colorado miners' laws' water rules express, I believe, two major principles or policy goals, which are really two sides of the same coin: the limitation of appropriation by each individual to the amount he could use, and the maximization of the number of owners able to stake claims to the water. The law gave practical effect to these principles through a number of rules: limitations on the size of an appropriation, whether by setting maximum amounts or by the use requirement, and the abolition of the riparian owners' exclusive hold on surface water sources, by recognizing the right of non-riparians to divert water and granting them rights of access to the water sources across riparian lands. The role of the priority principle in these codes was strictly supplementary, to prevent appropriations from the water source that would leave some without a viable share of water.

As we shall see, Colorado's water law in its first decades drew heavily upon the principles of the miners' laws, though, as has hopefully become apparent, not in the way that is usually assumed.

The Ideological and Legal Context of the Miners' Laws

Key to understanding the distributive norms of the Colorado miners' laws and water law is the realization that they did not materialize out of thin air as a spontaneous response to the conditions in the diggings, as was implied by many influential historians. They were, rather, expressions of an agrarian, populist world view widespread in the western United States in the nineteenth century, an ideology locked in a secular struggle with corporate capitalism and speculative investment, particularly in western lands.[38] Moreover, both the miners' codes and the Colorado appropriation doctrine were of a piece with certain laws and customs that had arisen in connection with the issue of acquisition of property on the public domain, a particularly important bone of contention between the opposing camps. Put simply, the issue was this: Would the lands of the public domain be disposed of to absentee speculators and corporations controlled by eastern and European investors, or to the archetypal "actual settler," a mainstay of agrarian political rhetoric and law? Colorado law came down largely in favor of the latter, as well as his relatives, the "actual miner" and, later, the "actual user" of water.[39]

The miners' codes reflected a world view with roots in republican ideology of the seventeenth and eighteenth centuries and the later Jacksonian Democracy, and identified in the mid- and late nineteenth century with land reform and agrarian movements such as National Reform, the Farmers Alliances, and the People's Party. Mid-nineteenth-century reform elements built on the Jeffersonian ideology favoring small, family-sized farms, arguing that every person should hold some land, both as a matter of right and in order to preserve the individual self-sufficiency and independence necessary for democracy to function.[40] These beliefs were at their pinnacle of popularity and influence in the mid-nineteenth century, when Colorado's miners' laws were being worked out, finding a particularly receptive audience in the West, which was viewed as the natural arena for making land available on such a widespread basis.[41]

Bound up in this view of land tenure was a "producerist" bias, a belief that "since the occupancy and use of the land are the true criteria of valid ownership, [only] labor expended in cultivating the earth confers title to it."[42] This idea had its roots in Locke's labor theory of private property, and its corollary, both in Locke and in republican ideology, was that no one could acquire more than he could make use of: "As much as any one can make use of to any advantage of life before it spoils, so much he may by his labor fix a property in; whatever is beyond this is more than his share and belongs to others."[43] Proposals for reform thus stressed the ideals of equality of landholdings, limitations on the maximum amount any individual might own, and limiting acquisition of public lands to actual settlers while forbidding purchase by absentee owners.[44]

The reverse face of this philosophy was the fear and loathing of monopoly, to the point where "monopoly" became something of an epithet for all the institutions agrarian reformers disliked or feared. "The word monopoly has an ominous sound to American ears," observed a prominent jurist, "and whenever the appellation fairly attaches itself to any thing, it is already condemned in the public mind."[45] It also had a more specific sense, referring to the accumulation of property on a scale beyond what was practical for personal use, particularly for purposes of speculation or deriving income from tenants. This was viewed as a violation of the natural-law, Lockean labor theory of property.[46] Anti-monopolism went hand in hand with a desire for limits to the private accumulation of land and the yeoman ideal of wide distribution to actual settlers.[47]

Anti-monopolism was also related to another aspect of agrarian ideology, its anti-corporate character. Corporations, in particular those created by legislative charter, were viewed as beneficiaries of unfairly granted privileges, as Jackson himself had made clear in his famous veto of the Second Bank of the United States:

> It is to be regretted that the rich and powerful too often bend the acts of government to their selfish purposes. . . . When the laws undertake . . . to grant titles, gratuities, and exclusive privileges, to make the rich richer and the potent more powerful, the humble members of society—the farmers,

mechanics and laborers—who have neither the time nor the means of securing like favors to themselves, have a right to complain of the injustice of their Government.[48]

Reformers accordingly advocated the passage of general incorporation laws, so that all businesses would be put on an equal footing.

It is important to note that this set of ideas, while egalitarian in nature, did not include socialism; rather, private property, widely distributed, was perceived as a bulwark of liberty and human dignity.[49] Most reformers did not oppose private ownership of property, only what they saw as undue concentration of ownership due to unequal distribution of the opportunity to acquire property.[50] Their ideology was part of the intellectual tradition of egalitarianism that has been termed "radical Lockeanism."[51]

Yet, radical Lockeans were not necessarily opposed to public or state ownership of property. In fact, private property was often seen as the antithesis not of these types of property, but of corporate ownership, itself held by some not to be private property at all. The opposition between private and corporate ownership was so strong that state ownership could be justified in terms of Lockean individualism as necessary to keep power out of the concentrated hands of capitalists and monopolies.[52]

Probably the best-known example of the nineteenth-century Jeffersonian ideal enacted into law is the famous Homestead Act of 1862, which contained all the core elements of radical Lockean thought: widespread distribution, use requirements, and limits on holdings.[53] Less well known today are the many other nineteenth-century American legal regimes, both official and informal, that provided precedents for the Colorado mining district laws, having as their primary concern the wide distribution of property rights to those actually working the resource in question and corresponding restriction of the ability of absentee capitalists to amass such property. These include the federal Preemption Act of 1841, which legalized squatting on the public domain, making permanent the hitherto sporadic policy of making up to 160 acres (a quarter-section) of public land available to actual inhabitants at a minimum price. Like the later doctrine of prior appropriation, this statute provided that in cases of two or more settlers claiming the same land, the right would belong to the party who had settled first; it also required the settler to improve the land and swear that the appropriation was not being made for speculative purposes.[54] The purpose of the law was clear: "It is by pre-emption policy that we secure these occupants, who have incorporated their labor with the soil, in their possessions, against the more wealthy who buy on speculation; and against whom they could not be expected successfully to compete, at public auction; and place the lands in the proper hands of those whose occupation is to cultivate them."[55]

Federal law actually reflected what already had become practice on the mid-century frontier, where settlers on the public domain had been forming clubs to enforce their claims against the paper titles of those who bought the same land from the government. These claim clubs, particularly prevalent in the territories of the Upper Mississippi Valley, generally set a maximum amount of land that could be claimed, and specified the value of improvements required to retain possession of the land.[56] This local "law" received some official sanction even before the Preemption Act, such as the decision of the Supreme Court of Iowa Territory affirming the validity of squatters' titles in derogation of federal statute.[57] Miners on public land in this period also adopted codes foreshadowing the later miners' rules of the Sierra Nevadas and Rockies, such as the regulations of the lead miners of Dubuque, Iowa, which set maximum claim sizes and minimum work requirements.[58]

The miners' codes of the California Forty-Niners, influential for the Colorado rules a decade later, are properly seen as part of this pro-settler trend in law, ensuring equal opportunity and preventing monopolization by speculators. That they were seen in their own time as advancing these values is evidenced by the testimony of contemporaries. Miner-turned-U.S. Senator William Stewart, in an influential speech, boasted that:

> These regulations were thoroughly democratic in their character, guarding against every form of monopoly, and requiring continued work and occupation in good faith to constitute a valid possession. . . . [The miners] look with jealous eyes upon every proposition for the sale of the mines which they have discovered and made valuable. . . . The reason for this is obvious. It is their all, secured through long years of incessant toil and privation, and they associate any sale with a sale at auction, where capital is to compete with poverty, fraud and intrigue with truth and honesty. It is

not because they do not desire a fee-simple title, for this they would prize above all else; but most of them are poor, and unable to purchase in competition with capitalists and speculators, which the adoption of any plan heretofore proposed would compel them to do; and for these reasons the opposition to the sale of the mineral lands has been unanimous in the mining States and Territories.[59]

Another former miner, Justice Stephen Field of the U.S. Supreme Court, wrote that the miners' laws "were so framed as to secure to all comers, within practicable limits, absolute equality of right and privilege in working the mines. Nothing but such equality would have been tolerated by the miners."[60] John Wesley Powell, reporting to Congress on the mining district laws, emphasized that "the association of a number of people prevents single individuals from having undue control of natural privileges, and secures an equitable division of mineral lands."[61] The radical land reformer Henry George described the California mining codes in his influential *Progress and Poverty* thus: "The miners in each district fixed the amount of ground an individual could take and the amount of work that must be done to constitute use. If this work were not done, any one could relocate the ground. Thus, no one was allowed to forestall or to lock up natural resources. Labor was acknowledged as the creator of wealth, was given a free field, and secured in its reward . . . all had an equal chance. No one was allowed to play the dog in the manger with the bounty of the Creator. The essential idea of the mining regulations was to prevent forestalling and monopoly."[62]

Colorado settlers, many of them from the Mississippi Valley states and territories where claim club law was widespread, and influenced as much by the principles of the Preemption Act as by California mining practice, early on established not only mining districts embodying the egalitarian and anti-speculation principles of preemption law, but also claim clubs for agricultural land in the valleys. These had many of the same general features as the mining codes, including limits on claim size (the iconic 160 acres for agricultural land) and work requirements.[63] Similar provisions for agricultural claims were also frequently a part of mining district codes, and were also enacted into law by Colorado's first territorial legislature, "by which," opined an observer, "millions of dollars [were] saved to actual settlers from the grasp of speculators."[64] Water claims were also part of agricultural claim club practice, with at least one setting limits measured in feet of fall similar to those found in the miners' codes.[65]

Therefore, rather than seeing Colorado water law as originating no further back than the mining camps, with the appropriation doctrine springing fully grown, Athena-like, from the heads of the miners; viewing it as a spontaneous response to the arid conditions of the Colorado plains; or describing it as a natural outgrowth of the Spanish and Mexican law formerly in force in the region, it would be more accurate to describe miners' laws, claim club regulations, and the appropriation doctrine as part of a complex of pro-settler and anti-speculator laws and rules prevalent in mid-nineteenth-century America, particularly in the West.[66] Viewed this way, the appropriation doctrine can be seen for the land-reform legislation it was, a sort of extension of the Homestead Act to water, aimed at preventing "monopoly" control of water supplies by allowing "actual settlers" to trespass on riparian lands and divest them of their common-law water rights. Aridity was important, of course, for whereas land retained its preeminence in the concerns of reformers in the well-watered east, where surface water was neither scarce nor particularly critical for agriculture, the value of water for agriculture in arid regions elevated its value to a level even beyond that of land in the West, making it a prime focus of agrarian agitation and lawmaking. As put by George Haight, a California lawyer, "Unlike the Eastern States, we have large areas threaded by a single stream of water. . . . If the local laws should permit these arteries of wealth and health to be monopolized by the few who chance to control their banks, to the entire exclusion of all other and adjacent land owners, they would be doing a great wrong under the shadow and protection of law."[67] Legal protections were needed to form "a perpetual barrier between that struggling agriculturist and those who would take advantage of our climatic conditions to reduce him to serfdom."[68]

The rules of the appropriation doctrine, as it developed in its pure, Colorado form, were thus shaped by the same ideology that favored the claims of settlers over speculators in the general debate over disposition of the public domain. The Lockean and Jeffersonian view of acquisition from the public domain, requiring work as a condition of appropriation and limiting the scope of rights to the amount a person could directly use, led directly to the use requirement for water claims, both in its direct form and indirectly through the miners' laws' limits on appropriations calibrated to the amount one person could reasonably use; and the abrogation of riparian ownership of surface waters was a manifestation of anti-monopolism and anti-speculation ideology, directed against the potential concentration of water wealth in the hands of those who could afford to buy up the riparian lands of the arid-country streams.

The water law of Colorado Territory, and subsequently of the State of Colorado, drew from the same sources as did the miners' laws. As we shall see in the next chapters, they expressed, too, the same agrarian, anti-monopoly, and anti-capitalist ideology.

CHAPTER 3

EARLY COLORADO WATER LAW AND *COFFIN V. LEFT HAND DITCH CO.*

Background

Coincident with the organization of the first mining districts at the Gregory Diggings and elsewhere in the "Pike's Peak" region, residents of the region were attempting to organize a territory that would gain federal recognition. The short-lived Territory of Jefferson, which held a legislative assembly in the winter of 1859–1860, failed in this respect, and was effectively terminated in 1860. Recognition of the Colorado Territory came in 1861, and with it the beginning of regular legislative sessions and territorial courts.[1]

As settlement of the territory intensified, agriculture began to replace mining as the sector principally concerned with and responsible for the use of water. It was at this point that the territorial legislature began to give shape to the Colorado Doctrine as a body of official law, moving beyond the view of water as a special sort of mining claim. Nearly every legislative session of the territorial and early statehood period added to the body of statutory law dealing with water rights and irrigation. The legislative acts, as well as the state constitutional convention in 1876, strove to regulate water use across multiple dimensions: property rights in the resource, provisions for access to water sources, the manner of use, and corporate regulation. Though water litigation in this period (from the territory's inception to the *Coffin* case in 1882) seems to have been relatively infrequent, the few reported cases help illuminate how Colorado water law was viewed by the judges who shaped it.

Territorial Legislation

The Jefferson Territory's first (and only) General Assembly met in Denver from November 1859 to January 1860. In a short "Act Concerning Irrigation," the legislature set out the law of water rights for irrigation, drawing upon all of the basic rules that characterized the mining laws. Non-riparian irrigators were explicitly given the right to divert water to their fields, as well as the necessary rights of way for entering riparian lands and building dams and ditches on them (with liability for damage thereby caused). Appropriation amounts were limited, in an indirect fashion, by a requirement that the water actually be used for irrigation and by limiting irrigated farm sizes to 160 acres. As in the mining codes, potential conflicts among irrigators were to be resolved by reference to the priority of appropriation.[2]

A year later, the new Colorado Territory also passed an irrigation statute at its first legislative session. This enactment for the most part remained the basic statute regulating the appropriation of water in Colorado during the territorial period and well into statehood.[3] The common-law riparian monopoly on stream waters was abolished, though the location of the irrigated land still seemed to retain some relevance:

> Section 1. That all persons who claim, own or hold a possessory right or title
> to any land or parcel of land within the boundary of Colorado Territory,
> ... when those claims are on the bank, margin or neighborhood of any
> stream of water, creek or river, shall be entitled to the use of the water of
> said stream, creek or river, for the purposes of irrigation, and making said
> claims available, to the full extent of the soil, for agricultural purposes.[4]

The circumscribing of the class of eligible claimants to those in the "neighborhood" of the watercourse may have reflected lingering riparian-law sentiment in favor of local use of the resource.[5] Nevertheless, the thrust of the section was the entitlement of all irrigators in the relevant region to divert water for irrigation, regardless of whether they possessed land directly adjacent to the stream, and regardless of their legal title to the land—nothing less than a direct (and uncompensated) attack on the vested rights of riparian owners. Other sections of the act reinforced this policy by legalizing trespass on riparian land, ensuring not only that those not situated directly adjacent to the stream or with too little waterfront along their claim would have a theoretical right to divert water, but also that they would not be disadvantaged by their location in the construction of diversion works:

> Sec. 2. That when any person, owning claims in such locality, has not sufficient length of area exposed to said stream in order to obtain a sufficient fall of water necessary to irrigate his land, or that his farm or land, used by him for agricultural purposes, is too far removed from said stream and that he has no water facilities on those lands, he shall be entitled to a right of way through the farms or tracts of land which lie between him and said stream, or the farms or tracts of land which lie above and below him on said stream, for the purposes as hereinbefore stated.
>
> Sec. 3. That such right of way shall extend only to a ditch, dyke or cutting, sufficient for the purpose required. . . .
>
> Sec. 8. That all persons on the margin, brink, neighborhood or precinct of any stream of water, shall have the right and power to place upon the bank of said stream a wheel, or other machine for the purpose of raising water to the level required for the purpose of irrigation, and that the right of way shall not be refused by the owner of any tract of land upon which it is required, subject, of course, to the like regulations as required for ditches, and laid down in sections hereinbefore enumerated.[6]

Here, as in the miners' codes, the law subjected riparian lands to easements of access and for construction of waterworks that non-riparians would require in order to realize their rights to the stream water. (Provision was also made for compensating the servient owners for damage caused by ditches running through their land.)[7] Here, too, the leitmotiv of sufficiency was evident: rights of way were created when an irrigator had insufficient riparian frontage to obtain the necessary fall or when his non-riparian lands had no other water source, and easements were to be only as extensive as necessary.

Perhaps most surprising in light of the conventional wisdom regarding Colorado water law is the section of the statute dealing with apportionment in times of scarcity:

> Sec. 4. That in case the volume of water in said stream or river shall not be sufficient to supply the continual wants of the entire country through which it passes, then the nearest justice of the peace shall appoint three commissioners as hereinafter provided, whose duty it shall be to apportion, in a just and equitable proportion, a certain amount of said water upon certain or alternate weekly days to different localities, as they may, in their judgment, think best for the interests of all parties concerned, and with a due regard to the legal rights of all.[8]

No hard-and-fast property rights according to priority or otherwise here; we find, rather, division of the resource "in a just and equitable proportion." While possibly adopted from the riparian law of the humid east, this standard more likely originated in the traditional Hispanic community ditches of southern Colorado, given the references to commissioners and rotation of water supply by days.[9]

The remainder of this section is also worthy of note:

> *Provided*, That this section shall not apply to persons occupying land on what is known as Hardscrabble Creek, a tributary of the Arkansas River; but upon said stream each occupant shall be allowed sufficient water to irrigate one hundred and sixty acres of land, if there shall be sufficient for that purpose; and if insufficient, then the occupant nearest the source of said stream shall be first supplied.[10]

Illumination of the historical reasons for this exception made for the proprietors along Hardscrabble Creek awaits further historical research. Yet there were two aspects of this special arrangement relevant to our larger discussion, both related to the ideal of sufficiency. First, the limitation of appropriation is again evident; as in the Jefferson Territory code, the amount necessary to irrigate a 160-acre homestead was a maximum. Second, in times of scarcity water was to be rationed according to a system of priority, so that at least everyone receiving water would receive the minimum amount necessary to irrigate. The apportionment, however, was based not on priority in *time of initial appropriation*, but on priority for the *upstream landowner*. This rule is worth keeping in mind as an alternative to the doctrine of prior appropriation, one that did not catch on.[11]

In the years leading up to and immediately following Colorado's statehood, the legislation dealing with water rights continued along the channels that had been carved out by the miners' laws and deepened by this foundational territorial statute: it both weakened the link between ownership of riparian lands and the ability to acquire water rights, and limited rights to the amount that could be beneficially used by an appropriator.

One apparent resurgence of riparianism begs examination. A statute enacted in 1870 declared liability for damage caused by return flow of water after its use to be "in the same manner as riparian owners along natural water courses."[12] This apparent revival of the preference for riparian owners was not, however, what it seemed; applying rather to all water users, it mandated only that liability be determined "in the same manner as" in riparian law, thus importing riparianism's principle of decision, but cut off from the context of exclusivity for riparian owners. Put another way, while Colorado rejected the eastern law's exclusive grant to riparian landowners of the privilege to own water, it limited the general applicability of priority by retaining the doctrine of reasonable use for disputes arising from damage to property caused by water use.

Much of the early regulation of water rights in Colorado arose in the context of corporate law. Lands lying adjacent to or near watercourses could be irrigated by an individual farmer, but those at a greater distance required larger and more heavily engineered projects, which in turn required investments of capital generally beyond the means of any individual farmer. To that end, ditch or canal corporations were formed, sometimes of the "mutual" or cooperative sort, in which the irrigators themselves were the shareholders and investors, sometimes as creatures of eastern or European capital, aiming to profit by selling water to farmers.[13]

Colorado's general incorporation statute of 1862 contained specific provisions dealing with ditch companies. In this statute, too, the diversion of water to non-riparian lands was permitted, yet the ambiguous language of Section 13 concerning priorities has caused historians (myself included) some confusion:

Nor shall the water of any stream be directed from its original channel to the detriment of any miner, millman or others along the line of said stream, and there shall be at all times left, sufficient water in said stream for the use of miners and farmers along said stream.[14]

This provision has been interpreted as reflecting vestigial sentiment in favor of riparian owners, a position that is consistent with the statutory language, but difficult to sustain in the wider legal-historical context: First, it is unclear why the legislature would (as discussed above) abolish priority for riparians in the 1861 session and then reverse itself the following year by giving them priority once again. Second, in the seminal *Coffin* decision (discussed later in this chapter), the state supreme court rejected the appellants' argument that Section 13 supported their contention that the riparian doctrine was in force in Colorado in the pre-statehood period. While it is possible to see the court as playing fast and loose with the statutory language in order to fit its preordained conclusion, its reading of the statute and its history seems more plausible than an anomalous riparian-tinted one: As explained by the court, Section 13 of the incorporation statute can reasonably be read as granting priority only to "any miner, millman or others" along the stream *already* using the water (as implied by "to the detriment of").[15] Moreover, the 1864 amendment to the statute, which added after "to the detriment of any miner, millman or others" the clause "who may have a priority of right," is probably best understood as a clarification, not a reversal, of the 1862 law. (In 1877 the language was completely cleaned up: "nor shall the water of any stream be diverted from its original channel to the detriment of any person or persons who may have priority of right.")[16]

It is also worth noting that under the 1862 statute, prior rights were recognized only as far as would be "sufficient" for mining or farming operations. The law gave prior appropriators a degree of preference, but, in keeping with the ethic of the miners' codes, they would not be allowed to "monopolize" the water by claiming more than necessary for their own use; the surplus would be available, for free, to other claimants.

The private acts by which the territorial legislature chartered a number of ditch companies took a mixed approach to riparian priority. Some of the early charters, while allowing the corporations to divert water to non-riparian lands, seemed to reserve a superior right for riparians if they needed the water for mining or irrigation. In others, the company's right to divert was subordinated only to those of prior appropriators, but prior claims were valid in many acts only when on lands with gold "in paying quantities."[17] The common denominator was that speculative holdings, whether by virtue of ownership of riparian land or of priority of appropriation, were not recognized; only water put to productive use supported a valid claim. The widespread provision of the miners' laws allowing persons "bringing water into the mines" a right of way over others' claims was also enacted into state law, further neutralizing the location of land holdings as a factor in the control of surface-water resources.[18]

Corporation law also addressed the issue of speculation in water. Here the legislature found itself in something of a bind. On the one hand, the developing ethic of water rights in Colorado was a commitment to spreading the use and ownership of the resource as widely as possible. On the other, as the very reason for creating a ditch company was to divert and convey more water than a single farmer could use, using economies of scale to lower the average cost to the individual, a rule limiting the amount of water that could be diverted would have frustrated these cooperative ventures. The law adapted to the exigencies of the situation without sacrificing its anti-monopoly principles by imposing two restrictions on the corporations: One was the establishment of maximum prices for water, whether by including such restrictions in the chartering acts of companies created in this way, or by delegating price-control authority to county governments.[19] The other was a requirement, the rationale and need for which might not at first glance be wholly apparent, that companies not refuse to sell at these terms to a willing buyer.[20] This was an attempt to prevent corporations from deriving rent from their control of the water by other means—for instance, by selling it only to settlers who would also buy land (a resource and market with no price controls) from the company. Commoditization of water was further discouraged by exempting from taxation ditches owned by individuals or mutual companies, but not those controlled by corporations selling water for profit.[21]

The anti-speculation and anti-hoarding aspects of Colorado water law were further reinforced at the hands of the territorial legislature through laws prohibiting waste and unnecessary diversions. An act of 1876 (still in force today), expanding an earlier law that had applied only to certain counties, required ditch owners to in general prevent the water in their ditches from going to waste, also ordering specifically:

> During the summer season, it shall not be lawful for any person or persons to run through his or their irrigating ditch any greater quantity of water than is absolutely necessary for irrigating his or their said land, and for domestic and stock purposes: it being the intent and meaning of this section to prevent the wasting and useless discharge and running away of water.[22]

This regulation, violation of which was a criminal offense punishable by fine,[23] is striking for its unequivocal shackling of the measure of the water right to the owner's needs. In effect, it reinforced and clarified the language of the irrigation statute of 1861 describing a water claim as entitling the holder to "the use of the water . . . for the purposes of irrigation."[24] It was now clear that what would come to be known as "beneficial use" was not only a condition specifying the types of uses for water that were included in the legal right (that is, irrigation) but also a measure of that right, limiting it to the amount necessary for essential uses. This limitation was notably described in terms consistent with the *Evans v. Merriweather* dictum on the possible application of the domestic-use right in arid regions.[25] More than frustration at seeing good water go to waste in an arid environment, the statute reflected a desire to stop speculative hoarding of water rights for the purpose of turning a profit.[26]

The law of water rights as laid down in the legislation of the Colorado Territory thus carried forward the main principles originating in the Colorado miners' laws: access to surface water for non-riparians and limitation of claim size. The constitution of the new state reiterated and developed these themes.

The Colorado Constitution

Colorado was admitted as the thirty-eighth state of the Union in the centennial year of 1876. Article 16 of its new constitution contained four sections dealing with water rights, under the heading "Irrigation."[27] These constitutional provisions reveal a "radical Lockean" scheme of acquisition based on use and limitations on the aggregation of private property.[28] Present were the by-now-familiar rules allowing ditch easements and providing for restraint of corporate power, as well as the priority principle, in what was a decidedly supporting role. Most importantly, the constitution set out clearly for the first time three central principles of the Colorado appropriation doctrine: public ownership of the state's surface waters, the beneficial use requirement, and the complete abolishment of riparian privileges.

Public Property

In general, the constitution enshrined the principles of Colorado water law that had been developed in the miners' codes and territorial legislation. The opening section, though, began with an innovation, declaring the waters of streams to be public property:[29]

> The water of every natural stream, not heretofore appropriated, within the state of Colorado, is hereby declared to be the property of the public, and the same is dedicated to the use of the people of the state, subject to appropriation as hereinafter provided.[30]

As noted by a U.S. Senate committee, this was the keystone of the whole edifice of Colorado water law: "Embedded deeply in constitution and statute, Colorado has recognized as fundamental the principle . . . [of] the public nature and property of all natural waters."[31]

In one respect the approach taken here is familiar. If the waters are the property of the public, they are, of course, not owned by riparian land owners; for this reason farmers had proposed a bill with similar language two years earlier.[32] Riparian rights were thus invalidated by implication, a clear invasion of private-property rights. As one delegate argued in opposition, the section "gave a man in Gilpin county the same right to the water of a stream in Weld county, as was possessed by those through whose lands it ran. This was an interference with the contract undertaken by the United States with individuals when they pre-empted land."[33] A little later, influential water lawyers put a more positive, but no less radical, cast on the matter, explaining, "The doctrine of water rights under our Constitution is a radical departure from the common law. At one stroke the aristocracy of 'riparian privilege' was swept away, and in its stead was established the *common right* of all our people to the beneficial use of water by appropriation. This was a great triumph of popular rights."[34] But why not suffice with replacing riparian title with ownership by appropriators? Why the communitarian public-property rhetoric, so at odds with the supposed frontier ethic of individualism and private property?

The conceptual punch of the section lies precisely in this public-property theory as the basis for the right of appropriation. Opening up the opportunity to acquire a water right to all members of the public was not, as one might have expected, based on a theory of the water being *res nullius,* unowned, and therefore freely available to all. It was, rather, as in riparian doctrine, the property of the public, *publici juris.*[35] Only the right to use could be acquired, and then only under conditions stipulated by the owner (through its agent, the state).[36] The recognition of public ownership, lobbied for by the territorial Grange,[37] was important for providing the theoretical and legal underpinnings for the limitations on appropriation that would be applied by the state to prevent the replacement of monopoly by riparian owners with monopoly by speculating appropriators. As explained by the economist Richard T. Ely, "the distinction between property in water itself and a private right to the use of public water . . . seems like a refinement, but experience shows it has important consequences, inasmuch as the treatment of water as public property to be appropriated by individuals for their beneficial use strengthens public control, making such control easier under American constitutional government than it is when the water itself is regarded as private property."[38]

The theoretical innovation of this section went yet one step further. The assertion of public ownership, as distinguished from state ownership, was significant for the framers, who evidently had something like the public-trust doctrine, with its limits on legislative power to dispose of a public resource, in mind for Colorado's water.[39] A proposal to have the constitution declare that "the primary right of ownership in the waters of the streams in this State is and shall be at all times in the State" was met with opposition from H. P. H. Bromwell, whose experience as a U.S. congressman and member of the radical 1870 Illinois Constitutional Convention lent him particular influence in the debates: "Bromwell was not in favor of giving an opportunity for pools to be formed to speculate in water, and did not want the Legislature to be surrounded by such crowds of monopolists. If the capitalists get hold of all the water, they will have the people by the throat. [He] did not want to see the Legislature free to do as they wanted to with all the water of the State."[40] His fellow leader of the agrarian "Granger" faction, and chair of the committee on irrigation, S. J. Plumb, agreed, saying "that the General Assembly could not be relied upon, and he wanted to get the matter as far from them as possible"; "Mr. Plumb urged that the stream should be under the control of the sovereign people, and not subject to the management and manipulations of the Legislature." The radicals' arguments carried the day.[41]

"Shall Never be Denied"

Once the question of ownership had been settled, the constitution proceeded to set the terms of acquisition of rights to use the water:

> The right to divert the unappropriated waters of any natural stream to beneficial uses shall never be denied. Priority of appropriation shall give the better right as between those using the water for the same purpose; but when the waters of any natural stream are not sufficient for the service of all those desiring the use of the same, those using the water for domestic purposes shall have the preference over those claiming for any other purpose, and those using the water for agricultural purposes shall have preference over those using the same for manufacturing purposes.[42]

The first sentence of this section, often ignored by commentators, appears as something of a puzzle. Is the directive that the right to divert water "shall never be denied" a manifestation of unbridled possessive individualism, an order that the individual's right to appropriate water never be subordinated to other societal values or principles? Such an interpretation would mark this section of the constitution as a radical break with Colorado's (albeit young) legal traditions, which, we have seen, were concerned more with widening the distribution of the water resource than with facilitating private aggrandizement of wealth.

While law has certainly known revolution, evolution is a more likely course of historical development. The initial sentence of Section 6 represented not the opening salvo of a capitalist manifesto of private ownership of natural resources, but a crystallization of one of the egalitarian principles that had been developing in the earlier miners' laws and territorial legislation: the power of any person to acquire water rights irrespective of the location of his land. The convention rejected as too friendly to speculators a proposal that the provision of the territorial legislation allowing appropriations by non-riparians, but preserving some preference for settlers within the valley, be made part of the new constitution. "Mr. Plumb said," it was reported, that "it was just this sort of thing that the committee desired to prevent. Many men had taken up lands along the streams, and done nothing with them, but were holding them in expectancy; were waiting to see if the Territory was to be a success, allowing their neighbors to do the work to insure that success. But they claimed the right to the water in the stream for the irrigation of all their lands. And the committee proposed to compel them to actually make their appropriations and go to work to help develop the resources of the Territory."[43] Or, as a Colorado lawyer explained a few years later:

> We contend that it is but natural right and justice, that the man, who in Colorado settled along the banks of a stream, and took no steps to divert the precious water to a beneficial use, *should* be subordinated to his neighbor who put his time, labor and money into ditches and reservoirs for the purpose of subduing and cultivating the arid plain; even though that neighbor may not have owned land directly on the banks of, or anywhere near the stream. That it is not right to encourage the "dog in the manger" spirit of the speculator on the banks of the stream, who will not make beneficial use of the water himself, and is not willing to allow the settler further back to get at one of the most precious gifts of the Creator—water. That it *is* right that the man further back should have the right of way given him by the law of the land to the water which he must have in order to cultivate his fields.[44]

Accordingly, the law's earlier hesitancy about totally abolishing the preference for riparian owners was now laid finally to rest, with the unequivocal declaration of the constitution that "the right to divert the unappropriated waters of any natural stream to beneficial uses shall never be denied"—even to the non-riparian proprietor.[45] Equal opportunity was the guiding principle: "Mr. Plumb said the committee desired to do away with the old doctrine of riparian ownership, so that those who should come here to settle would have equal rights in the unappropriated waters."[46]

Beneficial Use

The opening sentence of Section 6,[47] limiting the right of diversion to "beneficial uses," apparently marks the original use of this term in connection with western appropriation doctrine, but in this matter, too, the novelty was in the language, not in the underlying theory. Though in recent years some have focused on the requirement's potential as a doctrinal vehicle for invalidating socially and environmentally wasteful uses, it originally had little to do with this issue; practically all uses qualified as beneficial under the law, economical or not.[48] Rather, consistent with the distributive ideologies running through miners' and territorial law, the doctrine was a way of limiting speculation and concentration of wealth in water and encouraging its wide distribution: first, by preventing legislative giveaways of water rights; and second, by limiting the amount that could be acquired by any one irrigator to the amount actually needed to water his or her crops at the time of appropriation, as opposed to the amount the ditch was capable of carrying or the amount needed for all lands that could be watered by the ditch.[49] As the prominent California scholar John Norton Pomeroy explained:

> The system places an obstacle in the way of a prior appropriator's obtaining an exclusive control of the entire stream, no matter how large; and secures the rights of subsequent appropriators of the same stream; by requiring that a valid appropriation shall be made for some beneficial purpose, presently existing or contemplated; and by restricting the amount of water appropriated to the quantity needed for such purpose; and by forbidding any change or enlargement of the purpose, which should increase the quantity of the water diverted under the prior appropriation, to the injury of subsequent claimants; and by subjecting the prior appropriation to the effects of an abandonment, by which all prior and exclusive rights once obtained would be lost. By these means, a party is, in theory at least, prohibited from acquiring exclusive control of a stream or any part thereof, not for present and actual use, but for future, expected, and speculative profit or advantage; in other words, a party cannot obtain the

monopoly of a stream, in anticipation of its future use and value to miners, farmers and manufacturers.[50]

A Denver lawyer gave a similar explanation: "There must . . . be a present *bona fide* design or intention of applying the water to some immediate useful or beneficial purpose . . . otherwise no priority can be acquired, no matter how elaborate and complete the structures built by the would-be appropriator. An attempted appropriation for merely speculative purposes avails nothing."[51]

As we have seen earlier in this chapter and the previous one, earlier Colorado law had pushed hard on this front, with varying degrees of directness, through a variety of doctrines: not only the use requirement, but limits on claim sizes, prohibitions on waste, and the like. The beneficial use rule attempted to serve the same ends as these earlier doctrines through adoption of a flexible standard. In the absence of the use requirement, the first to arrive in a watershed could have monopolized all the river's water by diverting its entire flow, like Boone in Professor Freyfogle's fictional Aridia.[52] The use rule, however, as enforced by Colorado courts, prevented this by insisting upon the use requirement as an essential component of appropriation, ruling that diversion alone, without necessity and use, could not create or maintain a water right.[53]

Viewed in this light, beneficial use is a necessary derivative of the doctrine of appropriation. The right of any landowner to appropriate water, based as it was on the policy of preventing monopoly by riparian owners, could arise only if the appropriator meant to use the water, not hoard it for later resale; otherwise, the new regime of rights would just replace one monopoly with another.[54]

Beneficial use was not, as has been mistakenly argued, an exotic graft of eastern origin, but an organic part of western appropriation law from its inception.[55] It was a condition imposed by the owner of the water, the people.[56] Though some commentators, it should be noted, saw beneficial use as beginning to approximate the eastern law of reasonable use,[57] they saw this similarity as a convergence rather than as one doctrine deriving from another. Moreover, their view is another indication that the innovation of the Colorado Doctrine was seen as having little to do with creating clarity and certainty in water rights.

Priority

The next clause of Section 6, the one on which attention is generally focused, enacted the principle of priority of appropriation into Colorado's supreme law. As noted before, temporal priority was a feature of the distribution of water rights in many miners' codes and in territorial law, though in a supplementary capacity. Here, too, the auxiliary nature of priority in time as an element of water law is apparent on the face of the constitutional text, where it is relegated to half a sentence in the middle of the second of four sections dealing with water rights. Nonetheless, this element of the water law of Colorado has been given great prominence in subsequent writing—indeed, "prior appropriation" is today shorthand for the entire system of water law in the western United States—an anachronism when treating the legal history of the region.[58] The element of priority, though, has been sorely misunderstood.

To place the rule of priority in proper context, consider the alternatives available to the creators of a system of property rights in water. The doctrine of prior appropriation has been characterized as a rule of "capture."[59] The story usually told is that in privileging claims based on capture, western law opted to privatize public rights based on the morally dubious principle of priority in time, as opposed to the eastern system of riparian law, which preserved communal ownership of the water resource.

The focus on capture, however, obscures the true nature of the choice faced by Colorado's lawmakers, a choice between several versions of the capture rule. As Richard Epstein has pointed out, riparian doctrine, no less than western water law, also represents a regime of first possession, since under it a claim to water rights rests on ownership of riparian land, which in turn is acquired by first possession.[60] If Professor Epstein's argument seems overly theoretical when the imagined setting is a well-watered and long-settled area of New or Old England, it actually faithfully highlights the reality of settlement in the western United States. California law, for example, recognized riparian rights, but within a framework of priority: appropriative rights were acquired by use, riparian rights by settlement, but both were ranked by temporal priority.[61] The unjust, monopolistic holdings of Freyfogle's Boone, described earlier, would be impossible in a state hewing to the Colorado Doctrine, but they were a distinct possibility in an arid jurisdiction applying traditional riparian law. A contemporary observer made this point, contrasting Colorado law with riparianism: "Instead of having a right by priority of settlement to the whole of the stream, a man can only claim to have as much water as he has been in the habit of using."[62]

Given the widespread fear of wealthy capitalists and corporations monopolizing western water resources by laying claims to as much water-front land as possible, capture by riparians seemed like the more insidious of the two forms of first possession. Explorer and scientist John Wesley Powell warned in his survey of the western United States that a farmer obtaining title to land through which a brook ran "could practically occupy all the country adjacent by owning the water necessary to its use," and later exhorted the framers of North Dakota's constitution, "Think of a condition of affairs in which your agriculture . . . depending on irriga-tion, is at the mercy of twenty companies, who own all the water. They would laugh at ownership of land. What is ownership of land when the value is in the water?"[63] Instances abounded of ranchers and land companies controlling hundreds of thousands of acres by acquiring title to a few choice riverfront parcels. A Colorado rancher, for example, testi-fied to a federal commission that "wherever there is any water, there is a ranch. On my own ranch [of 320 acres] I have 2 miles of running water; that accounts for my ranch being where it is. The next water from me in one direction is 23 miles; now no man can have a ranch between these two places. I have control of the grass, the same as though I owned it."[64] It was estimated that another rancher's 80,000 acres of riparian land gave him de facto possession of half a million more.[65]

Contemporaries thus saw riparian rights as the tool of monopoly and oppression. One critic complained, "The land interests and water rights are necessarily connected. If the latter is in the hands of irrigation companies, and the land in the hands of individual farmers, the farmers will be at the mercy of stock companies, and monopoly will become a burden to the people. . . . When we permit a foreign rule of law to be applied to land tenure . . . that fosters greed, favors monopolies, gives to the few what nature intended for, and the law should give, to all, we permit an injustice to our people."[66] And another: "The English law . . .

has been justly denounced as 'an infamous law in an arid land.' There water is as gold. . . . The man who 'owns' or controls it by virtue of his ownership of riparian lands practically owns all the land within reach of the stream which might be made productive by the diversion of its waters. Through the power he derives from the English common law he may put an absolute veto upon the progress of the country, or, by permitting progress on terms of his own naming, may levy tribute upon his neighbors and unborn generations for himself and his heirs forever."[67]

The central thrust of Colorado water law was the abolition of this injustice, replacing the rule of capture of the resource by a limited group of landowners with a rule that gave equal opportunity to all to share in the resource. As one radical politician put it a little later, "It is a principle in equity that when all are equal in right, he who is prior in time is prior in right."[68]

Abolishment of the riparian privilege, however, opened the way for a different sort of monopolization by capture, the effective control of a watercourse by upstream owners, the form of priority one writer later called "higher-ority."[69] Some early northeastern cases had held the irrigation right of an upper riparian proprietor to be superior to that of his downstream neighbor, even if the downstream use had preceded the upstream by decades.[70] Though courts mainly rejected this view in favor of the reasonable use doctrine by mid-century, mainstream riparian law, as reflected in *Evans v. Merriweather*, continued to give absolute preference to the upstream owner as far as "domestic" uses were concerned.[71] A decade before *Coffin*, at least one western court had held that the common law of riparianism had been abrogated in favor of the right of upstream proprietors to divert water at the expense of lower users, regardless of temporal priority.[72] In Colorado itself, the special provision for Hardscrabble Creek in Colorado's irrigation statute of 1861 had similarly favored upstream users.[73] If the primary impetus for the adoption of the criterion of priority in time of initial appropriation was the desire to prevent monopoly by riparian landowners, a secondary concern was extracting streams from the grip of the upstream owners on whose lands the sources of the stream were located, who would be vested with de facto control of the entire stream, were no new system to replace the abolished riparian rules. As one early study noted, "Without some sort of general regulation and control the ditches farthest up the stream would take what they need, those lower down would take what was left."[74] This generally submerged current of concern rose to the surface in the Jefferson Territory irrigation statute, which recognized the rights of prior appropriators specifically as against a "person or persons making subsequent claims *above* said first claimant."[75]

Conflict between the priority and "higher-ority" principles broke out in several Colorado watersheds in the 1860s and 1870s. David Boyd, a member of the Union Colony at Greeley (see Fig. 5), described the clash with the settlers of Fort Collins, up the Cache La Poudre from Greeley: "The Collins parties were told that if their policy of the ditches highest up stream taking what they wanted was the one to be pursued, then we would go above them, and there would result an interminable and exhaustive race in which the greatest numbers and the largest purses would come out the winners. . . . It was finally agreed that they would let us down some water to save the most valuable things in Greeley. A promise they did not keep nor mean to keep. . . . A general rainstorm came in about a week afterwards and saved us; but from this day forth we had set our hearts on having some regulations looking towards a distribu-tion of the waters of the state in harmony with the principle of priority of appropriation."[76] Indeed, the experience of the influential settlers of Greeley and Fort Collins seems to have been a driving force behind the adoption of legislation for the enforcement of priorities a few years later.[77]

The final form of capture invalidated by the priority doctrine was a type commonly associated with the word "capture" today—capture of the resource by powerful interests, through political influence. In the earliest days of the Colorado Gold Rush, some companies had been given monopolies to be the exclusive suppliers of water in a certain area. This type of grant of special privileges to corporations was anathema to Jacksonian anti-corporation and anti-monopoly sentiment, running afoul too of the radical Lockean belief that property should be earned by labor, not by political connections (see Chapter 2). The adoption of priority of appropriation as the rule for acquiring water from the public domain meant that these types of giveaways would be proscribed (and even voided retroactively).[78]

Figure 5. Irrigation ditch leading into Greeley, Colorado, 1870. Courtesy
Denver Public Library, Western History Collection, X-9069.
The crisis created by diversions at Fort Collins, upstream, motivated leaders to
push for legislation clarifying water rights based on priority.

Having avoided the pitfalls of monopolization by riparian, upstream,
or well-connected owners, why, it might be asked, did Colorado law
adopt a rule of capture at all? Why not recognize the right of all citizens
to share in the valuable surface-water resources of the state? The answer
lies in the particular form of the distributive ideology expressed in
Colorado water law, discussed in the previous chapter—equality modified
by sufficiency. As in the miners' laws, equality of opportunity to claim
water rights was the rule so long as enough water remained to satisfy the
needs of all claimants, but not when it would dilute the water rights to
the point where they were too small to be sufficient for reasonable use.
This point was made clearly by Nathan Meeker, the influential journalist
who led the settlement of the cooperative Union Colony at Greeley, the
first large-scale irrigation undertaking in Colorado: "The Larimer *Express*
does not like the principle that is proposed for the new constitution that

'priority of appropriation' gives priority of right to water for irrigation. . . . Now, to divide the water among all who ask for it, is as all know who are used to irrigation, to reduce the supply so that no one will have sufficient to do any good, and this, in effect, destroys farming. . . . Thus, it would appear that there is no way in which the question can be settled so well as acknowledging the doctrine of priority of appropriation."[79]

A farmer's letter to the editor a few years later, opposing equal distribution of water, made a similar point: "Do you propose to destroy a section of natural farming and grass lands that is already improved, by directing the streams into the plains, in hopes of benefiting and making another farming section? . . . To say it is unjust does not fit the bill—it's first-class thievery. You had just as well follow the Platte and other streams down and burn everything in the form of improvements, for they will most assuredly be worthless to the owners if people and companies are encouraged to take out ditches with the assurance that there is to be a division of water to all ditches, no matter how much or little may be the supply."[80] So did the Colorado Court of Appeals, giving its account of the adoption of prior appropriation by the first Colorado settlers:

> The country was without law, but each individual brought with him the principles of equity and justice which were a part of his education. It was soon found that the water of the streams was inadequate to supply all the land. They found a new climate, new conditions calling for new laws applicable to the conditions. . . . In time . . . a series of rules or laws were adopted . . . embodying principles of equity and justice. They were recognized and obeyed, the settlers recognizing, as before stated, a fact which later corporations and settlers have not yet apparently recognized, or, if recognized, have disregarded, that the supply of water in the streams was not sufficient for all the land. Instead of parceling it out generally and making it practically valueless to any, following the course of California and other earlier settled territories where the same conditions existed, they adopted the only rule founded in equity that could be rightfully adopted in the premises, viz., that of prior appropriation, such appropriation to be controlled and limited. Such prior appropriation was so much as could be beneficially used upon the land for which the appropriation was made.[81]

Eastern common law avoided the necessity for seniority-based rationing only by restricting water-right ownership to those owning riparian land. The price of abolishing qualifications for entry to this club, thereby opening to all the opportunity to acquire a water right, though, was the imposition of an effective limit on the number of members through a different criterion.[82] "First in time" represented not a choice in favor of any ethos of capture particular to the western pioneers; it was rather, as in the miners' codes, an application of the traditional principle of equity favoring an earlier claimant over a later one in cases of conflicting property claims.[83] Though all had the right to use water, it was incumbent upon each to desist if his diversion conflicted with that of an earlier appropriator.[84]

The principle of priority, then, was not the cornerstone of Colorado water law at its foundation (though in practice it may have become dominant in later years). As late as 1892, the state supreme court could survey the differences between the Colorado Doctrine and riparian law and, while emphasizing public ownership of water in Colorado, fail to mention the rule of temporal priority.[85]

Nor was priority an absolute rule. The prior right of the earlier claimant was a severely restricted one, subject to the limitations of beneficial use. Moreover, the second half of the irrigation article's Section 6 further subordinated the principle of priority to that of necessity in the allocation of property rights in water, with more essential uses taking preference over those less so (domestic over agricultural, agricultural over industrial); priority of appropriation is the rule only "as between those using the water for the same purpose." Here was a particularly vivid expression of the law's concern for necessary uses, previously encountered in the miners' codes and in the territorial legislation (as well as in riparian law).[86]

As indicated by its place in the constitutional text, priority was an auxiliary principle, meant to ensure that the abolition of riparian and upstream privileges and concomitant opening to all of the opportunity to acquire water rights would not result in a tragic dilution of the resource to the point where no individual irrigator would be able to appropriate a right sufficient to irrigate his crops. Nor was it viewed as facilitating privatization of the resource. Rather, it was seen as an expression of public ownership, as indicated by Governor Elbert's message regarding desirable irrigation legislation to the Territorial Legislature two years before the state constitutional convention: "First.—That to the State should belong the water of its streams and the control of its distribution among canal owners. From this it would follow that no one would be allowed to divert the water from the natural bed of the stream to the injury of those having previously acquired and vested rights."[87]

Significantly, priority's most vocal supporters were the radical farmers, who would come to demand its enforcement as part of an agrarian and pro-labor program of government ownership of railroads and telegraphs, inflationary monetary policy, the secret "Australian" ballot, and the like.[88]

Rights of Access

In yet another example of the tendency to distill the rich brew of Colorado's water law into the simple proposition of priority, discussions of the state's constitutional appropriation doctrine usually refer only to the aforementioned Sections 5 and 6 of Article 16 (or Section 6 alone), while neglecting the following two sections.[89] This narrow view flies in the face of the structure of the constitutional text, in which these four sections are grouped together under the common heading of "Irrigation," and is lacking on the substantive plane as well. As previously discussed, territorial legislation, following in the footsteps of some of the miners' codes, had bundled the formal abolishment of the riparian monopoly on water rights together with the recognition of easements in favor of non-riparian claimants. The new state constitution followed suit, declaring:

> All persons and corporations shall have the right-of-way across public, private and corporate lands for the construction of ditches, canals and flumes for the purpose of conveying water for domestic purposes, for the irrigation of agricultural lands, and for mining and manufacturing purposes, and for drainage, upon payment of just compensation.[90]

As in the territorial water legislation, the right of way for ditches was a critical piece in the constitutional program of effecting a wide distribution of rights in surface water. Section 6's exhortation that the right to divert unappropriated water to beneficial uses "shall never be denied," aimed at breaking the monopoly of riparian ownership under the traditional common law, would have been a dead letter if those owners had retained the right to exclude other potential water users from their land.[91]

The threat was real, as indicated by a contemporary historian's description of the "water-grabbers" of Colorado, who "fenced off the rivers from the common use of the people."[92] Hence the constitution further invaded private-property rights by granting easements for the construction of water works to the general public, thereby guaranteeing that the policy of equal access to water for all would not be hobbled by impediments thrown up by recalcitrant riparian landowners.[93]

Control of Corporations

Though the constitutional convention failed to fully meet the Colorado Grange's demand that the legislature be prohibited from granting charters to water corporations other than those controlled by "actual settlers," it did enact a provision allowing the legislature to revoke or annul charters injurious to the citizens of the state, one of several "Granger" provisions limiting the power of corporations in general.[94] It was yet more aggressive on other issues.

Section 8 of Article 16, the final section of the chapter on irrigation, endorsed another element of territorial legislation, granting county commissioners the authority "to establish reasonable maximum rates to be charged for the use of water, whether furnished by individuals or corporations."[95] The elevation to constitutional status of maximum prices for water, like that of the preceding section, reflected an understanding that the abolition of monopoly control of surface waters required not only a formal statement of public ownership and the right of all to divert water to beneficial uses, but concrete regulatory steps that would prevent the concentration of control over the resource in the hands of a powerful few. The interests of settlers were also given preference over those of investors in the constitution's article on revenue, which constitutionalized the statutory exemption from taxation for only those ditches owned by individual irrigators or consumer-owned mutual corporations.[96]

With the rise in the early decades of statehood of increasingly ambitious irrigation schemes developed through corporate vehicles, issues connected with irrigation companies were litigated often before the state's supreme court. As will be discussed more fully in the next chapter, the court's jurisprudence in this area recognized the conceptual connection between the doctrine of appropriation and the regulation of corporate control over water, thereby affirming that the water-law subdivision of the Colorado Constitution was an integral whole, a unified reflection of a vision of egalitarian distribution of property in water. Let us turn now to an examination of the early water-law decisions of that court, including the leading case of *Coffin v. Left-Hand Ditch Co.*

Case Law Before *Coffin*

The first reported Colorado case dealing with the question of water rights was *Yunker v. Nichols*, decided in 1872 by the territorial supreme court.[97] At issue was neither the right to divert water nor the ranking of rights in terms of priority of appropriation, but the right of an irrigator to an easement for a ditch bringing water to his fields over the intervening lands of another. The immediate question presented to the court was whether a landowner's parol (that is, oral) grant of a ditch right of way was invalid under the statute of frauds. The supreme court held it was not, with each of the three justices resting his decision upon slightly different grounds. As the judicial pronouncements revealed much about the principles and purposes of Colorado's water law, I will quote from the opinions at some length.

The lead opinion was written by the respected Chief Justice Moses Hallett, who had left his Chicago law practice for an unsuccessful stint as a Colorado miner before establishing himself as one of Denver's first lawyers.[98] He based his decision on the territorial irrigation statute of 1861, which, as mentioned above, provided for private rights of way for the construction of water ditches.[99] Responding, it seems, to counsel's argument that the statute's imposition of rights of way amounted to an unconstitutional taking of the servient owners' property rights, the chief justice argued that the rights of way were, in effect, easements of necessity, to which all lands are inherently subject by law.[100] Though not mentioning *Evans v. Merriweather*, his reasoning in support of this contention was similar to the Illinois court's speculation on the possible extension of the domestic-use exception in arid lands:[101]

> In a dry and thirsty land it is necessary to divert the waters of streams from their natural channels, in order to obtain the fruits of the soil, and this

necessity is so universal and imperious that it claims recognition of the law. The value and usefulness of agricultural lands, in this territory, depend upon the supply of water for irrigation, and this can only be obtained by constructing artificial channels through which it may flow over adjacent lands. . . . In other lands, where the rain falls upon the just and the unjust, this necessity is unknown, and is not recognized by the law. But here the law [the 1861 statute] has made provision for this necessity, by withholding from the land-owner the absolute dominion of his estate, which would enable him to deny the right of others to enter upon it for the purpose of obtaining needed supplies of water. . . . It may be said, that all lands are held in subordination to the dominant right of others, who must necessarily pass over them to obtain a supply of water to irrigate their own lands, and this servitude arises, not by grant, but by operation of law.[102]

This earliest judicial exposition of the Colorado Doctrine thus focused not on the private-property right of exclusion, but on the limitations the law imposed upon private property (in land), subordinating it to the necessities of others.

Justice James Belford's opinion also explored the element of necessity. Analogizing the irrigation-ditch easement to the traditional way of necessity over the land of another, he found that the two institutions rested on a common moral foundation: "the good and salutary principle that the right of a man in the use of his property is restricted by a due regard to the equal rights of others."[103] Just as the way of necessity was necessary to ensure that all had access to their lands, this "due regard to the equal rights of others" dictated that privately held land be subject to an easement for a water ditch in order to secure to "all persons" in the neighborhood the use of water from a certain stream.[104] With the institution of private property harnessed to the goal of diffusion of the water resource among as many people as possible, the exclusionary aspect of property must give way.

The third justice, Ebenezer Wells, also justified the result in terms of necessity, and yet more decisively: "It seems to me . . . that the right springs out of the necessity, and existed before the statute was enacted, and would still survive though the statute were repealed. If we say that the statute confers the right, then the statute may take it away, which cannot be admitted."[105] The quasi-constitutional status he would have given the right of access to water is an indication of the seriousness with which Colorado jurists of the time took the goal of a broad distribution of property entitlements in water.

This was a radical decision, as noted by the great water scholar Samuel Wiel: "It is a rather socialistic doctrine, forgetting that we have constitutions guaranteeing private property rights, to say that if you want another man's property badly enough you have only to take it, or that a court will listen to an argument that you have a greater desire or necessity to possess my property than I have."[106]

It is worthwhile noting that while today the Colorado Doctrine of water rights is generally traced to the *Coffin* decision,[107] this was not always so; early commentators, as well as the author of *Coffin*, found its earliest expression in *Yunker*.[108] The issue is not one of mere pride of place, for on it depends our conception of what the Colorado Doctrine embraces. The convention that *Coffin*, decided ten years after *Yunker*, marks the beginning of the doctrine reflects a narrow conception of Colorado water law, focusing on appropriation. The older (and, it is submitted, sounder) view, recognizing *Yunker* as the foundational decision, gives the variety of rules embraced under the Colorado Doctrine their due, and recognizes that the primary aim of the law was to effect equal access to water resources, to which *Yunker* contributed by forcing riparian landowners to allow access over their lands to streams.

The foundational nature of the element of necessity in the Colorado water right was evident again a few years later in *Schilling v. Rominger*, a case noted for featuring the first reported judicial endorsement of the temporal priority principle in Colorado appropriation law (though the supreme court ruled against the prior appropriator, imputing to him a waiver of his rights).[109] Commentators, however, have not remarked upon the fact that the plaintiff saw it necessary to include in his complaint, and the court in its statement of the facts, the detail that the creek in dispute was the sole source of water for the parties, highlighting the assumption of Colorado's irrigation pioneers that appropriation alone, without need, could not establish a water right.

The case of *Crisman v. Heiderer*, decided a year before *Coffin*, is remarkable for its display of the staying power of riparian law principles in the prior appropriation environment.[110] Indeed, the facts were reminiscent of those typical of cases in the northeastern states a half-century before, in which disputes often centered around flooding and other damage caused by dams built by riparian owners.[111] Crisman, the owner of a flour mill, had erected obstructions in the South Platte, some way upstream from his land, in order to channel more water toward his mill race. As the changed flow of the river threatened to flood Heiderer's lands upstream, he himself built a dam in order to redirect the water away from his land. Each party sued to have the other's obstructions removed.

The state supreme court could have resolved the dispute in accordance with the norm of "first in time, first in right," supposedly the dominant ethic of western water law, wholly vindicating Crisman, who had been first to use the water as well as the first to place his obstructions in the stream. Such an approach had, in fact, been applied by English and American courts in similar cases before their adoption of the reasonable use doctrine.[112] Even Crisman, though, did not take an extreme position, arguing that the extent of his prior right was based on the amount necessary and sufficient to run his mill.[113]

The Colorado Supreme Court, too, ruled that prior rights were not absolute, holding that while Crisman, the prior appropriator, had been justified in taking steps to ensure a steady supply of water to his ditch, he had gone too far:

> The most reasonable mode of effecting the object must be adopted, and it must be done in such a manner as to occasion as little damage as possible to the owner of the adjoining premises. . . . The great maxim of the law 'sic utero tuo ut alienum non loedas,' applies with as much force to the enjoyment of water rights as to rights of any other description.[114]

The argument here, limiting the rights bundled into a water right to those strictly necessary for its enjoyment, is consistent with Colorado's "appropriation doctrine," harking back to the territorial irrigation statute's limitation of appropriators' ditch easements to the extent "sufficient for the purpose required" and even the miners' codes' definition of water rights in terms of the length necessary to get a certain measure of head.[115] In its attempt to harmonize the water use of the parties, and rejection of absolute priority for the earliest water user, it is also tellingly reminiscent of the reasonable use doctrine, which today's conventional wisdom teaches the Colorado Doctrine had abolished. This "eastern" approach was evident as well in the court's overturning of the lower court's injunction ordering Crisman to remove *all* obstructions from the river: "Such a rule," said the court, "is inequitable and would work hardship";[116] Crisman was allowed instead to divert the flow of water in a manner that would cause minimum damage to Heiderer. Furthermore, the elements of necessity and reasonableness are blended seamlessly in the opinion, an indication that for the Colorado Supreme Court a year before its seminal decision in *Coffin* there was no tension between the western water right and the norm of reasonable use.[117] In fact, by 1881 the reasonable use rule had a venerable Colorado pedigree for situations of this sort, with laws as far back as those of the Gregory Diggings calling for the application of riparian law to disputes over damage from water.[118]

Coffin v. Left Hand Ditch Co.

Coffin v. Left Hand Ditch Co.,[119] decided by the Colorado Supreme Court in 1882, is generally held to mark the full statement of the Colorado Doctrine of "pure" appropriation. As with some other examples of early Colorado law previously discussed, though, the modern focus on the judicial endorsement of priority of appropriation in this decision has obscured other facets of the judgment more important at the time.

Moreover, the efficiency school of property rights' view of *Coffin* as signaling a scarcity-driven shift from common to private property is based, it seems, on a misunderstanding, particularly of the following language in the decision:

> The climate is dry, and the soil, when moistened only by the usual rainfall, is arid and unproductive; except in a few favored sections, artificial irrigation for agriculture is an absolute necessity. Water in the various streams thus acquires a value unknown in moister climates. Instead of being a mere incident to the soil, it rises, when appropriated, to the dignity of a distinct usufructuary estate, or right of property.[120]

These lines have been cited as evidencing the connection between the increased value of water in Colorado's dry climate and the need for well-specified and thus marketable property rights.[121] What at first glance seems to be an argument by the court that the increased value of water in Colorado must lead to the creation of private-property rights, though, cannot be so, for the contemporary riparian doctrine of the "moister climates" of the East already viewed water as the object of private, usufructuary property—of riparian owners. No argument, geographic or otherwise, was required to convince that water should be considered private property. As Angell's leading treatise on riparian law explained, "The right of private property in a watercourse is derived, as a *corporeal right or hereditament,* from, or is embraced by, the ownership of the soil over which it naturally passes. The well-known maxim, *cujus est solum, ejus est usque ad coelum,* inculcates, that land, in its legal signification, has an indefinite extent upwards; . . . a *stream of water* is, therefore, as much the property of the owner of the soil over which it passes, as the stones scattered over it."[122] The claim in *Coffin* is, rather, that water's special value in the West elevates it to a *"distinct"* estate, that is, one not related to the rights of riparian landowners, not "a mere incident to the soil." This, the right of non-riparians to acquire water rights, was, we shall see, the real issue at hand.

Briefly stated, the case involved a conflict between the appellants, irrigators in the "neighborhood" of St. Vrain Creek (a tributary of the South Platte, on the eastern slope of the Continental Divide), and another group of irrigators who in 1863 had built a short ditch to divert water from the main branch of the creek to their lands near Left Hand Creek (itself a tributary of the St. Vrain, giving color to their claim to be in compliance with the statutory "bank, margin or neighborhood" requirement).[123]

In upholding the rights of the ditch company representing the earlier users, the court gave its approval to the rule of prior appropriation, arguing that it had always been the law in Colorado, by force of necessity, and prior to any legislation on the subject. This statement of the priority rule, though, was neither enough to decide the case nor the crux of the decision. The question on which the judgment turned was a variation on the one of whether one could divert water from a stream to non-riparian lands. Here, some of the appellants, while farming lands in the St. Vrain Valley, were themselves technically not riparians with respect to the creek, so the issue was presented in terms of the permissibility of diversion out of the watershed.[124] Appellants argued, based on a plausible reading of Colorado's territorial water legislation, that the statutes had modified the common law of riparian rights only in extending the right to appropriate water to non-riparians within the watershed, but no further.[125] In its decision, however, the Colorado court rejected any role at all for riparian or local use as a factor in water rights, making *Coffin* the seminal decision for the "pure appropriation" or "Colorado" doctrine.

The motivation for this radical approach is illuminated by developments in western water law in the years immediately preceding the case and the arguments made by appellants. Though appropriative rights on public land had been recognized throughout the West for some time,[126] including by a federal statute of 1866,[127] their validity with respect to privately held riparian lands was still unclear. State and federal courts in Nevada had held that appropriative rights could only be valid as against other squatters on the public domain, whereas lands that had passed from public to private ownership before the 1866 statute would include any riparian rights incident to them, regardless of any use previously established by non-riparians.[128] These decisions were also understood as implying that once riparian land had been sold by the federal government, any subsequent appropriation would be subject to the riparian rights of the landowner.[129] Put another way, the sale or grant by the federal government of riparian land would revoke all prior appropriations from streams passing through it (at least if the land passed into private ownership prior to 1866).[130] These decisions, much discussed in the 1870s, were highly unpopular,[131] yet the St. Vrain irrigators relied on this line of authority and took it one step further. They argued that since Colorado had not abolished the preference for local users until adoption of the 1876 constitution, the 1866 law recognizing appropriative rights would have effect in Colorado only from that date, and all lands patented before 1876 would carry water rights superior to any based on appropriation—even if the appropriation had been made years before the riparian owner arrived on the scene.[132]

The implications of this claim were far reaching: Not only would speculators and corporations be able to reserve water rights prospectively by gaining control of riparian lands before water had been appropriated from them, but they would also have the power to oust settlers retroactively from their prior water claims by buying up riparian lands even after the settlers had been irrigating for some time.

In the climate of fear over monopolization of public lands by railroad, ranching, and irrigation companies, this argument was too much for the Colorado court to bear. Its rejection was emphatic:

> The disastrous consequences of our adoption of the rule contended for, forbid our giving such a construction to the statutes as will concede the same, if they will properly bear a more reasonable and equitable one. . . . It might be utterly impossible, owing to the topography of the country, to get water upon [the irrigator's] farm from the adjacent stream; or if possible, it might be impracticable on account of the distance from the point where the diversion must take place and the attendant expense; or the quantity of water in such stream might be entirely insufficient to supply his wants. It sometimes happens that the most fertile soil is found along the margin or in the neighborhood of the small rivulet, and sandy and barren land beside the larger stream. To apply the rule contended for would prevent the useful and profitable cultivation of the productive soil, and sanction the waste of water upon the more sterile lands. It would have enabled a party to locate upon a stream in 1875, and destroy the value of thousands of acres, and the improvements thereon, in adjoining valleys, possessed and cultivated for the preceding decade. Under the principle contended for, a party owning land ten miles from the stream, but in the valley thereof, might deprive a prior appropriator of the water diverted therefrom whose lands are within a thousand yards, but just beyond an intervening divide.[133]

The Colorado rule was clear: riparian lands would have no water right incidental to them; all landowners could acquire water rights only by use, regardless of their land's location. This was the crux of the decision and of the Colorado Doctrine for which it is generally taken as the precedent: a total rejection of common-law riparian rights.[134]

The appellants had rested their claim on an alternative, contractual, basis as well, claiming that at the time of the ditch's construction, they had refrained from legal action against the Left Hand irrigators only upon the latter agreeing (orally) that in case of insufficient water for all, the riparian farmers would have priority. Curiously, though this claim was stricken by the trial court as insufficient under the Statute of Frauds, and the supreme court seems to have been skeptical as to whether any such agreement had really been made, archival evidence available today indicates that the riparian party could have made a related, seemingly stronger claim. The handwritten minutes of the Board of Boulder County Commissioners from 1863 contain the following entry:

> Then the Left hand Ditch Co's Certificate was taken up. Said ditch Co proposes to build or take a ditch to start at a point opposite the head of the west Branch of James Creek thence down said James Creek to Left hand Creek thence down said Left Hand Creek to St Vrains Creek, water to be used for mining milling and agricultural purposes. . . . Certificate approved with the following conditions That no water shall be taken out of St Vrains Creek when it is needed in its natural channel for milling mining or irrigating purposes above where it is conveyed back to its natural channel again.[135]

Given the probable state of county-government recordkeeping in the Colorado Territory, it is not unlikely that this documentation of the condition attached to the construction of Left Hand Ditch was overlooked by the parties.[136] Nonetheless, the supreme court probably would have ignored it anyway. After all, the language of the board's stipulation is similar to the rule of the territory's general incorporation statute, a provision which, as we have seen, the court had easily brushed aside in its rejection of any preference for in-watershed appropriators.[137] It would no doubt have done the same for the ruling by the county commissioners, had it been confronted with the issue.

Once the decision was made to open up the right of diversion to all irrigators, regardless of location, the adoption of the rule of prior appropriation was relatively trivial—for what were the alternatives? Equality for all comers would have led to the dilution of water rights beyond the point of usability. Failure to recognize any legal rights in future flows would have led to a disastrous race among irrigators going further and further upstream in an effort to capture the flows of the stream, and thus the abandonment of any possibility of reliance on future rights; ultimately it would have led to monopolization by upstream owners. Prior appropriation at least had the virtue of rewarding investment in ditch building and land cultivation, while spreading the wealth relatively widely.

Lest anyone misread its decision and think that the Colorado court had sanctioned an all-out rule of capture for the state's surface water resources, the court followed up *Coffin* four months later with another water rights case, *Thomas v. Guiraud,* in which some limitations on appropriation were spelled out. Here the justices pointed out that prior appropriation alone was not enough to give the better right:

> We concede that [the prior appropriator] could not appropriate more water than was necessary to irrigate his land; that he could not divert the same for the purpose of irrigating lands which he did not cultivate or own, or hold by possessory right or title, to the exclusion of a subsequent *bona fide* appropriator.[138]

These restrictions were of a kind with the anti-speculation ideology that had earlier been expressed in the miners' codes, territorial legislation, the constitution, and, as can now be seen, with *Coffin* itself.[139] They will be discussed further in the next two chapters.

CHAPTER 4

THE REGULATION OF COLORADO WATER CORPORATIONS

Background

While Colorado law in the territorial period and the first decade of statehood had not ignored the issue of water companies, its primary concern was the threat of water monopoly by riparian proprietors. In 1887, though, the state supreme court noted that a watershed had been reached:

> The subject of water rights has always been justly regarded as one of the most important dealt with in the legislation and jurisprudence of Colorado. Hitherto attention has been mainly directed to the adjustment of priorities and differences between individual consumers; but hereafter, owing to the rapid settlement of the eastern part of the state, the *status* of the carrier and its relations with the consumer will command the most earnest and thoughtful consideration.[1]

Indeed, until about 1870, Colorado irrigation projects had mostly been built as a result of individual effort or cooperation between neighboring farmers (see Figs. 6 and 7). Farmers organized for this purpose in cooperatively owned "mutual companies," sometimes incorporated, but often

Figure 6. George L. Beam, Irrigation in the Uncompahgre Valley, near
Montrose, Colorado, early twentieth century. Courtesy Denver Public Library,
Western History Collection, GB-8090.
Shows a simple headgate used to divert water from a main canal (on right)
to a smaller ditch.

not, due, at least in part, to the farmers being "prejudiced against stock
corporations."[2] The 1870s saw the advent of larger-scale cooperative
projects, pioneered by the Union Colony at Greeley. From around 1880,
though, large corporations began to dominate, financing large projects
with outside capital. These canals, benefiting from large capital investments and state-of-the-art engineering (see Fig. 8), and the economies of
scale these made possible, sped the development of irrigation in the state,
as explained in a legal brief on behalf of Benjamin Eaton, a local capitalist: "The settler soon realizes that the only way that he can render his
land productive is to cause the waters of neighboring streams to forsake
their channels and flow in new courses over field and farm. Great main
water-ways must be constructed for many miles and expensive appliances

HARPER'S WEEKLY.
JOURNAL OF CIVILIZATION

Vol. XVIII.—No. 912.]   NEW YORK, SATURDAY, JUNE 20, 1874.   [WITH A SUPPLEMENT. PRICE TEN CENTS.

Entered according to Act of Congress, in the Year 1874, by Harper & Brothers, in the Office of the Librarian of Congress, at Washington.

IRRIGATION IN COLORADO—LETTING WATER INTO A SIDE SLUICE-WAY.—[SEE PAGE 514.]

Figure 7. Frenzeny & Tavernier, Irrigation in Colorado—Letting Water into a Side Sluice-Way, cover of Harper's Weekly, June 20, 1874. Courtesy Denver Public Library, Western History Collection, Z-4031.

The large image shows a simple headgate operable by a farmer and his hand. The wooden flume shown inset at bottom right is a more impressive feat of engineering, presumably built by some kind of collective effort, but not as massive or sophisticated as the one shown in Figure 8.

67

Figure 8. William Henry Jackson, Platte High Line Canal, after 1882.
Courtesy Denver Public Library, Western History Collection, WHJ-1403.
The High Line Canal near Denver, financed by British investors, was the focus
of much anti-corporate agitation, and its practices the catalyst for litigation that
resulted in limitations on the power of water corporations.

and management must be devised and inaugurated, before the vision is
realized. This the settler alone or in aggregation cannot usually accomplish. Capital, the hope and helper of labor must be induced to undertake the enterprise."[3]

Such investor-financed corporate canals quickly became the largest and
most important in the state.[4] Contemporaries recognized this corporate
dominance of the irrigation infrastructure as an explosive issue, part of a
larger concern over the postwar growth of corporate influence on the
economy and politics in general.[5] Some saw it in a positive light:
"Colorado is a State of corporations. In fact, without them it would be
little more to-day than an unimproved wilderness."[6]

But others recognized the potential for conflict posed by corporate
control of irrigation and viewed any attempt to profit from this control as
immoral. "Next to bottling the air and sunshine," wrote one influential

publicist, "no monopoly of natural resources could be fraught with more possibilities of abuse than the attempt to make merchandise of water in an arid land."[7] Moreover, corporate control of water posed a grave threat to hopes for western irrigation as a boon to the smallholding, independent yeoman ideal. Many influential Americans saw irrigation as a panacea for the social and economic ills plaguing Gilded Age America, with its rapid industrialization and urbanization: "The future belongs to Arid America. There alone can the population safely expand; there alone can labor win independence; there alone can a new and better civilization be erected under the impulse of the new century about to be born."[8] Irrigation, its enthusiasts believed, would reinvigorate the homestead ideal, banish monopoly, and "save the nation and the state for democracy—making possible small-scale autonomous communities, egalitarian harmony and justice."[9] It would "guarantee industrial independence, and the small farm unit, the equality of man,"[10] while breaking up large landholdings and the power of the corporations, returning power to the people.[11] Cooperative ditch-building and ownership, through the vehicle of mutual companies, would bring to these farmers the benefits of independence, self-sufficiency, and social equality, obviating the need for outside capital.[12]

To many, development of irrigation infrastructure by capitalists threatened this vision: "The water, as a matter of right, belongs to the men who till the soil, and rich corporations should not be allowed to take it from those to whom it properly and of right belongs."[13] Since land in the arid west without water was essentially without value, outside capital's control of water meant, economically and practically speaking, control of the land. As Alfred Deakin, an influential Australian irrigation official and politician, explained, "In the West, all value may be said to inhere in the water. Land is plentiful; and almost worthless. The owner of the water really owns the land, for it is useless without his supply. The quantity of available water, and not the area of a territory, defines its agricultural extent; consequently, where capitalists have built canals to lands which they do not own, and have secured the water, they have really acquired the land too. They have the farmers absolutely at their mercy, and enjoy a monopoly of the most arbitrary kind."[14] Levi Booth, head of the Colorado Grange, also warned against this danger: "These companies are taking possession of our waters, without any regard to prior rights or prior use of such waters. And if we do not look well to our rights we shall soon find to our sorrow, that we have allowed them to even rob us of our lands, for if they can take the water they thus deprive us of the use of our lands, for without water they are useless."[15]

And indeed, despite the ideals and efforts of the "irrigation movement," speculative investment capital flowed from the East and from Europe into western irrigation infrastructure. "Men began to dream," wrote Elwood Mead, an influential civil servant and one of the movement's leaders, "of a new race of millionaires, created by making merchandise of the melting snows, by selling 'rights' to the 'renting' of water, and collecting annual toll from a new class of society, to be known as 'water tenants.'"[16] During his tenure as assistant state engineer in Colorado, he colorfully described this threat of a new, corporate feudalism in a speech to Colorado farmers: "Six hundred years ago when a King of France wanted to reward a noble he gave him the waters of a stream. To-day for the noble, who was a man and could be reached and treated as such, we have substituted that pulpy individuality called a corporation, and have said here is a fertile and bounteous land; the ditch which provides its water supply holds the key to its value. Build the ditch; the water you can have for nothing; and at the same time virtually own the land."[17]

William Smythe, another of the movement's leaders, played upon a similar theme. "This attempt to fasten a water monopoly upon the budding civilization of the arid region," he wrote,

> . . . if successful, would create a system essentially feudal, since ownership of the water in an arid region is practically equivalent to ownership of the land. In this feudal system the man who owns the water is the great proprietor; those who use that water and pay him tribute are the peasants. The political influences which might grow out of such a system, and their far-reaching effect upon the future, may be readily imagined.[18]

The new fear of water tenancy played into the traditional radical invocation of "the ghosts of monarchy, aristocracy, and feudalism," already by mid-century an established trope in arguing for agrarian land policies in general.[19] Now, in the post-bellum period, the threat of feudalism was most immediately identified with the "immense and powerful corporations" of the age, as argued by a Grange leader in 1873: "Men came to see that it was only a question of time when these monopoly interests should be as absolute in their ownership of the agricultural and producing classes of the country as the nobles of Russia are of the serfs."[20]

One source of agrarian sentiment against the big canal companies was their foreignness. Xenophobia in the context of Colorado's water was intensified by the fact that most of the state's large irrigation works were built and controlled by outside capital, "from Boston, New York, and from over the sea."[21] Travellers Insurance Company of Connecticut built some of the biggest projects, especially in the south and west of the state. In the Denver and Front Range areas of the northeast, where the earlier ditches had been mostly small-scale or cooperative efforts, many of the major canals were built by the British-owned Northern Colorado Irrigation Company, usually referred to locally as the "English Company."[22] European ownership stoked locals' fears that corporate control of water would lead to renewed feudalism, with tenant farmers working the lands of absentee owners, leaving the Colorado farmer "in the position of a peon or tenant."[23] Critics made dire comparisons to the situations in Ireland and "Asiatic countries," where absentee landlords were held to oppress a downtrodden peasantry.[24] Less bombastically, Master Booth of the Grange argued, "Vast ditch companies are being formed, controlling a large amount of foreign capital—capital that has no sympathy for us or ours."[25] As one historian notes, "Even if British enterprises behaved as any American capitalistic concern would, and even if their activities were not such as to press upon every one of the exposed nerves of western agrarian anti-British feeling, their British character could never be forgotten, and it embittered any conflict. The building of irrigation works on the High Plains in the 1880s provided a rich matrix in which these animosities might luxuriate."[26]

Hostility to the canal companies and fear of feudal tenancy were heightened by the contractual terms on which the canals sold water. These standard-form contracts took one of two forms: either the sale of a perpetual "water right" or annual "rental" of water from the company.[27] Under both plans, the irrigator was bound to pay and the company was held free of liability, regardless of how much water was actually delivered, or whether any was even delivered at all, an arrangement the governor was to call "a monopoly that only the cheek of a paid lobbyist can defend."[28] In addition, the farmer's land was usually made security for his obligation.[29] Given that the farmer relied on the supply of water to grow the crops from the sale of which he planned to pay the water company, the combined effect of these terms was to make the canal company the practical owner of the farmer's land. Even the President of the United States inveighed against the dangers that this type of corporate landlordism posed to irrigators: "If this matter is much longer neglected private corporations will have unrestricted control of one of the elements of life, and the patentees of arid lands will be tenants at will of the water companies."[30]

Giving this arrangement yet greater draconian force was the water companies' practice of selling water rights based on the theoretical capacity of the ditch, usually significantly in excess of the actual available supply. Their contractual guarantee of payment in full regardless of quantity delivered was obviously an incentive to do so.[31] The farmer, in contrast, when forced to irrigate a smaller acreage than he had planned for, nonetheless had to make his payments to the company from the proceeds of his reduced yield, often an impossible proposition. This imbalance was a major source of friction between the farmers and the big canal companies. One local leader attributed nefarious motives to the companies: "An irrigation company can destroy a settler in two or three days, if it chooses. It can sell him the land, give him plenty of water for two or three years, till he gets it well improved. Then at the critical moment it can withhold the water for a few days, destroy his crops for that season, and ruin him. He is unable to meet his payments. The company takes his land, rendered more valuable by the improvements he has put on it, sells it over again, and makes money by the transaction. I am sorry to say that is being done all the time."[32] Elwood Mead, too, decried the deleterious effects of the lopsided contracts: "We need . . . to correct the abuses which have fastened themselves on our methods of distributing water, and which for the past five years have operated as a bar to immigration and threatened the very prosperity of our agriculture. I refer to the inequitable water contracts and oppressive charges of many of the canals engaged in the business of selling water. . . . I have yet to find a contract for the sale of water whose provisions are fair toward the buyer, or that offers any incentive or inducement to secure its economical use."[33] And Denver's *Rocky Mountain News*, reflecting classic Jacksonian anti-corporate rhetoric, editorialized against "corporations which, through the ownership or control of water, seek to absorb the farm lands of Colorado": "No Irish absentee landlord ever required his tenants to sign a more infamous contract than this company forced on the farmers under their canal. . . . To collect pay for water they do not carry, to demand six months' pay for two months' work, to require royalties and bonuses before they will sell water at all, to set themselves up as privileged individuals or organizations not subject to commercial losses like other people—all these assumptions are part and parcel of the arrogance which characterizes corporations, and which has been borne long enough."[34] If water were to be kept from becoming "an instrument of monopoly and extortion,"[35] it would have to be subject to the same wide distribution that the yeoman ideal required of land.

The dominance of the corporation in irrigation was thus of unambiguous legal significance, as pointed out by early irrigation economist R. P. Teele: "The number of farmers who own their own ditches and take water direct from streams, subject to no conditions but those imposed by the laws and by nature, is so small that it can be neglected. The forms of organizations and the conditions prescribed by them are almost wholly independent of irrigation law, but have fully as much influence on the development of an arid region as the laws, or perhaps more, and have a much more direct relation to the everyday affairs of the farmer. . . . The farmer is much more directly affected by the rules of his company than by the water laws of his state."[36] More specifically, the question of ownership was paramount. When ditches were owned by the farmers who used them, it mattered little whether the law recognized the user or the ditch owner as the owner of the diverted water. The advent of the outsider-owned canal corporation, however, meant that the question could no longer be avoided: Who owned the irrigation water, the canal company or the end-user?[37]

As it did for the prior appropriation doctrine in general, Colorado also pioneered the law of irrigation companies. In 1893, when the West Publishing Company issued a posthumous, revised edition of the influential John Norton Pomeroy's treatise on water rights, updated by Henry Campbell Black (of *Black's Law Dictionary* fame), not only did the added chapter on "Irrigation and Ditch Companies" cite mostly Colorado cases, but Black stated that "the laws of [Colorado] contain one of the most complete and detailed systems for the regulation of irrigation companies. And as these regulations were adopted, in part, as early as 1868, they must be regarded as constituting the original system, from which those in force in the other states were copied or imitated with greater or less closeness."[38] Other treatises, too, recognized Colorado as the leader in this field.[39]

How did Colorado law deal with the issues related to corporations and their control of irrigation water? Conventional wisdom has it that the Colorado government in this period was "dominated by a strongly entrenched business interest which dictated legislation, influenced the courts, and controlled the economic life of the state," that the prior appropriation doctrine paved the way for corporate development, and that "canal corporations were fostered rather than controlled by State law."[40] A dictum of Colorado's supreme court, though, reveals its perception of the law's bias in the controversies surrounding canal corporations:

> The courts should protect the consumer in the full enjoyment of his constitutional and statutory rights; but they should also jealously guard the rights of the carrier; and so deal with it (*the constitution and statutes permitting*) as to encourage the investment of capital in the construction of reservoirs and canals for the storage and transportation of water.[41]

In the eyes of their final arbiter, at least, the state's constitution and legislative acts were so strongly anti-capital that an extra measure of caution was called for to prevent undue deterrence of investment in irrigation facilities.[42]

But significant for this study is not only the fact that Colorado law came down consistently on the side of the yeoman farmer and the consumer in their struggle against big business, but also the doctrinal and theoretical bases on which it relied. While other American courts tended to view the issue of control of the ascendant corporations through the prism of the police power or regulation of a business impressed with a public trust, Colorado courts argued for limitations on the power of water companies based on the state's principles of property rights in water, especially the constitutional tenets of public ownership and the use requirement.

This observation about public ownership requires some clarification. Some Coloradans proposed to fight corporate control by instituting state ownership of all ditches. As early as 1874, the *Rocky Mountain News* was writing that it would "prefer a state control of all irrigation companies, since in this country the ditch owners will control the land, and, consequently all large ditch companies should be controlled at some point by the people."[43] Throughout the irrigation controversies of the 1880s and 1890s, some continued to advocate for this solution.[44] As we shall see, though, this was not the path Colorado took; instead it acted to ensure a wide distribution of the benefits of the state's scarce water by other means, consonant with the agrarian ideology of prior appropriation.

The Law of Water Corporations

How did Colorado counter the power of water companies over the state's yeoman irrigators in the closing decades of the nineteenth century? One legal tool to prevent speculative water appropriations, to be discussed more extensively in the next chapter, was the strict application of the beneficial use principle in a variety of contexts. Though the limitations beneficial use imposed on property rights in water applied equally to all appropriators, whether corporate or individual, it primarily affected—as intended—the investor-owned canal companies.

Alongside this general anti-speculation doctrine of appropriation law targeting big water corporations in practice, a number of issues considered by Colorado courts in this period pertained specifically to corporate control of water. The most significant and salient of these, to be discussed first, was the legitimacy of the rates charged by canal corporations for water supplied to farmer-consumers. Throughout the 1880s and 1890s, in both the legal and public opinion arenas, farmers and their supporters waged a bitter battle with water companies over the latter's attempts to evade price controls imposed on them by law. In several of the highest-profile American water-law cases of the period, the state's high court sided with the farmers, applying the principles of public ownership and beneficial use, discussed in the previous chapter, to limit the power of canal corporations over the water they diverted. The principles of the supreme court's water-price jurisprudence served as important precedents for the other major water-corporation issue facing the court in this period, discussed next: the power of the corporations to prorate water shortages among their consumers. Beneficial use was again the guiding principle in the next issue: the validity of legislative grants of water rights to corporations. Finally, this section notes the Colorado Court of Appeals' peculiar application of the law regarding ditch easements to canal companies, another context in which the law vindicated consumer interests.

Controversies over Water Pricing

From its inception, Colorado law imposed or allowed for price limits on water, restraining the ability of water companies to profit from the territory's water. As early as October 1861, a month before any general water-law legislation was passed, private acts chartering ditch companies included in their terms price caps on the water sold.[45] The next year, Colorado enacted its first general incorporation law, giving the power to set water rates to "the tribunal transacting county business" (later amended to the county commissioners).[46] Some later company charters also gave the commissioners the power to set a "reasonable price" for their water.[47] The state constitution, in 1876, affirmed the policy of "reasonable maximum rates" to be set by the county commissioners.[48]

Lawmakers realized, however, that price caps alone were insufficient to prevent companies from profiteering in water. Companies could easily evade the rules by keeping prices within the legal limit, but tying water supply to the purchase of land—the price of which was not controlled—from the company. To prevent this, the General Incorporation Act of 1862 required that:

> Any company constructing a ditch under the provisions of this act shall furnish water to the class of persons using water in the way named in the certificate [of incorporation] as the way the water is designated to be used . . . whenever they shall have water in their ditch unsold.[49]

This rule, too, had been preceded by similar provisions in company charters.[50]

The law requiring water companies to sell water to all, regardless of whether the buyer bought land, was criticized by some for "transferring to landowners who had invested nothing in canals part of the profit to be made by those who had so invested."[51] However, from the agrarian point of view, allowing companies to leverage water in their canals to derive profits from land would have been unacceptable: "A monopoly sought to be secured in [water] for the purpose of selling lands held for speculation would be a crying injustice."[52] A canal company was entitled to a fair return on its investment, but not to economic rents deriving from its control of the water, since the water in its ditch was not really its own.

The new General Incorporation Act passed in Colorado's first year of statehood carried over these provisions, while also attacking the hoarding issue from another angle: The law subjected companies' water rights to forfeiture if work on the ditch were not commenced and completed within specified periods, thereby limiting the ability of companies to gain control of water supplies in advance of settlement. This statute, along with the water-law sections of the state constitution, laid the groundwork for resolution of the major controversies that erupted in the 1880s and 1890s over corporate development of Colorado's water.[53]

THE 1879 IRRIGATION ACT AND THE RIGHT TO
PURCHASE WATER

Colorado's groundbreaking 1879 Irrigation Act, passed under pressure from agrarian interests (and discussed extensively in the next chapter), had as its primary goal the institution of an administrative system for determining the validity and priority of water rights, but it opened by restating the price-regulation power of county commissioners.[54] A new twist on this old theme appeared in Section 3 of the law, which granted irrigators the right to continue purchasing water at the price set by the commissioners if the price had been so set; if it had not, then the consumer could demand the sale of water at the price at which the ditch owners were then selling the water or had done so in the preceding year.[55]

In *Golden Canal Co. v. Bright*, a test case brought by farmers to challenge the power of canal companies to set what they saw as unreasonable contractual conditions, the state supreme court explained that the purpose of Section 3 was indeed to protect consumers from having to submit to onerous contractual conditions that companies might try to force on them.[56] The customer cannot be required, the court said, as a condition precedent of exercising his right to continue purchasing water, to acknowledge the equity of all the rules adopted by the ditch owner; to say that he could, would be, in a measure, to place him at the mercy of such proprietor, for he could thus be coerced into compliance with the most oppressive and unjust regulation. If the rule is fair and reasonable, and in harmony with law, his obedience thereto will probably be enforced regardless of prior approval; but the reasonableness thereof is a matter to be determined in some proper tribunal.[57]

Notably, the court justified the commissioners' power not in terms of the law of business regulation, but against the background of the public's property right in Colorado's water:

If these persons or corporations [furnishing water to farmers] were entirely uncontrolled in the matter of prices, it requires no prophetic vision to see that injustice and trouble would follow. If allowed to speculate upon that which is properly a part of the public domain and protected in the possession thereof, it is exceedingly appropriate that they should be subjected to reasonable regulations in connection therewith. Hence, the wisdom and justice of section 8 of the constitution above quoted [giving county commissioners power to set rates].[58]

Public control of water prices was thus explained in terms of the resource's being "properly a part of the public domain." Private rights were recognized, but only to the extent they served the public purpose of water distribution to as many irrigators as possible. Beyond that, public control was retained.

THE ROYALTY CONTROVERSY

Faced with public control of the rates they could charge farmers for water on the one hand, and the reservation of most federal lands for actual settlers, canal companies hit upon a new way to structure their relationships with consumers so as to increase profits: selling water only to farmers who first purchased from them what they called a "water right."[59] The holder of such a right would still have to pay on an annual basis for the water he needed,[60] but while the latter transaction was subject to the maximum prices set by county commissioners, the former was not.[61] Thus, even without technically owning any land, the companies, through their ownership of the water, would be able to force the settlers to share with them the expected profits of irrigated agriculture, in effect capturing the increased value of the land due to irrigation.[62] The investors justified their demand for economic rents on the basis of the increased value they imparted to surrounding lands,[63] and may have also felt this type of deal was necessary to help the companies recoup the large up-front capital investments necessary for the large canal systems.[64]

Though this sort of profit division might seem unobjectionable, it was seen at the time as contradicting the agrarian ethos, according to which public land should be reserved to actual settlers. While Coloradans agreed that canal companies should be compensated at a rate sufficient to pay shareholders a market rate of return on their investment,[65] the new surcharge, termed by opponents a "royalty" or "bonus," appeared to represent the monopolists' "arrogant claim of ownership in that most vital of natural elements to an arid land" and an illegitimate attempt to profit from the settlement of the public domain.[66] "Why should a royalty near Denver be worth $30 and a royalty a certain distance from Denver be worth only $5?" asked one opponent.[67] The royalty, said a Grange leader, was depriving irrigators of "their bread of life—their water rights."[68]

Farmers reacted angrily to the new contracts offered by the "evilly disposed ditch companies and their agents."[69] A particular target of their ire was the "foreign method of doing business" of the "English Company."[70] "The idea of a royalty upon water was un-American," it was said. "It was not the idea of an American brain or an American heart."[71] Opponents whipped up "folk memories of 1776,"[72] invoking the Stamp Act and Boston Tea Party,[73] with Denver's *Tribune Republican* protesting that "John Bull had lots of cheek, and that it seemed as if the old days of English tyranny were coming back."[74] When the company's foes, led by prominent members of the state Grange and other farmers' organizations, introduced an "Anti-Royalty Bill" in the state legislature, anti-corporate invective in support of the bill rose to new heights. The Grangers claimed that the corporations were working to make slaves of the industrial classes.[75] One legislator proclaimed, "There is an insolence about a corporation that I never could understand, and more so than in any in these corporations which claim to own water. They don't own a drop of it."[76] The *Rocky Mountain News* opined:

If this bill becomes a law, the death knell of the water monopolists will have been sounded. Having grown rich upon the larceny of water—the constitutional property of the people—they now hope to be allowed to continue their robbery until the people's heritage shall have been exhausted, and the entire waters of the state shall have passed into the hands of corporations as soulless as their gains are ill-gotten. . . . The anti-royalty bill has but one purpose, and that is to put an end to this larceny of water. . . . Senators . . . must vote to free the people from this outrage and oppression, or to bind them more tightly in the hands of the monopolists. Gentlemen of the senate, are you for English royalties or for the rights of American farmers? Your vote on this bill will determine.[77]

Opponents of the companies played not only upon fear of corporations and Anglophobia, but also upon other core elements of the farmers' agrarian ideology discussed earlier. In keeping with the radical Lockean or Jeffersonian ideals of property—that is, based on labor and widely distributed—they saw the state constitution's declaration of public ownership of water as guaranteeing the resource's availability for actual users, not profit-making corporations. The *News* editorialized that it "has advocated free water as a natural right. . . . It is labor that gives value to nearly everything. . . . Ditches in themselves imply no water rights."[78] It also reported speeches by supporters of the anti-royalty bill sounding on the same themes:

It was a fundamental law of the state that the natural streams were the common property of the state. Let anyone read the provisions of the constitution of Colorado and he will see that we have upset the common law. No man has a right to sell an inch of water in this state from a natural stream. A corporation doesn't own one drop of it. It belongs to the people. . . . It is repugnant to the constitution that any man should practice extortion in regard to this water. . . . Surplus water does not belong to any company. That surplus water belongs to the natural stream.[79]

Water, [even] before the laws of 1876, was clearly regarded as public property. Every person in the land has a right to that which the constitution declares he is entitled to. . . . If [charging for water rights] continues, we will have in the free state of Colorado a tenant system which has all the incipient elements of all the worst tenant systems of other and older countries. The greatest evil that threatens our nation to-day is the danger of great landed corporations and other monopolies.

Mr. Wright insisted . . . that the water, according to the constitution of Colorado, belonged to the people. It was simply the right to use the water that was granted to companies or individuals and not the right to own a single inch of it. It belongs to all of us, thank God. (Applause.) It is one of the free things in this country.[80]

If the people were the true owners of the water, it was argued, it followed that the canal companies were nothing more than common carriers, and subject to regulation as such. As put slightly later by the editor of the influential *Irrigation Age*, "We believe the water, like the air and the sunshine, belongs to the public. When a company of men 'appropriate' it and build ditches to distribute it over the land, they merely take charge of it for the public and handle it as common carriers. For this service they should be reasonably paid."[81]

Proponents of the legislation passed a resolution tying all these issues together:

Whereas . . . the lands, and what is much worse, the waters, of the state are rapidly passing into the control of corporations and syndicates, both domestic and foreign; and speculation in the unused water of the state is openly claimed as a right . . . and is exercised as such in defiance of the sense of the community and against common right; and . . .

Whereas, We are not only threatened but actually confronted by the presence of organized syndicates, taking up and intending to hold for their own gain, the waters of the state, which are the life blood of the common welfare; and keeping the public waters from the use of the people, until their own profits can be secured; therefore, be it. . . .

Resolved, That monopoly and its promoters under whatever pretext must be overthrown together, and the country rescued from the designs of such, whether cloaked under the pretense of claiming water for the future appropriation of stockholders in the pool, or of watering lands at a future day—as all such and other claims for seizing and holding the public waters for future speculation are in fraud of the common right.

Resolved, That the recent awakening of the entire people of the United States to a proper understanding of the enormous evils of monopoly in the case of the railroad management, as shown by the passage of the "Inter-state Commerce Bill," should not be despised by the legislative bodies of Colorado, who now hold in their power the future welfare of the state, that the people must be heard and not the agents of speculators.

Resolved, That the passage of necessary legislation for the protection of the people from the designs of those who are now preparing to take advantage of the looseness of the corporation law and other enactments supposed to permit unlimited aggression on the public interests is demanded now;. . .

Resolved, That the ownership of land by corporate bodies, except for the purpose of sufficient grounds for buildings and enclosures and right of way necessary for the transaction of business, is an intolerable evil fraught with ruin to the welfare of the state, and contrary to the intent of the constitution, and of the statutes of this state concerning corporations.[82]

The farmers' lobbying efforts met with success in the 1887 Anti-Royalty Act, which criminalized charging for any royalty, bonus, or premium over and above the rates set by the county commissioners, and gave the attorney general power to initiate *quo warranto* proceedings for dissolution of violators.[83]

THE *WHEELER* LITIGATION: THE ROYALTY CONTROVERSY IN COURT

In parallel, the farmers also pursued litigation in an attempt to have the courts declare the new contract structure illegal. Dr. Byron Wheeler, a prominent member of the state Grange and the new Farmers' Protective Association, had tendered to the owners of the High Line Canal (the "English Company"; see Fig. 8, p.68) their annual water rental price of $1.50 per acre for his farm near Denver, but refused to pay the further sum of $10 per acre demanded as a precondition for the annual rental.[84] When the company, as expected, refused to supply him with water, Wheeler instituted mandamus proceedings to compel them to do so. Upon losing in the district court, he appealed to the state supreme court. Wheeler apparently conceded that the up-front charges by a water company might be justifiably considered part of the legal water rates if related to the company's expenses in furnishing the water, but argued that this was not the case for the High Line's charges. As the "royalty" demanded varied not with the distance of the irrigated land from the head of the ditch or other cost-related factors, but with the supposed value of the land, the company clearly was trying to profit from the sale, not just earn a reasonable return on its investment.[85]

In its 1888 ruling in favor of the farmers' movement activist, the court's discussion ranged considerably beyond the narrow grounds on which it ultimately rested its decision—that the General Incorporation Act, requiring companies to sell unsold water at the established rate, prevented the company from charging a fee for the water beyond the rate quoted for the water rental itself.[86] Its arguments reflected those made by the anti-royalty bill's supporters, quoted above. First, the court explained, under the Colorado Constitution the canal corporation was not the owner of the water it sold:

> Our constitution dedicates all unappropriated water in the natural streams of the state "to the use of the people," the ownership thereof being vested in "the public." The same instrument guaranties in the strongest terms the right of diversion and appropriation for beneficial uses. . . .
>
> The constitutional convention . . . , in its wisdom, ordained that the ownership of water should remain in the public, with a perpetual right to its use, free of charge, in the people.[87]

Caught between the paramount ownership of the public on the one hand, and the use right of the actual user (that is, the consumer) on the other, the water company essentially had no "salable interest"[88] in the water and thus could not demand payment for the right to receive it. Such was the decree of the state's fundamental law, in particular its public ownership and beneficial use provisions. The company, the court stated, had the status of a "*quasi*-public servant or agent," a common carrier, and as such would have been subject to public control even absent the constitutional authorization of water-corporation regulation and relevant statutes.[89]

For this last strand of its reasoning the court cited the recent *Granger Cases,* in which the U.S. Supreme Court had upheld state regulation of railroads, as well as Illinois precedents on the same issue.[90] It also referred to a California case upholding regulation of canal companies.[91] Though California law recognized the water company as the owner of the water it was selling, it justified restrictions on the business as deriving from the corporation's exercise of public power, especially that of eminent domain.[92] A canal company was, in *Granger Cases* terms, a business "affected with a public interest," or, as the California Supreme Court put it, one that had "impressed upon it a public trust."[93]

The Colorado Supreme Court, in contrast, while nodding in the direction of the public-service precedents, really provided an entirely different theoretical basis for its decision: the public's constitutionally protected property right in the water. As state engineer J. S. Greene later pointed out, this principle seemed to rule out any charge by the canal companies, other than for the expense of distributing the water:

> The constitutional provision declaring "the water . . . not heretofore appropriated . . . to be the property of the public . . . subject to appropriation" is the striking feature of our water laws. It is generally admitted that what is thus *declared* law *was* law before such declaration and even from the first, so that at no time were the waters of the streams other than the property of the public. To this fundamental declaration the constitutional provision recognizing the right to charge for the use of water furnished offers an apparent contradiction; and seemingly affords a basis for the claim that the lease or sale of the waters of the streams is legitimate, since it apparently recognizes a right in water almost equivalent to ownership in the person effecting the diversion and conveyance thereof. But in giving to those portions of the Constitution relating to water the interpretations which make of them a complete and consistent whole, it becomes evident that this provision is designed to permit a charge for the *furnishing* of water rather than for the *water* which is furnished.[94]

The court relied on similar reasoning, ruling, moreover, that the principles of public ownership and beneficial use, and the ideal of broad distribution, meant that the company was powerless to impose oppressive conditions on the consumer:

> The [Constitution's] primary objects were to encourage and protect the beneficial use of water; and while recognizing the carrier's right to reasonable compensation for its carriage, collectible in a reasonable manner, the constitution also unequivocally asserts the consumer's right to its use, upon payment of such compensation. Any unreasonable regulations or demands that operate to withhold or prevent the exercise of this constitutional right by the consumer must be held illegal, even though there be no express legislative declaration on the subject. . . .

We must declare the $10 exaction illegal. Respondent [company] cannot collect of [Wheeler] the sum of $10, or any other sum, for the privilege of exercising his constitutional right to use water. . . .

In fact, the majority of those who till the soil are too poor to comply with such a demand; to say that they must do so or have no water is to deprive them of their right to its use just as effectually as though the right itself had no existence. It is true these people would not themselves be able to bring water from the natural streams to their farms, and without the carrier they might be compelled to abandon their attempts at agriculture. This consideration, however, only reinforces the position that a reasonable control was intended. The carrier must be regarded as an intermediate agency existing for the purpose of aiding consumers in the exercise of their constitutional right, as well as a private enterprise prosecuted for the benefit of its owners. Yet, if such exactions as the one we are now considering are legal, the carrier might, at its option, in the absence of legislation, effectuate or defeat the exercise of this right; and we would have a constitutional provision conferring an affirmative right, subject for its efficacy in a given section to the greed or caprice of a single individual or corporation.

Besides the extraordinary power mentioned, the carrier would also, under counsel's view, be able to consummate a most unreasonable and unjust discrimination. B. could have water because he can pay for its carriage twenty years in advance; C. could not have water because he is unable to pay in advance for its carriage beyond a season or two.[95]

Furthermore, the constitutional status of the beneficial use doctrine meant that even the legislature would be powerless to authorize oppressive company regulations:

The legislature itself cannot establish the unreasonable rule we have been considering, which enables the carrier to accomplish a wholesale discrimination between consumers, and deny, if it chooses, to a majority of them, the rights secured them by the constitution. A regulation or rule entailing such results, whether established by the legislature or carrier, must be regarded as within a constitutional inhibition. This conclusion is not based merely upon the ground of private inconvenience or hardship; it rests, as will be observed, upon the higher and stronger ground of conflict with the beneficent purpose of our fundamental law."[96]

The *Wheeler* decision was understandably hailed by farmers as a decisive victory, which struck down the canal companies' "monstrous plea" to be recognized as the appropriators of the water they diverted.[97] As long as the law prevented corporations from gaining ownership of the water, opined the *Denver Republican,* there was no danger of them gaining a "monopoly" of the region's water or land.[98] Elwood Mead elaborated on *Wheeler*'s significance, commenting that prior to the decision, "Between 1880 and 1885 many parts of the state were gridironed with canals built in advance of their need, simply and solely because of the belief that by thus securing possession of the water supply they controlled the values of all the land tributary to their ditch. You all know the results; the price of water rose steadily with the value of the land; $10, $12, $15, $20 per acre for water rights were the prices marked up each year, as the increasing tide of settlement made land more scarce and dear, until at last the charges became for most prohibitive. A fortune was necessary to begin farming in this new state; with its free land and state water. The poor man of the East seeking a home could not find it here, however much it was desired."[99] *Wheeler,* he felt, by stopping these corporate practices, would put an end to the excessive charges. In fact, it actually did even more than that, setting in motion a process by which most investor-owned canals passed into the hands of the water users.[100]

Soon after, the court took its pro-consumer stance on price regulation a step further, ruling that the maximum price set by county commissioners applied even when consumers had petitioned the commissioners for the rate after having previously contracted for water with a canal company at a higher price—despite a statutory proviso to the effect that the commissioners' action should not affect existing contracts.[101] Chief Justice Helm engaged in some dubious interpretation of the statute and contract at hand, ruling that as the contract with the water company was terminable at will by consumers, the proviso did not apply to the case. Nor was any effect given to the contractual language according to which failure of the consumer to pay the specified annual charge led to forfeiture of all claims to water in the ditch; this was explained as applying only to claims under the contract, not the consumer's constitutional right to water, which existed independently of any contract and so survived its termination. The court intimated that a consumer might not have the power to waive

his constitutional right to water in any case.[102] Once again, what is significant here is not only the court's aggressive advancement of the irrigators'
interests at the expense of the corporations', but also the legal basis for its
ruling: Colorado's water jurisprudence rested on the agrarian ideology of
wide distribution of property to individuals, as expressed in the state
constitution.

STOCK OWNERSHIP AS A CONDITION OF RECEIVING WATER

With their "royalties" banned on both statutory and constitutional
grounds, the canal companies tried once again to achieve the same result
by other means. Now their method was to require that the customer buy
stock in the company, with a certain number of shares representing a
water right.[103] Since there was no legal limit on the price that might be
charged for company shares, the irrigation companies could remain in
compliance with legal price limits on the water itself while capturing the
rents generated by irrigation through the share price. By the late 1880s,
prices had apparently gone up; while the "English Company" in *Wheeler*
had demanded a "royalty" of $10 an acre for water rights, the water
company in *Combs v. Agricultural Ditch Co.* was selling shares for $50 per
acre—prompting the observation that "truly 'John Bull' is as far behind
his 'Yankee Cousin' in this matter as in many others that we brag of!"[104]
Here, as in the royalty controversy, the Colorado Supreme Court invalidated the companies' new rules, explaining that the element of use was
not only necessary, but also sufficient, for the acquisition of a water right,
and that stock ownership was neither:

> Priority of appropriation to actual beneficial use, and not mere ownership
> of stock in a ditch company, gives the better right to such use. Individuals
> may organize a company, either by or without incorporation, for the
> construction of an irrigating ditch, and may by such means divert the
> unappropriated waters of a natural stream. They may provide that their
> several interests in such enterprise shall be represented by shares of stock.
> But neither the company nor any stockholder of the company can thus
> withhold the water from beneficial use, nor reserve it for the future use of
> junior appropriators to the prejudice of prior appropriators, nor to the
> exclusion of those who in the mean time may undertake, in good faith, to
> make a valid appropriation thereof.[105]

The policy considerations behind this ruling were made explicit by Justice Elliott:

> If the law were to be declared otherwise,—if ditch companies were at liberty to divert water without limit, and at the same time make the owner-ship of stock an absolute condition precedent to the right to procure water from their irrigating canals,—water-rights would soon become a matter of speculation and monopoly. . . . The constitution provides that the water of natural streams may be diverted to beneficial use; but the privilege of diversion is granted only for uses truly beneficial, and not for purposes of speculation.[106]

Authority for this proposition was found in *Wheeler*'s dictum that unrea-sonable regulations imposed by a water company that operated to frus-trate the consumer's constitutional right to water would be illegal, even in the absence of legislation on the subject.[107]

Interestingly, Chief Justice Helm added in his concurrence that this ruling would not apply to cooperative mutual companies, who could continue to supply water to shareholders only. Justice Elliott also implied that this might be his view, and later decisions seem to have accorded with this position.[108] From a doctrinal point of view, this qualification seems difficult to square with the invalidation of this practice when carried out by for-profit corporations, since the use requirement and priority rule should have applied equally to rights acquired from both sorts of companies. Yet the differential treatment of mutual and for-profit companies was supported by the deeper foundations of the decision. Since mutual companies were organized and controlled by settlers them-selves, and charged for shares at a level sufficient only to cover costs, there was no capture of economic rents or indirect ownership of public-domain land in their limiting sales to shareholders, and hence no need to insist upon enforcement of priorities. Here, too, the influence of radical Lockean ideology is clearly visible in the formative stage of Colorado's water law.

Also noteworthy is the fact that while the court required companies to sell unused water to non-shareholders, it let stand the practice of bundling water rights into company stock, with shares representing water rights, and control of the corporation passing to its customers when capacity (or some proportion thereof) had been reached.[109] Though economically similar to the outlawed royalty, this new practice was allowed, probably because the customers would in due course be the owners of the entire works.[110] With control of the water ultimately removed from the ownership of outside investors and placed in the hands of users, the courts felt that there was no need to intervene to prevent monopoly and to ensure broad distribution to actual settlers.

CONCLUSION: PUBLIC OWNERSHIP OF WATER

In summary, it is important to note not only that Colorado law clearly took the side of the farmers in their disputes with big canal companies over the sale of water, but also the doctrinal basis on which it did so. The power of the state to impose price controls was seen as a necessary derivative of public ownership of water, as enshrined in the state constitution. Writing of the state's reservation of the power to regulate water rates, Henry Campbell Black opined that "Such a reservation, in view of the important interests affected by such corporations, and in view of the frequent opportunities they would otherwise have of almost unlimited extortion and oppression, as well as in view of the valuable rights and franchises conceded to them, must be regarded as eminently just and reasonable."[111]

The justification was found not only in the important interests at stake, but in the view that the companies were being granted concessions or franchises in what was properly understood as public property.

Priority, Prorating, and Overselling

The 1879 Irrigation Act had among its provisions one that, though seemingly unremarkable, was to be the source of considerable mischief and litigation. The statute declared that when a canal did not receive the full amount of its water right, so that there was not enough water in a ditch to satisfy all rights holders, the water should be divided pro rata among the irrigators, "so that all owners and purchasers shall suffer from the deficiency arising from the cause aforesaid each in proportion to the amount of water to which he, she or they should have received in case no such deficiency of water had occurred."[112] Here was a partial return to one of the principles of riparianism: sharing of shortages. While not mandating that all users from a stream share the water without regard to priorities, the legislature did order sharing among the users taking water from the new, massive artificial streams that were being constructed in this period to deliver water to customers.

Prorating to share losses is arguably a fairer system than one of absolute temporal priority—if equality is the principle applied. It is also, due to decreasing marginal returns from water use at the individual irrigator level, likely more efficient in terms of aggregate wealth. Put another way, by distributing shortages as widely as possible (loss spreading), it might be possible to avoid total ruin for all.[113] The intense hostility this rule provoked among small-scale farmers and the organizations that advocated on their behalf, like the Grange and Farmers' Protective Association, thus puzzles at first glance. The 1890 platform of the farmers' Independent Party, for instance, demanded in its leading plank the recognition of priorities among co-consumers, and the Colorado Grange warned of attempts to abolish the rule of priority, which it felt was "just and should be maintained."[114] The farmers' opposition is yet more surprising in light of numerous contemporary reports to the effect that they often shared their water, in disregard of legal priorities, as well as through devices such as the mutual irrigation company.[115]

The radicals' hostility to prorating may be understood, though, on the background of the sufficiency principle, discussed in earlier chapters, and in light of the corporate-canal controversy. As in the miners' codes and the priority principle expressed in the constitution, the fear was that forced application of the equality principle would lead to the dilution of water rights beyond the point where they had any significant value for the individual user (here, the yeoman farmer). In the context of corporate ditches, this fear was heightened by the contractual terms offered by the companies, which, as discussed above, required payment by the consumer regardless of whether water was actually delivered or not. With canal companies typically selling water rights beyond their ability to deliver, the effect of the prorating rule was that the addition of each new customer to a canal directly harmed existing customers by shrinking the amount of water that would be supplied to them. At the same time, the increased revenue for the company was pure profit, since no additional costs need be incurred as a result of adding the additional customer.

Evidence of opposition to prorating appears as early as 1879, when a bill introduced in the state legislature by farming interests provided that water in a ditch would be first divided according to priority of use, and only then, among equal priorities, divided pro rata.[116] In the 1884 *Bright* test case, discussed above, the farmers argued that prorating rules in a water contract were unreasonable, and therefore void under the statute granting irrigators the right to purchase water.[117] Though the farmers won this case, the supreme court did not reach the prorating issue in its decision, and so the farmers continued to agitate. In 1887, the legislation committee of the Denver-area Farmers' Protective Association reported through Dr. Wheeler that the "Law regulating water *pro rata* should be repealed."[118] The meeting to which Wheeler reported was chaired by R. A. Southworth, an officer in the state Grange and general anti-corporate activist on behalf of small-scale irrigators.[119] The farmers decided that another test case would be their vehicle for attacking prorating, and so Southworth brought suit against the High Line Canal, alleging that it was violating his right to the quantity of water he had been using since 1881 by threatening to cut back his water allotment, in accordance with the prorating statute, if there were not enough in the ditch for all customers. This, it was alleged, was an unconstitutional taking of private property.[120] Judge Victor Elliott ruled for Southworth, and the canal company appealed to the supreme court.[121]

State Senator Isaac E. Barnum, who had been active in the fight against the "royalty" charges as well, argued the farmers' case against prorating, relying on the sufficiency principle of distributive justice:

> When a farmer has gained his priority, if the doctrine of prorating distri-
> bution is to be allowed he will have no certainty of his crops for any year,
> because the greed of ditch owners and the pressure of the claimants of
> subsequent priorities may at any time reduce his amount of water so that it
> will be practically useless for the saving of his crops. The appellants urge
> that prorating should be enforced on the theory of the "greatest good to
> the greatest number," but that theory can have no application where, as in
> this case, it would result in the destruction and burning up of everybody.
> . . . There is just so much water in the creek, and it will irrigate just so
> much land profitably and well, and it is folly to undertake to make it do
> three times that amount of irrigation. That ruins everybody. If there is not

enough water in the creek for subsequent purchasers they must not buy; they have no right to seek to establish priorities and attempt to make prior appropriators sacrifice one-third or one-half their crops.[122]

Though it rejected Southworth's suit on the grounds of defective pleadings,[123] the state supreme court this time took up the opportunity to address the apparent conflict between the principles of prorating and priority, with the justices differing on whether a carrier could legally prorate among consumers whose use had commenced at different times. Two of three justices felt it could not: since, as explained in *Wheeler*,[124] the Colorado Constitution decreed that the consumer's use, not the company's diversion, created the water right, that right of necessity must date from the time such use began. Applying the prorating statute to any rights other than those the use of which began at the same time would therefore be unconstitutional.[125] Even though under the law of common carriers the carrier must serve additional customers even if the result is a reduction in service to prior customers,[126] *Wheeler*'s reliance on the theory of ownership of the water by the public and the users, on top of the law of common carriers, allowed the court in *Southworth* to ignore this arm of common-carrier law.[127]

The court accepted Barnum's argument from sufficiency, warning of the "disastrous consequences which would ensue if the prorating statute should be made the rule for the distribution of water for purposes of irrigation, instead of the rule of priority": The earliest irrigators would be compelled "to prorate with all subsequent consumers until the amount of water that each would receive would become so infinitesimally small as to be of no practical value, and would eventually be entirely wasted before it could be applied."[128] The majority's adoption of the Grangers' legal position was thus motivated by the same concern behind the adoption of the priority principle in general: ensuring settlers a sufficient quantity of water for irrigating their land, and preventing later (and better-funded) comers from taking away their water under color of equal rights to the water.

In the minority on this point, though concurring in the judgment, was Chief Justice Helm, erstwhile herald of priority,[129] who felt that the prorating statute, though in derogation of the priority rule, was constitutional. While agreeing with the majority that the water right was created by the consumer's use, he accepted the water company's argument that a water right's priority date "related back" to the date of diversion by the corporation acting as the consumer's agent, so that the rights of all consumers from a given canal effectively had the same priority, regardless of when their actual use began.[130] Though in the minority, Helm's opinion seems to have been accepted as the applicable rule in some circumstances, as will be seen presently. Perhaps this was due to the administrative difficulties inherent in determining and enforcing priorities among irrigators from a canal, as would have been required by the opinions of the other justices.[131] In any case, Chief Justice Helm's approach of allowing prorating did not mean corporations would be allowed to oversell water rights to the detriment of their existing customers. Recognizing, rather, the potential of the prorating rule to facilitate oppression of smallholding farmers, he suggested that sales beyond the amount diverted would be unlawful and trigger appropriate (though as-yet unspecified) remedies.[132]

The prorating issue arose again soon enough. In *Wyatt v. Larimer & Weld Irrigation Co.*, a conflict between farmers using water from the Cache la Poudre River, in northern Colorado, and the canal that supplied their water (predictably enough owned by the "English Company").[133] Because of over-appropriation of the river, the company was already unable to supply the full quantity of water due to its customers, and with their cooperation it had been prorating the available water among them. Now, though, the company had plans to sell a large number of new water rights to Benjamin Eaton, one of its directors and a local representative of the British owners, as part of a deal also involving the transfer of thousands of acres of land to Eaton, to be irrigated by the new water rights.[134] (Some indication of Eaton's wealth and stature is given by his house in Greeley; Fig. 9.) The other farmers sued to enjoin the deal, as it would further dilute the value of their water rights by increasing the number of shares among which the available water would have to be divided. For its defense, the company relied on its standard contract terms, which not only provided for prorating and absolved the company of liability for shortages, but allowed it to sell water rights up to "the estimated capacity of the company's canal to furnish water."[135]

Figure 9. A. E. Dickerson, Home of ex-Governor Eaton, Greeley, Colo. 1902. Courtesy Denver Public Library, Western History Collection, X-9023.

The state court of appeals ruled in favor of Eaton and the company, basing its decision in part on the theory that the company was the owner of the water it carried in its canal. On this point it was roundly rebuked by the state supreme court, which pointed out that it had already ruled otherwise in a series of decisions, including several of those discussed above, and that this issue was in any case irrelevant to the proceedings at hand.[136]

The case, rather, turned on the interpretation of the contractual clause limiting the number of water rights the company could sell to those covered by the "estimated capacity" of the canal. The company claimed, plausibly enough, that it was entitled to sell water rights up to the physical capacity of the ditch, as seems to have been the general practice.[137] Any difference between this capacity and the amount to which it was entitled during any given irrigation season, argued the company, would have to be split among the rights holders on a proportional basis. Wyatt and the other appellants, however, claimed that the "estimated capacity" referred to in the contract should be interpreted as the canal's ability to furnish water to its customers in practice (under typical conditions), a function not only of physical capacity but also of available water in the river and the priority dates of the canal's appropriations. They argued that the prorating clause was meant to apply only under conditions of unusual drought or accident among the original stockholders, not to foreseeable shortages resulting from the sale of new water rights that the canal could not reasonably be expected to cover, given the size and seniority of its own rights.[138]

In keeping with its prior decisions, the court sided with the farmers in this case, highlighting again the importance of the sufficiency principle in its water jurisprudence:

> If appellees' contention is correct, and the irrigation company by the terms of these contracts have the right to dispose of definite water rights, and by ambiguous expressions in subsequent provisions reserve the power to render them uncertain and indefinite in quantity, by disposing of water rights admittedly in excess of its ability to furnish water, they are not only inequitable and unfair, but clearly illegal under the decision of this court in *F.H.L.C. & R. Co. v. Southworth*, ... wherein it is said:

> "A contract to carry more water than has been lawfully diverted would be unlawful; and to prevent injuries resulting therefrom, or to recover damages in case the injuries are suffered, ample legal remedies exist."[139]

The citation from *Southworth* is from Chief Justice Helm's minority opinion,[140] and it gives some indication of what type of remedy his approach envisioned. The *Wyatt* rule allowed prorating of true shortages when agreed to by consumers, but prohibited dilution of water rights on a grander scale by refusing to give effect to contracts for water rights beyond the ability of the carrier to furnish. This combination of the prorating and priority rules is interesting from a theoretical point of view, as it displays a resolution of the tension between two distributive-justice principles, equality and sufficiency, similar to that encountered earlier in the miners' codes. As in those codes, where the basic principle of water rights was proportional division between the claimants, with priority kicking in when division would lead to diminution of rights beyond the point sufficient for a miner to carry out his work, the regime proposed by Helm in *Southworth* and adopted by the majority in *Wyatt* encouraged sharing of unusual shortages, but drew the line where equal division would lead to the shrinking of water rights beyond the point necessary for irrigation. While the earlier customers of a water company, who had bought their rights when the canal's typical water supply was sufficient to fulfill its contracts, had to share shortages among themselves, they could invoke the priority principle to enjoin sales beyond that level.[141]

Special Charters

As noted in Chapter 2, one of the pet causes of Jacksonian Democracy and related groups had been attacking monopoly power created by the grant of special privileges and powers to corporations. The primary legal vehicle for doing so was the enactment of general incorporation acts, a trend that accelerated after the Civil War.[142] Colorado's territorial legislature failed to enact such a law in its first session, in 1861, meanwhile creating a number of corporations, including ditch companies, by private act.[143] Before the next session, though, Governor Evans told the General Assembly, "To facilitate the organization of corporate companies ... I would advise the passage of general laws, so that all persons may enjoy equal rights and privileges under them. ... The granting of exclusive rights and privileges—always of doubtful propriety—cannot be too sedulously guarded against."[144] Responding to this call, the legislature enacted a general incorporation act in 1862, though it created some companies by special legislative act as late as 1867.[145]

The issue of special privileges granted to corporations took on particular urgency in the case of water companies, given the extreme sensitivity of farmers to attempts by capitalists to gain control of water, and through it, land. As discussed earlier, the prior appropriation doctrine had been aimed in part at the threat to widespread distribution posed by legislative grants of water to corporations. Such special privileges were anathema to Jacksonian anti-corporation and anti-monopoly sentiment, and ran afoul too of the radical Lockean belief that property should be earned by labor, not by political connections. Though, as noted, the issue of such charters had already fallen into disfavor in the territorial period, some such corporations, such as the Consolidated Ditch Company of the Gregory Diggings area (see Fig. 10), had been granted exclusive rights to streams by legislative charter, and remained in business into the statehood period.[146] These companies sometimes claimed exclusive control of certain bodies of water on the basis of their chartering acts.

The Colorado Supreme Court faced such a claim in 1889, in *Platte Water Co. v. Northern Colorado Irrigation Co.* In 1860, with much of what was to become Colorado still part of the Kansas Territory, the legislature of that territory had granted a charter to the Capitol Hydraulic Company, predecessor of the appellant, which included a grant of exclusive rights to the water in Cherry Creek and the South Platte in the Denver area

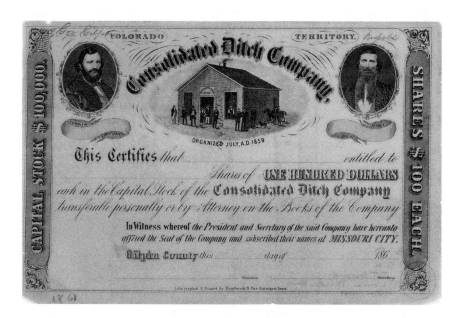

Figure 10. Stock certificate of Consolidated Ditch Company. Courtesy Denver Public Library, Western History Collection, C338.762234; C763co; 1861.

(see Fig. 11). In 1883, the Colorado district court adjudicating the water rights in the area based the parties' rights on the dates of actual appropriation, ignoring the charter's grant of exclusive rights to the area water. Platte Water appealed this decision, claiming that its predecessor's charter had vested it with the exclusive right not only to the water necessary for agricultural and other uses in 1860, but to the water needed for irrigating all lands that might be settled under the area "for all times thereafter." Its rights acquired under the charter, it claimed, were vested rights, and therefore immune to impairment under the U.S. Constitution as well as the federal Mineral Lands Act of 1866.[147]

But, as the state supreme court pointed out, the Mineral Lands Act said nothing about the protection of rights acquired by legislative grant, recognizing instead only rights acquired by "priority of possession."[148] Under Colorado law, "from the earliest times," the court explained, water rights

Figure 11. Stock certificate of Capitol Hydraulic Company, Incorporated by the Legislature of Kansas Territory. Courtesy Denver Public Library, Western History Collection, C628.109788; C172cap; 1860.

The inset map shows the line of the canal and a series of reservoirs, beginning (on the left) from the South Platte north of Denver and paralleling the river (through company lands), and ending at the city reservoir on Cherry Creek.

could be acquired by one method only: diversion with beneficial use. Such was the rule set down in Colorado's constitution and statutes, and reinforced in judicial decisions from the foundational *Yunker v. Nichols* and *Coffin v. Left Hand Ditch Co.* to the recent *Wheeler* decision, where the court had ruled that an appropriation's validity was dependent on consumer use.[149] The law of prior appropriation, thus correctly understood as protecting "actual appropriation," was "a refuge to all *bona fide* appropriators of water from the natural streams of Colorado,"[150] but not to those claiming under legislative grant. The latter would be subordinated to the rights of actual settlers acquired through use.

Ditch Easements

As discussed in the previous chapters, one of the legal invasions of private property in the name of universalizing access to water, associated from the beginning with prior appropriation, was the grant of ditch easements to irrigators over lands between their land and the water source. The point of this statutory right of way was to prevent riparian owners from monopolizing water sources by using their land to block non-riparians from gaining access to the water. Later, in 1881, the legislature had acted to mitigate the burden this rule placed on servient lands by prohibiting the construction of more than one canal over any parcel if one canal would be sufficient.[151]

However, when litigation arose over one company's attempt to enjoin another from constructing a canal across its land, a project that would compete with the first company's canal, the state's court of appeals ruled that the anti-monopoly principles of the state's water law made the 1881 statute inapplicable when the burdened land was that of another canal company:

> No authorities are presented which intimate that the construction of one canal is sufficient reason to prohibit the construction of another because it runs parallel with the first. If that rule would obtain it would result in the creation and continuation of a monopoly against which the constitution of our state and the statutes are directly aimed. And even if there were no provisions of the constitution and statute, no court has yet held or would hold that such contention should prevail.[152]

The statute's protection of private property was thus held to apply only to private landowners, not canal companies. This discrimination can be understood only as an expression of agrarian, radical Lockean ideology, which stressed the importance of private property when widely distributed but opposed it when held by speculators or corporations to the detriment of actual users.

Discussion

Corporate Regulation in the Gilded Age

The common image of Gilded Age America, a land of corporations run amok and lawmakers and judges all too willing to do their bidding, is commonly assumed to have been particularly valid with regard to the development of Colorado's water resources in the closing decades of the nineteenth century. Yet, looking at the legal developments regarding corporate ditches in this period, we can see clearly that in the conflict between absentee capital and local settlers, Colorado law came down firmly on the side of the latter. Informed contemporaries had much the same opinion; so much so that in 1893 the editor of *Irrigation Age* could laugh at the suggestion by eastern journalist Julian Ralph that Colorado water corporations were "milking" its settlers:[153] "To those who are familiar with Colorado legislation and court decisions, Mr. Ralph's discovery that the corporations have the people by the throat is very entertaining. At last accounts the people had the corporations by the throat. . . . The fact is that many of the corporations complain bitterly of the tyranny of the people in making laws which hamper enterprise and discourage investment."[154]

John Wesley Powell had made a similar observation about the West in general: "There is a sentiment in the land that the farmer must be free, that the laborer in the field should be the owner of the field. Hence by unfriendly legislation and by judicial decision—which ultimately reflect the sentiment of the people—these farming corporations and water corporations of the West have often failed to secure brilliant financial results, and many have been almost destroyed. Thus there is a war in the West between capital and labor—a bitter, relentless war."[155]

A few years later, a history of Colorado agriculture could sum up this period by saying that "For a time threat of corporate monopoly of water hung over the agricultural industry, but court decisions and legislative action ended this menace."[156]

Private, Public, and Corporate Property

As shown above, many of the state supreme court's decisions favoring consumer interests over those of canal companies rested on the doctrinal basis of public ownership of all surface water and the use requirement as an element of water rights that could be satisfied by the consumer only, not the canal company.[157] An editorial in *Irrigation Age* summed up well the connection between these issues: "Water, sunshine and air are natural elements, existing for the benefit and essential to the life of all. . . . The universal law that water must be applied to 'a beneficial use' is in itself a denial of the right of ownership. What a man owns he may apply as he pleases. Water is public property. . . . When any other view of water ownership is admitted it will be time not merely for a king but for a slave-driver. Private investment in works will always be protected, but private ownership of water will not be conceded until air and sunshine are sold in bottles."[158]

The public-ownership theory of corporate regulation, advanced first and most forcefully by the Colorado Supreme Court, was a bold one, going beyond the more widespread theory legitimating regulation based on the common-carrier theory of a business affected with a public interest. But in the agrarian jurisprudence of the day, public ownership of water did not mean a negation of private rights—it was, rather, wholly consistent with private water rights, as long as they were acquired by actual use. The theory seems to have been that water was the common property of the public, with the use regime for its owners based on the amount needed for their beneficial use: "Equity demands that flowing water shall be considered as a common stock or fund, the right to the use of which shall be regulated, and beneficial use shall be the measure and the limit of such right."[159]

Some, such as the chief of the U.S. Bureau of Statistics, saw the relationship between public ownership and private rights as a two-stage process, with the latter deriving from the former: "The idea appears to have taken deep hold upon the public mind in Colorado and Wyoming, that while in the beginning the State or Territorial Government must assert its control of all running water as the common property of the people, yet that the ownership and control of water rights . . . must eventually be vested in the people who are to use such works, subject to the supervisory power of Government."[160]

But others saw public ownership and private use as a seamless whole. As explained earlier, jurists of the Jeffersonian and Jacksonian persuasions tended to distinguish between corporate property and what they considered true private property—that is, property distributed widely among individuals. Private property was not seen as antithetical to the public sort, but could be wholly consistent with it, even a logical expression or consequence of it. Property was "public" when controlled by the broad population, regardless of whether it took the legal form of widely distributed private property or more concretely state or public assets. The important distinction was between property in the hands of the broad public and property concentrated in the hands of a powerful few—typically through corporations and "monopolies." Following this Jacksonian conception of property, Samuel Wiel, the great Progressive-era scholar of western water law, completely conflated private and public rights in his analysis of Colorado water law. As he pointed out, the law's recognition of the public-private property of appropriative rights was aimed at defeating corporate control: The constitutional declaration of state ownership, he wrote, "has been tacitly taken for what it says—State or public proprietorship or ownership of waters the same as in a public building. The result has been in Colorado and the interior States to build a system of law of water distribution upon the basis that consumers from a distributing system are the real proprietors of the system, and the distributor or canal company but their agent to care for the works and bring the water to the consumers' land."[161] Wiel described the law of appropriation as "resulting in an approach to public ownership" and "closely approaching public ownership of irrigation systems."[162] Similarly, federal irrigation expert Richard Hinton explained state control of water companies as deriving from the doctrine of prior appropriation: "It must be borne in mind that the miners' doctrine of prior appropriation underlies all legislation and judicial decisions within the arid region. As the state is the owner of all natural waters, it follows that corporations or other conveyors of water, take rank with the railroads as common carriers."[163]

In early Colorado water law the formal distinctions among private, common, corporate, and public property were thus far less clear than they seem to be today. What was important was not the classification of the property right or its nominal owner, but the distribution of its costs and benefits. This point will be discussed further in the final chapter.

CHAPTER 5

BENEFICIAL USE AND LIMITS ON TRANSFER

The three previous chapters began the exploration of the connection between distributive justice and the evolution of property institutions in the historical context of the development of the appropriation doctrine. We saw that the development of water law in Colorado (the leading water-law jurisdiction in this period) in the initial decades of white settlement was guided primarily by a concern to ensure as broad a distribution as possible of the crucial resource, and a desire to prevent its monopolization by capitalists and speculators. The adoption of a property regime based on appropriative rights was aimed firstly at preventing monopolization of water (and through it—land) by speculators buying up riverfront (riparian) property. When outside capitalists attempted to gain control of the region's waters by laying claim to the water diverted by the corporations they formed, Colorado law stymied their plans by ruling that property rights could be acquired only by actual users; investor-owned companies were relegated to the status of common carriers, entitled to earn a reasonable rate of return on their investments, but not the profits generated by irrigated agriculture.

To further illuminate the relationship between distributive justice and the evolution of property institutions, this chapter will focus on an issue that occupied irrigators, businessmen, and lawyers in late-nineteenth-century Colorado, and that continues to occupy policy makers, scholars, and water users today: the issue of water transfers. It will also deal with the more general property-theory issue thereby implicated, the question of alienability. We will see that the restrictions on transfer of water rights imposed by the classic appropriation doctrine in effect created an anti-commons, in which welfare-enhancing transfers and assembly of property rights were severely limited. While water rights were in theory transferable to others, and in practice some transfers were carried out, the effect of this anticommons was to move property in water closer to inalienability than to the relatively full alienability usually associated with private property. More importantly, we shall see that this development was anticipated—and nonetheless consciously chosen—by the judges and officials who created the appropriation system, who preferred a property regime that encouraged broadly distributed rights over one that maximized value. Normative implications of this history, and some contemporary applications of the insights garnered from it, will be taken up in the final chapter.

Beneficial Use: An Inefficient Principle of Law

The appropriation doctrine's use requirement, anchored in the Colorado constitution's provision that "the right to divert the unappropriated waters of any natural stream to beneficial uses shall never be denied,"[1] is notoriously inefficient. While seen by some detractors as a fly in the ointment of an otherwise efficient system of private property, and by the conservation-minded as a prototype for limiting the power of rights holders under that same system, all seem to agree that it is an anomaly, so much so that scholars have tried to explain it away as a foreign import.[2]

In a system of water law based on private-property rights, it is difficult to understand why the right's validity would be conditioned on the appropriated water being put to actual use. The use requirement encourages wasteful, low-value use for the purpose of acquiring or holding rights; worse, as outlined presently, it forms very high barriers to transfers of water rights to more efficient uses and users. Why not allow free appropriation and transfer of water rights, and let the market guide the water to its best and most beneficial uses?[3]

In order to appreciate the high transaction costs created by the beneficial use rule, it is necessary to understand a bit of irrigation hydrology, as well as what precisely is meant by "use" in western water law. First, one must bear in mind that from the point of view of a water basin, under traditional irrigation technologies (such as furrow irrigation) a significant proportion of the water diverted to the field is not consumed (that is to say, taken up by the crops or evaporated into the atmosphere). Some, sometimes most, of the water (the proportion depends on the type of crop, climate, and so on) returns to the water source as difficult-to-measure "return flow," either as surface runoff or by subsurface percolation and flow.[4] To give a numerical example, an irrigator might divert water from a river at a rate of 4 cubic feet per second (c.f.s.), in accordance with her recorded right, in order to irrigate her fields, but have 3 c.f.s. of that quantity return to the river, available to downstream irrigators to use for their own purposes. Her consumptive use would be only 1 c.f.s.

The legal definition of use derives from these physical circumstances— from the large gap between what is diverted and what is actually consumed, and from the fact that the difference is largely available for new appropriations by downstream users. While western water law has typically provided for the recordation of rights based on quantities diverted, it has also consistently held that an appropriative right is valid only to the extent the water claimed is put to beneficial use. This is the meaning of the oft-quoted maxim "Beneficial use is the basis, the measure, and the limit of right to the use of water."[5] Though, as the next section of this chapter will show, several possibilities for measuring use were discussed in the period in question, the standard ultimately adopted by all jurisdictions was about as narrow as possible. Water "used" (and thus appropriated) was not water *diverted* from the stream, but the amount of water *necessary* for the purpose for which the appropriation had been made. Moreover, if an appropriator wished to sell her right to another, her right was effectively cut back even further—to the amount actually consumed.

In day-to-day practice, the difference between an irrigator's recorded right and his right measured by the beneficial use standard is of little consequence, since water diverted in excess of "use" returns to the stream, and is available to other appropriators. (This explains why western water law traditionally has been unconcerned with encouraging

efficiency in water use, often even discouraging it.)[6] The practical importance of beneficial use arises primarily in the context of transfers of
water rights to new locations or uses. In these situations, beneficial use
has motivated the adoption of the "no-injury" rule, which has proved to
be a major impediment to the effective functioning of water markets.
Moreover, it has ruled out an efficient solution to what has come to be
seen as a major policy problem. While its disadvantages are clear, the
reasons for the rule's adoption have remained something of a puzzle.

To illustrate the rule's effect using our example, our irrigator (Irrigator
A) would have the right, grounded in her initial appropriation, to
continue diverting the full 4 c.f.s. to her fields, regardless of the effect on
junior appropriators. Yet if she wished to sell her right to Irrigator B,
located elsewhere (whether downstream, below intervening junior appropriators, or in another watershed), transferring the full quantity of her
recorded right would result in an impairment of the return flow, thereby
impinging on the property rights of downstream appropriators, whether
junior or senior to her. The "no-injury" rule adopted by western courts in
the late nineteenth century forbade any such impairment, even if the
rights of those harmed were junior to those of the transferor, and in
effect adopted consumptive use as the true measure of A's right in this
situation: she would be allowed to transfer to B only 1 c.f.s., and would
have to refrain from using the remaining 3 c.f.s. of her original right.
That way, intervening appropriators would continue to receive the 3 c.f.s.
of water previously sent downstream as return flow. Similarly, if A wished
not to transfer the right, but simply to use her right for a different
purpose (such as drinking water for a town), she would be allowed to
consume only 1 c.f.s. in the new use, and obligated to ensure that 3 c.f.s.
continued to be available to downstream juniors.

Though this system has the advantage of forcing parties to a transfer to
internalize the effects of their change on third-party appropriators, it also
places severe limitations on the ability to conduct efficiency-enhancing
transfers of water to new uses or locations.[7] The difference in the quantity
used at the original location and that able to be applied at the new location is often great enough to prevent efficient transfers from taking place.

Transaction costs are further inflated by the procedure mandated
for water transfers. In all appropriation states, holders of a water right

wishing to execute a transfer must first petition the authorities (typically the state engineer, in Colorado a court of law); approval is granted only upon a showing of no injury to other appropriators. Thus, beyond the costs imposed by the no-injury rule itself, parties wishing to effect a transfer have to incur the significant costs of hydrological research to determine the extent of possible injury to third parties, as well as the costs of legal and engineering counsel for the proceedings, in which the petitioning party has the burden of proving no injury.[8]

Now, one might argue that the no-injury rule need not prevent efficient transfers from taking place. If the potential productivity gains of the new use truly cancel out the losses to downstream juniors, it would seem that the parties to the transfer should be able to share some of their profits with these appropriators, paying them to forgo their rights to the return flow. Yet this type of deal is rare. Especially in Colorado, with its court proceedings potentially involving all appropriators in the watershed, the no-injury principle creates high transaction costs, to the point where it is "practically impossible to bring about such a change in the face of any vigorous protest."[9] Given that relatively cost-free transfers are generally thought to be the preferred mechanism for ensuring allocation of water to its most productive uses, the result upon the efficiency of the water market of the no-injury restriction, based on beneficial use, has been termed "disastrous."[10] An indication of the efficiency gains forgone due to impediments to transfer can be obtained by comparing the price of water for agriculture and that for urban uses in the West; the difference often reaches several orders of magnitude.[11]

In essence, the beneficial use doctrine created what property theorists today call an anticommons. As with the Moscow storefronts made famous (in property law circles) by Michael Heller, property rights in any given stream are typically divided among scores of users, and intertwined with one another, due to rights of even junior appropriators in the return flow produced by upstream rights holders at the time of appropriation. The resulting restrictions on transfer make reallocations of water extremely difficult; in some cases, impossible, even when the efficiency gains are great. The multiplicity of interconnected private-property rights (see Figs. 12–14) tends to lock water into suboptimal uses, as predicted by theory.[12]

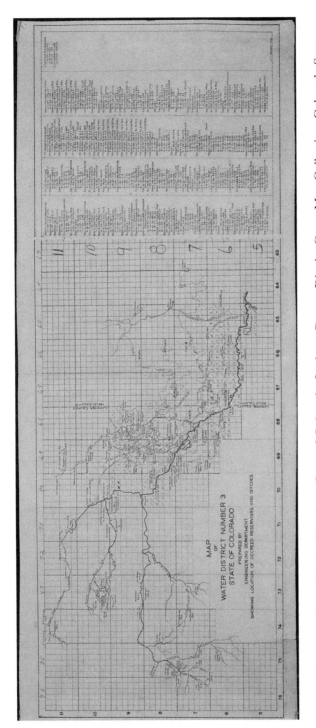

Figure 12. Water District Number 3 State of Colorado, Larimer County District Court Map Collection, Colorado State University, Archives and Special Collections.

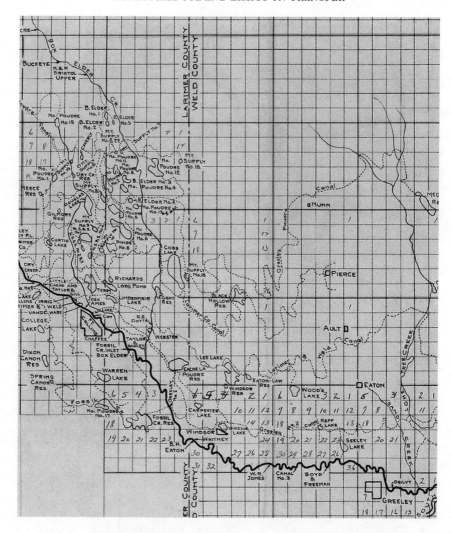

Figure 13. Detail, Water District Number 3, showing the complex of canals
and reservoirs in the neighborhood of
Greeley and Fort Collins.

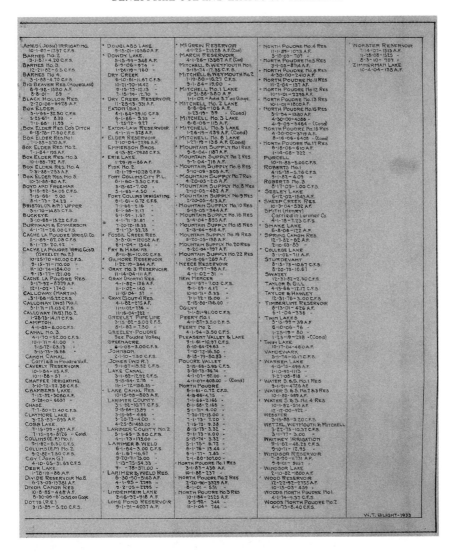

Figure 14. Detail, Water District Number 3, showing the decreed water rights. The ditch rights are mostly dated to the 1860s and 1870s, while the reservoir rights are nearly all from the 1880s through the first decade of the twentieth century.

Yet the prior-appropriation anticommons was not inevitable. As economics-oriented lawyers such as Charles Meyers and Richard Posner have recognized, efficient transfers could have been facilitated by a modified (actually simplified) appropriation system, one that gave third-party appropriators no rights in the return flows of upstream users.[13] With this simplification of property rights in water, Irrigator A would be able to transfer the entire amount of her diversion to Irrigator B, without the need to subtract return flow or compensate downstream users harmed by the transfer. Of course, such a transfer might harm downstream users, but only if A had been letting her unconsumed water run back to the stream without recapturing it. Under the rule proposed by Meyers and Posner, she likely would have recaptured her return flow and either put it to further use herself or leased it to others, leading to internalization of the effects of transfer on the return flow.

Even had she had been allowing downstream appropriators to make uncompensated use of her return flow, and even were their uses more valuable than B's proposed use, the Meyers and Posner rule would likely be more efficient than the current one. First, because users of the return flow would have been on notice that the return flow could be sold at any time by A, they would have either planned accordingly or contracted with A to prevent this from happening. Second, even would they not have done so, the collective-action obstacles that would have stood in their way would have likely been less intractable than the holdout problem created by the current rule: Under the Meyers and Posner rule, downstream appropriators threatened with a combined loss significantly greater than the supposed profits of the proposed transfer would often be able to offer Irrigator A sufficient inducement to not go through with the transfer, even with significant free-riding by other downstream irrigators. In contrast, under the no-injury rule, even one holdout can be enough to prevent even an extremely profitable transfer from going forward.

Under a rule giving senior appropriators full rights to their diversions, then, water would have flowed more easily to its highest and best use, rather than be frozen in old and inefficient uses, as under the appropriation doctrine.[14] It is striking to note that this efficient solution was not first suggested in the ivory tower; it was, rather, advocated loudly by many in the late nineteenth-century West. Defining appropriative rights in terms of the amounts diverted, giving the first to divert the water full property rights in all the water diverted, was the preferred approach of the canal corporations in particular.

Even so, the lawmakers who created the appropriation system and beneficial use rule chose the inefficient option—basing the water right on beneficial use rather than diversion—and did so knowingly. It is often said that in the West water flows uphill to money and power, yet the impediments to transfer have often led to water being frozen in old uses, stymieing the plans of the monied and the powerful. Why? The answer to this question, to be found in the early legal history of the appropriation doctrine, raises questions about whether such a choice should be made by contemporary law and policy makers.

The History of the Beneficial Use Doctrine

The Measure of Use

From the appropriation system's inception in the informal laws of the mining districts, beneficial use provided the measure and limit of a water right acquired from the public domain. The linchpin of the agrarian program for western water law, the rule was essential to prevent undue aggregation of water in the hands of the few, and ensure its wide distribution to actual users. As William Smythe, one of the influential leaders of the irrigation movement, explained, "[Water] is a natural element, like sunshine and air. Every human being is entitled to receive as much of it as he can apply to a beneficial use. No person may hold it out of use for speculation to exploit the necessities of others or to levy tribute upon his fellow men. . . . Wherever there is more land than water, it is true public policy to have the water so conserved and distributed as to reclaim the utmost number of acres, create the utmost number of homes, and sustain the utmost number of families."[15]

Unfortunately, since the term "use" suffered from a certain amount of vagueness, the extent to which Colorado's use requirement would actually succeed in preventing speculation was, for a time, unclear. All agreed that an actual "appropriation," as opposed to a mere claim based on location, as in the "feudal" riparian-rights system, was a *sine qua non* of a valid property right in water. But what constituted an appropriation? Several interpretations were possible. One minimalist position was that only the volume or flow of water put to actual use at a given date would be considered appropriated as of that date. The other relatively minimalist interpretation would base the quantity appropriated on the amount of water objectively considered necessary for the task for which the water was put to use. A bill introduced by farmers' representatives in the state legislature, for instance, provided that in time of shortage "no ditch, in such time of scarcity, be allowed, whatever its capacity or priority of rights, to draw any more water from the stream than shall be necessary to irrigate the trees and crops then growing under it and needing further irrigation."[16]

At the other extreme, some claimed that construction of a canal effectively appropriated sufficient water to irrigate all of the lands under the ditch (that is, the lands capable of being irrigated from it) or even water sufficient for all the lands that might be irrigated by extension and enlargement of the ditch.[17] Positions slightly less ambitious, but still generous to the early claimant, included recognizing as appropriated the quantity diverted through the canal's headgate (regardless of actual application to a useful purpose)[18] and basing the appropriation on the capacity of the canal as constructed.[19]

The stakes in this controversy were high, since the more maximalist positions would allow corporations to gain control of large amounts of water in advance of settlement (and use), while the minimalist stance would allow farmers to claim water rights superior to those of corporate canals that may have been constructed first, but had not yet put the water to actual use. The issue arose already in the territorial (pre-state) period, with the *Rocky Mountain News* warning that the right acquired by priority of use "should be limited to the amount of water actually necessary. Thus, if A has acquired a vested right to the use of water from any stream for purposes of irrigation and needs only fifty inches for his farm, he should not be permitted to take one hundred or one hundred and fifty inches and waste it about his premises to the detriment of B C and D, his neighbors, who would be deprived of water by A's wastefulness. In a dry season A would be entitled to be supplied from the stream first, and if it only furnished enough for his purpose he would be entitled to all of it. If there was a slight surplus it would go to B, who had the next vested right. . . . [The priority rule] should be guarded by all necessary provisions to prevent a monopoly or a wasteful or unnecessary use of water."[20]

Yet as late as 1886, the issue was clearly unresolved, as indicated by Carpenter's treatise on Colorado water law published that year:

The question may well be raised whether there can be a valid appropriation, which could be maintained as a priority against a subsequent *bona fide*
appropriation, by persons or corporations, who, owning no lands themselves, build a ditch and . . . attempt to monopolize the water of a stream
for the purpose of speculating in the needs of those who afterwards may
settle on lands naturally irrigable from such stream; or who, owning *some*
lands, attempt to claim by appropriation more water than is needed for
those lands, with the speculative intent aforementioned. . . .

Let us now suppose that a corporation constructs a large ditch, and claims
to appropriate the entire volume of water ordinarily flowing in it, in order
to convey such water above a large unsettled tract over which it has no
control; and that afterwards, and before such lands are settled up suffi-
ciently to use such a volume of water, a settler near such a stream take out
a ditch from it to irrigate his lands. Could that company deny him priority
as against their claim, on account of their indefinite prospect of an ultimate settlement of all the lands under their line? Or would their claim not
be limited as against such settler, to the amount of water actually needed
for such lands as were actually occupied under their line at the time of his
settlement?[21]

As discussed earlier in this book, in Colorado's early years, with the
primary threat of water monopolies coming from speculators trying to
exploit riparian rights to control the state's water and land, the courts had
focused on that issue, clarifying in their decisions that the right to appropriate water was open to all. Now that this principle of freedom of appropriation had been firmly established, the new threat to broadly distributed
water rights came from the opposite direction, speculative diversions of
water claiming appropriative rights.[22] Agrarian elements complained that
"the lands, and what is much worse, the waters, of the state are rapidly
passing into the control of corporations and syndicates, both domestic and
foreign; and speculation in the unused water of the state is openly claimed
as a right . . . and is exercised as such in defiance of the sense of the
community and against common right; . . . We are not only threatened
but actually confronted by the presence of organized syndicates, taking up
and intending to hold for their own gain, the waters of the state, which are
the life blood of the common welfare; and keeping the public waters from
the use of the people, until their own profits can be secured."[23]

In tandem and interwoven with their jurisprudence of water companies discussed in the previous chapter, Colorado's courts (particularly the
supreme court) worked out the law of beneficial use in a way designed to
meet this challenge (leading the way for other western jurisdictions).[24]
The first case to tackle the issue was *Thomas v. Guiraud,* handed down just
a few months after the great *Coffin* decision.[25] The defendants in error had
sued to enjoin diversions by Thomas, who was upstream from them, but
who had begun diverting water after their predecessor had done so.
Thomas conceded that the Guirauds' diversion had antedated his own,
but argued that their claimed appropriation was larger than the amount
their predecessor possibly could have used, given the size of the land in
his possession on the date of his initial appropriation.[26] The supreme
court, while ruling that Thomas had not proved that his adversaries'
claim was "greater in quantity than was reasonably necessary for the
purpose designed," agreed with him as a matter of law, ruling that
"Guiraud could not appropriate more water than was necessary to irrigate his land." Neither could he appropriate more than was necessary
for himself with the hope of selling it at a profit to others: "He could
not divert [water] for the purpose of irrigating lands which he did not
cultivate or own, or hold by possessory right or title, to the exclusion of a
subsequent *bona fide* appropriator."[27] This case became the seminal one
establishing the element of beneficial use as an essential requirement of a
valid appropriation.

The principle of beneficial use thus established as a limiting factor on
appropriations, the supreme court moved later that year to apply it in
limiting the size of an appropriation. *Sieber v. Frink* involved a ditch that
had been built in 1871, with only a portion of the water diverted actually
having been applied to irrigation before 1876. Though conceding that
absent intent to abandon, the lack of use in the interim had not technically constituted an abandonment, the court ruled that the quantity that
had been applied only beginning in 1876 could not be considered part of
the 1871 appropriation, and therefore would be ranked junior in time to
intervening appropriations: "One of the essential elements of a valid
appropriation of water is the application thereof to some useful industry.
To acquire a right to water from the date of the diversion thereof, one
must within a reasonable time employ the same in the business for which

the appropriation is made." In other words, there had been no abandon-ment because, absent the requisite use, the quantity of water in question had never been appropriated in the first place. Priority gave the better right, but appropriators were "only entitled to priority for the quantity . . . used," not the full amount diverted.[28]

Sieber was the first in a line of decisions in which the state supreme court applied the beneficial use requirement to limit or invalidate appropriations.[29] In *Platte Water Co. v. Northern Colorado Irrigation Co.*,[30] for instance, the appellant's appropriation was limited to the amount it had acquired through actual use, and its claimed appropriation based on legislative grant nullified. Particularly far reaching was *Combs v. Agricultural Ditch Co.*, in which the court ruled that farmer Combs could not be denied water by the appellee company on the grounds that he held no shares in the company.[31] The fact that the company's 200 shares of capital stock were all sold did not mean each shareholder had the right to 1/200 of the canal's water; each shareholder, rather, was limited to the amount of water actually necessary to irrigate his land, and any surplus in the ditch would be available to non-shareholding appropriators. Priority as a guiding rule went only so far; it was limited by the use doctrine and the necessity principle it was designed to advance and protect:

> It is plain that the quantity of land and the character of the soil which the appropriators of water from the ditch have under cultivation, as well as their actual prior appropriations of water to the irrigation of such lands, and not the number of shares of stock they may own, are the important matters to be considered in determining such a controversy. In the trial of such an issue it is also important to observe that, no matter how early a person's priority of appropriation may be, he is not entitled to receive more water than is necessary for his actual use. An excessive diversion of water cannot be regarded as a diversion to beneficial use, within the meaning of the constitution. Water, in this country, is too scarce, and consequently too precious, to admit of waste. The constitutional rule of distribution, "first come, first served," does not imply that the prior appro-priator may be extravagantly prodigal in dealing with this peculiar bounty of nature.[32]

Necessity here was held to trump even actual use, when the latter measure would give the appropriator more than he really needed.

Similarly, the state court of appeals explained that in a lawsuit over water rights, facts essential for the pleadings included not just the amount of water claimed to be diverted, or even used:

> Under the constitution and laws of Colorado, the right to the use of water for irrigation is dependent upon its diversion and actual and continuous appropriation to such beneficial use, and then only to such extent as is necessary for the use intended. . . . An additional fact, equally essential to be known and stated, is the quantity of land for the irrigation of which the water is used. No right can be secured either by diversion or appropriation to more water than is necessary for the proper irrigation of the land to which it is applied.[33]

Necessity was also recognized as a limiting factor, along with the use requirement, in *Nichols v. McIntosh:*

> No one is entitled to have a priority adjudged for more water than he has actually appropriated, nor for more than he actually needs. His priority of right must be limited by each of these considerations. Proof of present need is not of itself proof of prior appropriation; and *vice versa.*[34]

The implication here and in other cases[35] was that necessity and the use requirement were to act in tandem as a continuing check on the size of appropriations, limiting not only the initial size of an appropriation, but potentially shrinking it at any time if the user's need for the water decreased for some reason, whether reduced needs due to moistening of the soil or improved methods.[36] As one irrigator-turned-water commissioner explained, "Whoever has acquired a legal vested right to the use of the water, and has need for the same, must be protected at all times in the enjoyment of its use. But whenever that need ceases then it becomes the property of the public."[37]

Requiring proof of necessity was also a way for the law to prevent excessive claims of use. Stretching a water right out to irrigate more land than originally irrigated might seem wholly unobjectionable, a pure efficiency gain; nevertheless, this practice was frowned upon by Colorado courts. The reason seems to be their awareness that water claimants had frequently obtained excessive decrees, whether due to lack of evidence, interested or ill-informed witnesses, or courts ignorant of the engineering and mathematical issues at hand.[38] The claimant would then hold the surplus water, possibly many times the amount actually needed for his own use, for sale or use at a later date on other lands.[39] Measuring the water right in terms of necessity, objectively determined, as well as supposed actual use, prevented this type of speculative hoarding of water rights.[40]

Water Decrees

The issue of the use requirement's effects on appropriations was presented squarely by Colorado's groundbreaking legislation of 1879–1881, setting up an administrative and judicial system to enforce priority rights.[41] The statutes were drafted and pushed through by several representatives of the irrigator community, including H. P. H. Bromwell, who had been active in drafting the water-law provisions of the state constitution.[42] This legislation came in response to pressure by farmers, especially small-scale ones, who, through their Grange representatives, had been pushing for such an administrative system to protect them against exploitation by capitalists since the territorial period.[43]

The issue the new statutes were meant to address was that the seniorities of the several appropriation rights on any stream were terribly difficult to know and enforce. Since there was no central registry of water rights, irrigators could determine their relative priority only by expensive and time-consuming lawsuits on a case-by-case basis, with courts even then taking jurisdiction only when specific relief was sought.[44] Each time an appropriator felt his right was being infringed by a water user with rights junior to his, he would have to bring a claim against the supposed offender, and take his chances on judicial proceedings that found it notoriously hard to determine with any sort of accuracy the quantities and priorities of the rights involved.[45] If he won, he would have at his disposal for implementation of the ruling only the usual machinery for enforcement of judicial rulings. Obviously, the whole process could take several years; "many irrigating seasons would pass and many crops be lost before litigants could secure their rights."[46] Worse, any such court proceedings would determine the relative rights only of the immediate parties to the controversy, leaving unresolved the question of relative priorities with other irrigators in the watershed. The lack of clarity and enforcement of property rights hit small farmers particularly hard, due to the relatively high costs of litigating and enforcing relatively small rights.[47] "The verdict on the part of many," wrote the director of the U.S. Department of Agriculture's Irrigation Inquiry, "is too much lawyer and court; too little engineer and irrigator."[48]

The new legislation aimed to solve these problems, first by calling for special adjudications to determine all the water rights in each area. As demanded by the Grangers, Colorado was divided into water divisions based on its major river basins, with these further subdivided into water districts, each covering the drainage area of a stream or stream section (see, for example, Fig. 12, p.109). Once the water rights for each district had been adjudicated (see, for example, Fig. 15), water commissioners, answering to the state engineer, would be responsible for enforcing the decrees, opening and closing headgates as necessary to ensure that each irrigator received the water due him at the proper time.[49]

So much for the judicial and administrative machinery to determine and enforce water rights, in which Colorado was the pioneer. The new laws also attempted to grapple with the substantive issue of determining the extent of a water right, defining how much water had been applied to a

TABLE GIVING DITCH AND RESERVOIR DECREES IN DISTRICT NO. 3.

From Certified Copies Decrees Furnished Irrigation Division Engineer, Division No. 1, by Clerk District Court Issuing Such Decrees.

ORDER OF PRIORITY IN DISTRICT	NAME OF DITCH OR CANAL	SOURCE OF APPROPRIATION	DATE OF APPROPRIATION	AMOUNT IN SEC. FT. DECREED TO EACH PRIORITY	TOTAL AMOUNT PREV'SLY DECREED IN DISTRICT
1	Yeager Ditch	Cache La Poudre river	June 1, 1860	24.80	0
2	Ditch of Watrous, Whedbee & Secord	Cache La Poudre river	June 1, 1861	1.44	24.8
3	Dry Creek Ditch	Cache La Poudre river	June 10, 1861	11.07	26.24
4	Pleasant Valley and Lake Canal	Cache La Poudre river	Sept. 1, 1861	10.97	37.91
5	Pioneer Ditch	Cache La Poudre river	Mch. 1, 1862	12.93	48.88
6	Boyd & Freeman Ditch	Cache La Poudre river	Mch. 15, 1862	66.05	61.80
7	Whitney Irrigating Ditch	Cache La Poudre river	Sept. 1, 1862	48.23	127.85
8	Yeager Ditch (upper branch), first enlargement	Cache La Poudre river	June 1, 1863	8.70	176.08
9	B. H. Eaton Ditch	Cache La Poudre river	Apr. 1, 1864	29.10	184.78
10	Larimer & Weld Irrigating Canal	Cache La Poudre river	June 1, 1864	3.00	213.88
11	Pleasant Valley & Lake Canal, first enlargement	Cache La Poudre river	June 10, 1864	29.63	216.88
12	Pioneer Ditch, first enlargement	Cache La Poudre river	Sept. 15, 1864	16.67	246.51
13	John G. Coy Ditch	Cache La Poudre river	Apr. 10, 1865	31.63	263.18
14	Ditch of John R. Brown	Cache La Poudre river	May 1, 1865	8.00	294.81
15	Box Elder Ditch	Cache La Poudre river	Mch. 1, 1866	33.50	302.81
16	Chamberlin Private Ditch	Cache La Poudre river	Apr. 1, 1866	14.85	335.31
17	Taylor & Gill Ditch	Cache La Poudre river	Apr. 15, 1866	18.48	350.14
18	B. H. Eaton Ditch, first enlargement	Cache La Poudre river	June 1, 1866	3.33	308.62

Figure 15. Table Giving Ditch and Reservoir Decrees in District No. 3 (first page), from Decree in the Matter of Priorities of Water Rights in Water District No. 3, Entered by the Hon. Victor Elliott, Judge of the Second Judicial District, April 11th, 1882, Colorado State University, Archives and Special Collections.

beneficial use. Delegates to an 1878 conference of irrigators agreed that only actual use created a valid water right, but split over the pragmatic question of how to administer these rights in practice. One party maintained that as only actual use on the land created a valid right, each new or expanded application of water should be considered a separate appropriation, with its own priority. The quantity of the appropriation would be variable, depending on the amount needed for the parcel in question; lands irrigated, rather than amounts of water diverted, is what would appear in each water district's registry. The other faction, however, contended that it would be impracticable to measure and administer so many water rights, or to base their size on the amount actually used or needed. Their proposal was that construction of a ditch would entitle the owners to water to the extent of its capacity, with the appropriation dating from the time the work commenced. The amount of the appropriation could be easily determined and easily regulated, by opening and closing the headgates, rather than by checking how much water was needed at any time for each parcel.

The convention adopted the position that water rights should be tied to the land on which they were used and dated from the time of use, and a bill to that effect was drafted: "It shall . . . be the duty of . . . water commissioners to divide the water in the natural stream or streams of their district among the several ditches taking water from the same, according to *the prior rights of the different claimants taking water through such ditches respectively*"—not according to the construction of the ditches.[50] The state legislature, however, whether bowing to what it likely saw as administrative necessity, or to pressure from ditch companies, redrafted the bill, and the bill enacted into law provided that water rights would belong to ditches, not users.[51] It bears emphasis that had the law been implemented as written, it should have created the conditions necessary for an efficient market in water rights. As in the system advocated more recently by law and economics scholars, in which appropriators would retain the rights to their return flows, appropriators under the 1879 Colorado law would have been freed from the restrictions imposed by the rule of no injury to third-party appropriators, thus allowing water rights to move smoothly to more valuable uses when they existed.[52]

Yet the law was not implemented as written. Fair distribution, not maximization of productivity, was the reigning value of the time, and the view that water rights should be tied to land and users, not to canals and diversions, was therefore not vanquished. It found an influential supporter in assistant state engineer Elwood Mead, who criticized the law as effectively granting the water to corporations instead of its users, "sacrific[ing] the principles of justice to present or prospective gain, [and] augment[ing] the power of the rich at the expense of the poor." Mead took his views with him to neighboring Wyoming, where, as state engineer, he was able to have them incorporated in the state constitution. (He later achieved national and worldwide influence as a leader of the so-called irrigation movement and head of the federal Bureau of Reclamation.)[53]

Meanwhile, in Colorado, it turned out that the irrigators' view was not vanquished either—it found powerful support from another source, the state supreme court. The first blow to basing water rights on ditch construction, rather than actual use, came in the leading case of *Wheeler v. Northern Colorado Irrigation Co.*, discussed in the previous chapter, in which the state supreme court based its invalidation of "royalty" charges imposed by the company on the theory that property in water was created by the irrigator's use, not the canal owner's construction of the canal.[54] A year later, the majority in the *Farmers' Highline Canal & Reservoir Co. v. Southworth* seemed to practically annul the ditch-based system of the irrigation statutes, ruling that prorating was unconstitutional, so that consumers taking from one ditch could insist on the enforcement of their relative priorities vis-à-vis each other.[55] While thus ruling in favor of the agrarian position as far as substantive rights were concerned, the court nonetheless left intact the administrative and judicial procedures created by the act, and in particular its direction to record the priorities of ditches (not users), based on the date of construction, rather than that of use.[56] This may have been a concession to administrative considerations, as it would have been far more difficult to determine the dates and quantities of farmers' use than the dates of ditches' construction and their capacities, but it also severely limited the utility of the decrees worked out under the statutory procedure: Under *Southworth*, while decrees issued under the statutory procedure would have legal force in disputes between one canal and another, they would leave the relative rights of individual appropriators undetermined, open again to case-by-case litigation.

At stake in this seemingly technical dispute over water rights administration was actually whether speculators and capitalists would be able to get control of Colorado's water, as the agrarian elements feared, or whether the ownership of water would be reserved for actual users, as they hoped. The application of the 1879–1881 acts was thus inextricably tied up in the issues of corporate versus individual control discussed in the preceding chapter.[57] The state supreme court's rulings on this issue, as in so many others, were clearly on the side of the farmers. So noted legal scholar William Russell Thomas in his praise of the court: "In no [other] state had the courts exercised a more decided and wholesome influence over the development of irrigation practice, supplying by suggestion apparent defects in statutes and ruling wisely and liberally on those which admitted of a double construction. Thus, under the statutes of 1879–1881, it might have been held that the great ditch companies were the real appropriators and proprietors of the water carried in their canals, but in two controlling cases, decided in 1888 and 1889, the supreme court declared that they were common carriers only, and that the carrier cannot become the proprietor of the water diverted. The far-reaching effect of this opinion in preventing a monopoly of water in Colorado has hardly yet been appreciated by the people of the state."[58]

The view that actual use, rather than ditch construction, should create the water right, received further support when the supreme court consistently ruled that beneficial use was the measure of a water right, regardless of court decrees based on other measures. In *Greer v. Heiser*,[59] a lower court's decree in the general adjudication for Water District No. 8, granting a water right based on the capacity of the ditch in question, was invalidated. The ditch was found to have a capacity to carry nearly enough water for 160 acres, but as only fifteen to twenty acres were "under ditch" (that is, capable of being irrigated from it), the supreme court held the water right limited to the latter amount, since that was all that it was possible to apply to actual use. In support of its basing the size of the water right on actual use, the court cited *Wheeler* and *Southworth*, the major water-corporation decisions that had emphasized consumer use as an essential element of appropriation, as well as *Sieber* and *Platte Water Co.*, leading cases applying the use requirement to limit appropriations.[60]

A similar situation presented itself soon after in *Ft. Morgan Land & Canal Co. v. South Platte Ditch Co.*[61] At issue in this case was the adjudication for Water District No. 1, in which, once again, the district court had based its decrees on the capacities of the various ditches, instead of on actual use:

> The capacity of the several ditches enumerated in the decree to convey water seems to have been the criterion by which the [district] court was governed. . . . Such capacity having once been established, together with proof of diversion and the use of a limited portion of water, with a promise to increase such use up to the limit of the ditch within a reasonable time, was sufficient to procure for the ditch a priority for an amount of water equal to such capacity. Such priority dating from the inception of the work of construction upon the ditch [*sic*].[62]

The state supreme court invalidated this decree, remanding it to the trial court for a new decree based on actual use, instead of capacity. This time, the court explained its reasoning a little more extensively:

> From the first, this court has recognized and emphasized the idea that a priority could only be legally acquired by the application of the water to some beneficial use. Hence, there must be not only a diversion of the water from the natural stream, but an actual application of it to the soil, to constitute the constitutional appropriation recognized for irrigation. Farmers' Canal & R. Co. v. Southworth, . . . and cases cited. This may now be considered as one of the fundamental principles underlying our system of irrigation. It is too well established to be open to controversy. A diversion unaccompanied by an application gives no right. This principle applied to the record in this case is fatal to the decree rendered by the district court.[63]

The court also illustrated the type of speculative dealing in water that the capacity rule would encourage, and which it was hoping to stamp out by requiring that decrees be based on actual use:

> For instance: It appears from the testimony in the case that the Platte & Beaver Improvement Company was the owner of more than thirty thousand acres of land adjacent to their ditch. And finding it impracticable to obtain either tenants or purchasers for this land they were about to consummate an arrangement at the time this decree was rendered in the

spring of 1887, whereby the same [that is, the water decree] could be divided among its stockholders with the object in view [*sic*] of accomplishing a more rapid development of the lands and a more extended application of water to the soil.[64]

By reading the beneficial use requirement as an implied condition into decreed water rights, the court solved the problem of excess decrees, rendering any "excessive previous appropriations[s] comparatively harmless."[65]

Ft. Morgan and *Greer*[66] had been appeals to the supreme court of a district court's decree for a water district, attacking them directly for awarding excessive appropriations without due regard to actual use. *New Mercer Ditch Co. v. Armstrong*[67] came up to the court under different circumstances: John L. Armstrong, water commissioner for District No. 3, had refused to allow the appellant company to take the 33.5 cubic feet per second of water that it claimed under the very senior rights to which its predecessor, Joshua Yeager (the earliest appropriator in the district), was entitled according to a decree of 1882 (see Fig. 15, lines 1 and 8). The official's reasoning was that while the decree had declared Yeager to be entitled to this amount based on diversions made in the early 1860s, he had never been able to actually use more than a few c.f.s. for the 120 acres he irrigated. When New Mercer sued to enjoin the water commissioner from interfering with the flow of water into its ditch, the trial court found that Yeager had, in fact, never used more than 3.5 c.f.s., and that after selling his decreed rights to 33.5 c.f.s. to the company in 1891, the company had conveyed back to him 3.5 c.f.s.. In effect, the company's claimed water right consisted of water that had never been applied to any beneficial use before 1891.

Now under the Irrigation Act of 1881 review of a water decree was supposed to be limited to two years from its entry, and all parties affected by it were considered to have acquiesced to it after four years.[68] Unlike the earlier direct attacks on decrees, the posture of this case presented the court with a situation in which the use doctrine was in conflict with the values of certainty and repose embodied in this statute. These competing values did not deter the court from its relentless application of the beneficial use doctrine, to the point where it seemed to eviscerate the limitations clauses of the law. It did so based on the (arguably question-begging) reasoning that as any decreed rights were implicitly conditioned on actual use, the decree itself was not being challenged in any way.[69] Accordingly, the court argued,

> Neither Yaeger nor his grantee can be heard to assert a claim to the full quantity fixed in this decree, not because the decree is in any way set aside, but because . . . no claimant of any of the priorities therein established can maintain a claim to an excessive quantity of water. There is an entire failure of proof that either Yaeger or any one in his behalf has made any beneficial use of the excess of water to which now the plaintiff asserts his right.[70]

The court thus ruled that the decree was no indication of Yeager's true appropriation, and cut back his right to 3.5 c.f.s.[71]

This decision struck a powerful blow at speculative appropriations, but at a cost. The judicial adherence to the beneficial use measure of water rights practically abolished the certainty and finality of clear property rights that were supposed to be afforded the appropriator by the statutory scheme of general stream adjudications. Now, just as before the enactment of the Irrigation Act, an appropriator's rights on paper bore little relation to those that would be enforced by the legal system. Even rights judicially decreed—what lawyers call *res judicata*—could be challenged again in court, at any time, for deviance from the use requirement.

Instead of providing sellers in the water market with an inexpensive tool for demonstrating their ownership, and buyers with the ability to easily determine the salient elements of the right and decide on its value, Colorado law practically nullified the utility of water-rights records. Since these records usually reflected the amount claimed, typically based on the amount diverted or canal capacity, while the true right (under case law) was only the amount actually used, the records were next to useless.[72] A prospective buyer or junior appropriator, in order to know the true extent of the rights, could not rely on the official record of water rights in the district, but would have to conduct extensive research in order to determine the actual pattern of use in the watershed.[73] Furthermore, as each water right was constantly subject to contraction based on lessened use or need, irrigators could not rely even on the quantities previously determined in lawsuits (based on actual use). Since a court decision could only declare the extent of a right at the time of litigation, non-use in the inter-vening time could render even the more accurate measures obsolete.[74] The irrigator, wrote a Colorado state engineer, "is surrounded by an atmosphere of doubt as to the exact status of his title and the rights upon which the success or failure of his efforts depend."[75]

The Law of Water Transfers

Most challenges to water rights (and thus most of the Colorado case law on water in the last decades of the nineteenth century) arose in the context of cases in which a water right had been ostensibly transferred from the original appropriator to another.[76] Appropriators attempting to convey the full extent of their claimed appropriations were required to show that they had in fact used, and thus truly appropriated, the water right they presumed to transfer to another.

Actually, the first issue that arose in connection with transfers of water rights was whether they should even be allowed at all. This question was a subset of the larger issue of alienability of real property, a topic that had presented a dilemma for antebellum agrarian reformers.[77] On the one hand, as discussed in Chapter 2, they were committed to the broad distri-bution of property for use, not sale or speculation. This consideration called for limiting the alienability of land, especially homesteads, as these property rights were meant to fortify the independence of the yeoman, not turn him into a speculator.[78] On the other hand, the prospect of limiting alienation was redolent of feudal tenures, threatening the very independence, freedom, and opportunity to benefit from his labor the homestead ideal was supposed to give the actual settler.[79] Consequently even the free homesteads granted by the federal government were allowed to be sold or otherwise alienated by their settlers.[80]

This internal contradiction in reformist thought played itself out again with the water issue. Prominent reformers, including John Wesley Powell and Elwood Mead, as well as Colorado farmers' organizations, advocated tying water rights to the land for which they had been appropriated.[81] It was also argued that since water rights depended on necessity, a transfer of rights should be impossible, since it would reveal that the grantor no longer had any use for his water, and thus void his right.[82] Advocating tying rights to specific parcels of land was part and parcel of the position denying corporate ownership of water rights. "The spirit of the [Colorado] Constitution, to be maintained," argued a former state engineer and member of a blue-ribbon commission on irrigation law reform, "requires that the sale or lease of the water of the streams, or any traffic therein or charge connected therewith, save a lawful charge for the carriage thereof, should be effectively prohibited by the statutes."[83] This, it was thought, would prevent the commodification of water, as well as the third-party and distributive effects to be discussed shortly.[84]

Alienability was necessary, however, to allow the settler to buy his water right on credit or pledge it as security for the capital necessary to develop his farm, as well as to give him flexibility in use and to let him cash out on his investment when it made sense. It also gave him independence from the canal corporation that delivered his water.[85]

The state supreme court was clearly sympathetic to the latter line of thinking in its seminal *Strickler* decision, holding that a water right could be sold separately from the land on which it had been used:

> If A. is the owner of one hundred and sixty acres of land with a water-right for only eighty acres, it may be of great benefit to him to change the place of use as the soil upon a portion of the tract becomes exhausted or impoverished by the raising of crops. To deny the right to change the place of use under such circumstances would result in injury to the prior appropriator with no corresponding benefit to others. . . . And no reason is perceived why, if the place of use may be changed to a tract adjoining the one in connection with which the priority came into existence, it may not as well be changed to a piece of land at a greater distance. . . . The authority for changing the place of use from one part of a quarter section of land to another place upon the same quarter section will permit the purchase of land elsewhere and utilizing the water in its cultivation. . . . To limit its transfer . . . would in many instances destroy much of its value. It may happen that the soil for which the original appropriation was made has been washed away and lost to the owner, as the result of a freshet or otherwise. To say under such circumstances that he could not sell the water-right to be used upon other land would be to deprive him of all benefits from such right.[86]

Soon after, though, fearing that it had opened a Pandora's box of speculation with its ruling that a water right "may be sold and transferred separately from the land in connection with which the right ripened,"[87] the court reassured:

> It must not be inferred from this language that such priority may be secured by the mere acquisition of stock in an irrigating company, without applying the water to beneficial use. An owner of irrigating stock cannot thus carry prior rights to the use of water in his pocket for an indefinite or unreasonable time, and thereby prevent others from acquiring a bona fide priority by actual use. . . . A stockholder in an irrigating company . . . may transfer his stock to whom he will, but he can only transfer his priority to some one who will continue to use the water.[88]

This at least partially addressed the concerns of those favoring restrictions on alienability, since it clarified that water rights could be transferred only to other users. Of course, this would also impair the robustness and efficiency of the market for water rights, but allowing the bona fide water user to benefit from his right, not efficiency, was the goal here.

With sale of water rights legalized, the permissible scope of these transfers needed to be determined. The *Strickler* court, while allowing transfers, had not gone nearly as far as canal corporations would have liked, stressing throughout its decision that transfers would be allowed only to the extent that they did not injure other (junior) appropriators.[89] In doing so, it implicitly rejected the position that appropriators owned the rights to their return flows.

New Mercer Ditch Co. v. Armstrong[90] provided Colorado's highest court with an opportunity to face square on the issue of how an appropriative right was to be quantified for purposes of transfer. As discussed above, it seems that Yeager, the original appropriator and the company's predecessor in title of the water right, had an official right of 33.5 c.f.s., though he used at most one-tenth of that amount. As long as he continued to water only his small farm, his excessive claim was of little import. The excess portion of his claim was presumably left in the stream; even if diverted, it probably returned directly to it. When Yeager sold his right to a ditch company, however, his paper right posed a threat, since the company planned to make use of his entire decreed allotment. Most immediately threatened would have been his downstream neighbors, whose appropriations all along effectively would have been using the

30 c.f.s. or so of his paper right that he had not been applying. Transferring his full 33.5 c.f.s. to another location, or even making use of the full allotment in place, would have taken away water upon which these other appropriators had until now relied.[91]

The issue of externalities was only one of the problems presented by transfers and changes in use, though. The more important problem was a distributive one, the opportunity that transfers and changes offered for solidifying a claimant's grip on an excessive water decree.[92] Allowing the original appropriator to sell the full 33.5 c.f.s. of his decree to another user would have been equivalent to abolishing the use requirement as a necessary element of a valid appropriation, effectively making diversion or some other maximalist criterion the measure of a water right, thereby endorsing speculative and monopolistic claims on public-domain water. How to deal with the distributive issue posed by the discrepancy between water decreed or diverted and the water actually used was a major issue facing Colorado lawmakers and courts. Elwood Mead felt this problem justified prohibiting transfers altogether: "If in these transfers . . . water [were] applied to no greater acreage elsewhere but simply in a more saving matter, there would be no objection; but so far as the writer's observation has gone this is not the moving purpose of these sales. In every instance investigated the real purpose has been to make money out of excess appropriations. The parties who have acquired surplus rights are unable to use the water themselves, and seek to sell to some one who can. The primary object is not economy, although this sometimes results. The usual result is to take as much water away from one user as is supplied to another."[93]

An appropriator, wrote another expert, "primarily takes water for a specific purpose for a definite tract of land, and is granted as much as is necessary for his use, with a fixed maximum also conditioned on its beneficial and economic use. Thus in the very beginning unused or surplus water does not belong to him; and why, then, should he be permitted to sell and transfer what is not his? Where would be the hardship in permitting him to continue the use of water as he had always used it?"[94]

The court took a more moderate position, allowing transfer but at the same time ruling that a water decree inherently limited each water right in it to the amount actually put to beneficial use, regardless of the quantity specified in the decree:

One may not, as against subsequent appropriators, divert, and indefinitely or for an unreasonable length of time hold, water for purposes of mere speculation, and make no beneficial use of it, while so holding; nor may he divert more than he needs for the purpose of which the diversion was made, though he may change the use or sell his right to another. So that this decree as to a claimant thereunder—no more than does a deed of conveyance to a grantee from one unquestionably the owner—affords no protection as to the waters thus diverted, if they are not within a reasonable time applied to a beneficial use.[95]

Apparent here was concern over externalities (the harm to "subsequent appropriators"), but also over the distributive issue (holding water "for purposes of mere speculation"). The court's decision met both of these concerns by allowing the transfer only of that portion of the original claim that had been put to actual use. Cases like this, with claimants threatening to exploit excessive and speculative claims that hitherto had not been fully used, is where the beneficial use and no-injury rules did their real work. The rule, enforced in transfer proceedings by other private appropriators on the stream demanding no impairment in the applicant's return flow, effectively voided speculative claims.

With the *New Mercer* decision apparently catalyzing recognition that the excessive and speculative amounts recognized in the original decrees would be of critical importance when it came to transfers of water rights,[96] the General Assembly passed a law in 1899 requiring that changes in the point of diversion be made only after petitioning the district court for permission. The court would conduct a hearing similar to that for the original decree for the water district, and allow the change only if it did not injure others.[97] In other words, the amount subject to transfer would be not the decreed amount, but the quantity that had been put to actual, consumptive use before other appropriations had been made. This was really the ultimate anti-speculation trump; speculators might build ditches to divert more water than they could use, and even succeed in gaining recognition for their excessive claim in a general stream adjudication, but when it came time for them to profit from their speculation by sale, their efforts would be neutralized in these new proceedings, where rigorous proof of use would be required, and the no-injury rule would allow them to sell no more than they had been consuming in practice. This law was rightfully hailed as neutralizing speculative excess appropriations.[98]

Here, again, speculation was stymied and the broad distribution of water rights among actual users was enforced. And again, this distributive goal was accomplished at the expense of significant losses in terms of efficiency. Not only were many efficient transfers ruled out by the protection given to dispersed third parties and the costs of legal and other expert counsel necessary to complete transfer proceedings, as discussed in the first portion of this chapter, but the uncertainty created by the need to enter into these expensive proceedings in order to determine the transferable component of a water right probably deterred many owners from even beginning the process, even when from an objective point of view the transfers were legally possible and financially worthwhile.[99]

Storage Rights

The evolution of the legal treatment of reservoirs and water storage in this period further illustrates the extent to which the beneficial use principle was used to subordinate efficiency interests to anti-speculation and anti-monopoly considerations. The flow in Colorado streams rose and fell with the seasons each year, with peak flows in the late spring and early summer as water melted off the Rocky Mountain snowpack, and water slowing to a trickle or less by the late summer and autumn. Since some crops needed to be watered late in the season, some water storage was practically imperative for efficient use of the resource.[100] Further efficiency gains could be achieved by storing water from year to year, helping to smooth out annual variations in precipitation. The idea of storing water for later use, however, smacked of speculation in water, since stored water was *ipso facto* not being put to beneficial use.[101] This led to complications in the recognition of storage rights.

The Irrigation Act of 1879 had explicitly allowed for the construction of reservoirs, with the right to take "any unappropriated water not needed for immediate use for domestic or irrigation purposes."[102] The meaning of this phrase was ambiguous, however: Did it mean that reservoirs could appropriate for future use any water *as yet* unappropriated, or did it imply that the rights to stored water would always be subordinate to the rights of even *later* appropriators to put the water to direct and immediate use (that is, without intervening storage)? The latter interpretation would seriously impair the utility and value of "storage rights," since they could always be preempted later by irrigators putting the water directly to use. However, the very idea of storage for later use seemed anathema to the principle that had been developed and clarified in the cases discussed in the previous section—namely, that use for current necessity, not construction or other attempt to reserve a right, was the essence of appropriation. As the court in *Combs* later said, a company could not "withhold the water from beneficial use, nor reserve it for the future use of junior appropriators to the prejudice of prior appropriators, nor to the exclusion of those who in the mean time may undertake, in good faith, to make a valid appropriation thereof."[103] Recognition of storage rights raised the specter of monopoly; well-funded corporations, it was feared, would build massive storage works and appropriate all the state's water to themselves, and then force settlers to buy water from them at inflated prices.

In 1882, two new reservoir companies were incorporated with the goal of building reservoirs on the Cache La Poudre (a tributary of the South Platte) at the base of the Rockies, upstream from the important and influential agricultural settlements of the valley (including Fort Collins and Greeley). The farmers feared that all the unappropriated water of the river would be taken by these companies, forcing the farmers to buy from them the water for any future expansion of their farms:

> If these two reservoir companies are allowed what they claim none of these enlargements can avail these farmers anything, for every inch of the water would have to be purchased at such price as may be determined by these reservoir companies—and $1000 for eighty acres seems to be the rate now charged. Now, what has either of these reservoir companies done to entitle them to a monopoly of all the water of the stream not already appropriated? Suppose they cannot sell it, is there no power which can step in and appropriate a portion of that which is allowed to run to waste? Certainly there cannot be if this claim to all the unappropriated water is once admitted. And thus the constitutional provision that all the appropriated waters of the streams of this State belong to the people, would be set at naught.[104]

Farmers feared that these new projects signaled a new trend, a "first and insidious attempt of a corporation to control and monopolize the supply of water, and so to bring under tribute the whole of the agricultural interest in the State of Colorado."[105] The district attorney for Larimer County accordingly filed suit for the dissolution of the Larimer County Reservoir Company, claiming that by building a reservoir, without diversion of the water to a beneficial use, the company had violated the law.[106]

There was, of course, a possible intermediate position on storage rights, one that recognized the validity of water storage for use late in the season, giving these rights security against later appropriations by direct irrigators, without allowing reservoirs to appropriate water for speculative future uses. That was to recognize storage as a valid diversion like any other, while requiring application to beneficial use within a reasonable time. This was the position the Colorado Supreme Court took in the case against Larimer County Reservoir, in which it ruled that storage, even without diversion, was constitutional, as long as it was followed by diversion and use within a reasonable time, with the rights so acquired subordinate only to previously acquired rights.[107]

The decision was criticized, however, as being too friendly to corporations, giving them water rights without the requisite use.[108] In practice, storage rights were subordinated to later diversions for direct use, and when presented again with the issue in *Water Supply & Storage Co. v. Tenney*, the supreme court adopted the anti-storage position, ruling that a storage right was inferior to a later appropriation for direct irrigation, "even though the priority of the latter was junior in time to the construction of the reservoir."[109] The legislature followed suit, declaring in a 1901 law that a reservoir could not impound water "during the time that such water is required in ditches for direct irrigation or for reservoirs holding senior rights."[110] This rule clearly interfered with the allocation of water to its best and most productive uses, as immediate use during the high-flow season would always take precedence over irrigation later in the year, even when the latter was for more valuable crops. It also radically impaired the certainty and security, and thus the economic feasibility, of storage rights; investments in these expensive works would be forever vulnerable to the actions of later appropriators for direct use. Here is yet another example of Colorado water law subordinating productivity or wealth creation to the anti-speculation ideology.

Conclusion: Tragedy, Comedy or Morality Play?

While beneficial use has been criticized by the economic-minded as pointless (since in a free market unused water would naturally be bought and sold until it ended up being put to the use most beneficial to society),[111] this type of criticism—focusing on the allocative features of the law while ignoring its distributive implications—is completely beside the point, as far as the use doctrine's historic purposes go. As this chapter has shown, and even modern jurisprudence has recognized, the intent behind the Colorado use rule was to make the appropriation for speculation in unused water a legal impossibility.[112] The critics are right that the market would have allocated water to its most productive use on its own, but that was not the concern of the Colorado Doctrine's creators. The use rule was not intended to regulate the types of use to which water could be put, but rather to limit the amount of water that could be appropriated from nature, as well as the amount that could be subsequently held by an appropriator. In keeping with the radical Lockean ideology of Colorado's early settlers, this doctrine helped ensure that this valuable property was distributed as widely as possible to actual users, and speculation in it inhibited. As prominent water lawyers of the time argued:

> While each bona fide appropriator is to be protected in the particular interest which he lawfully acquires to the extent of his actual user, nevertheless, his rights are to be restricted to the limits of his appropriation—that is, to the limits of his actual diversion and actual use. This must be the rule, lest the rights of other bona fide appropriators be invaded or impaired. It is only by the strict enforcement of prior rights and by rigid economy in the distribution of water that "the greatest good to the greatest number" can be assured among the good people of this commonwealth.[113]

Not only was achieving allocative efficiency through freely conveyable private-property rights not a goal of the farmers, lawyers, and publicists who advocated and developed the rules that made up the Colorado Doctrine, but they even created an anticommons, in which fragmented and intertwined private-property rights made efficiency-enhancing transfers difficult to impossible. The inefficiencies of limits on transfer of water rights were recognized even at the time, as in this criticism by state engineer John E. Field:

A valid objection against a law which puts obstacles in the way of transfer is that all such changes tend to more economical use of water, or to its application to more productive land, and should be encouraged. Any legitimate transfer has one of these for its object. The abandonment of the old bottom lands and the redemption of warm, productive mesas is [*sic*] of benefit to the community as a whole. The application of water to more productive land, producing as it does a greater return, enhances the value of the water, and the more valuable the water the more carefully and economically it is used, and the greater its duty. By transfer several ditches can be consolidated into one; the cost of repairs and maintenance diminished, as well as the loss by seepage and evaporation. This saving by lessening seepage and evaporation is more considerable than appears at first glance, for not only is the exposed surface diminished, but as transfers are almost always upstream the waste encountered by traversing a broad, sandy river bed to the lower head gates is eliminated entirely.[114]

Yet lawmakers nonetheless embraced draconian restrictions on transfer, in order to prevent speculators from grabbing water rights beyond what they needed for their use. They did so with awareness of the cost. Elwood Mead, for instance, recognized that transfers of water rights could lead to "economy," or more efficient use of the resource, yet this icon of the supposedly efficiency-oriented conservation movement advocated outlawing them outright, in order to prevent appropriators from profiting from excess appropriations.[115]

As discussed above, the costs imposed by the beneficial use rule could have been avoided by adopting the rule advocated by the canal companies: giving each user full ownership of his diversion, including the return flow. This would have dissolved the anticommons at a stroke, as transferors would be accountable to no one for any reduced return flow caused by the transfer. But the more efficient regime would have had distributive consequences at odds with the Lockean ethic of use-based property rights. Giving an appropriator the rights to transfer or sell his return flow would have turned the water right from a use right to a purely economic asset, and this option was never really on the table. Inefficiency in allocation of water was a price Colorado was willing to pay to prevent speculators from gaining economic rents from water rights and to keep the water in the hands of its actual users.

The aim of this book as a whole is to highlight a different way of thinking about and classifying property regimes: Rather than the classical private/common taxonomy, with its focus on the relationship between the legal powers of the actors with regard to the resource and its optimal allocation, the distributive lens would suggest that property regimes might be more usefully categorized based on the effective distribution of the resource and its benefits: any form of property—private, commons, public, or anticommons—might result in a narrower or broader distribution of the resource, depending on circumstances and the particular way in which the legal rules are constituted and applied. Looked at this way, a property regime like the appropriation system, in which fragmented rights make transfer and assembly of rights very difficult, might be viewed not as a tragedy, but as a comedy, with the near-freezing of ownership and use patterns having salutary effects.

Claims for a positive role for the anticommons (or "antiproperty") have been raised before, but, as with the private/commons literature in general, these have been arguments from utility, focusing on how this institution might, in some situations, succeed in allocating a resource to its socially optimum use. That might be the case with regard to appropriative water rights, too; for instance, as the anticommons created by a multiplicity of private rights retards the transfer of some unprofitable rights to more lucrative uses, the effect may be to leave water in the stream, thereby allowing it to serve ecosystem and other functions that benefit the diffuse interests of the public. Or the opposite may have been true; as Henry Smith has argued, the low transferability of rights may have increased use of the resource.[116]

What has as yet gone little noted, however, is the way heavy restrictions on transfers of private property (effectively creating an anticommons) might be used to achieve not allocative purposes, but distributive ones. An ancient example of this phenomenon is the agrarian law of Leviticus, under which transfer of ownership in an Israelite's field was impossible; only leaseholds expiring in the jubilee year were allowed. Similarly, the framers of nineteenth-century American agrarian land-settlement legislation had toyed with the idea of freezing the broad distribution of land acquired from the public domain under laws such as the Homestead Act of 1862 by severely limiting its alienability, but only moderate restrictions were adopted.[117] In the water context, however, while appropriative rights typically could be transferred in theory, the legal impediments to doing so effectively prevented transfer in most cases. The result, while inefficient (that is, having a negative effect on aggregate wealth), appears to have ensured that water rights remained distributed widely among actual users, rather than accumulated by well-capitalized corporations and speculators.

This property drama was thus, properly speaking, neither a Hardinian tragedy (since the law brought about the desired outcome with regard to the water resource) nor a Roseate comedy (since satisfaction of these distributional goals came at the cost of preventing the resource's allocation to its most valuable uses), but rather a "morality play," in which legal institutions were effectively aimed at advancing ideals of justice.[118] Thus, on the level of positive property theory, distributive factors may be an overlooked dimension that can help explain the evolution and outlines of various property regimes that defy the efficiency-based logic of mainstream theory. When a prominent scholar implicitly took this position, arguing that the restricted alienability of homesteads under the Homestead Act may have served distributive purposes, she was attacked by another on the basis of the system's inefficiency.[119] Yet his criticism, like criticisms of the inefficiency of the beneficial use rule, is inapposite. It may be that the distributive policies of homesteading or the appropriation doctrine sacrificed efficiency, but that is precisely the point—the law may choose to prefer fair distribution of property over efficient allocation, and did so frequently in the context of the mines, farms, and water sources of the American West.

This historical drama might have normative implications for contemporary property issues as well, as will be discussed in the final chapter.

CHAPTER 6

CONCLUSION

To conclude this study, several aspects of the relationship between the early history of Colorado water law and property theory will be examined. After a review of the distributive-justice principles reflected in the appropriation doctrine, the classic claim that the adoption of the prior appropriation regime was a transition to a system of more specified private-property rights, driven by considerations of economic efficiency, will be examined. Next to be considered will be other economic explanations for the transition in property rights, especially those highlighting the inefficient institutions that may result from interest group pressure. The fourth section will highlight some practical, modern implications of this study. Finally, the insights gained into the history of the Colorado Doctrine will be used to question conventional classifications of property regimes.

The Appropriation Doctrine and Distributive Justice

As intimated earlier, there is a dominant, narrow view of Colorado water law, in which its varied and interconnected doctrines and rules have come to be obscured (and to some degree replaced) by one particular rule, the rule of priority.[1] Yet, as we have seen, this synecdochic view of the law is unfortunately more than a simplification; it is misleading.[2] Standing in for the whole is not just one rule among many, but an auxiliary, unrepresentative one at that. This book has labored to show that the rule of priority was but a small piece in a larger puzzle of rules, principles, and policies concerned primarily to allocate surface water rights in accordance with contemporary principles of distributive justice.

The principles of distributive justice advanced by Colorado water law, discussed extensively in earlier chapters, were not, on their surface, entirely the same as those advocated by modern property theorists who advocate favoring the less well-off in various doctrinal contexts.[3] The thrust of the legal regime was rather to distribute rights in a specific resource as widely as possible among actual users, without regard to their relative wealth. This was accomplished by making water rights available to all (abolition of riparian rights and imposition of ditch easements) and by employing the requirement of beneficial use both to restrict ownership to actual users and to limit the extent of the rights. With the amount needed for actual use the measure of the appropriative right in the mines and for irrigation, water rights were thus limited to the amount reasonably used by the individual miner or settler; excessive or speculative appropriations were not protected by law. As explained in Chapter 2, these rules of water law acted in tandem with legal limits on land and mine holdings to limit the amount of water that could be held by any one person. The heavy property-based regulation of water corporations (discussed in Chapter 4), along with the crippling restrictions imposed on efforts to create a market of easily alienable water rights (discussed in Chapter 5), further impeded attempts to accumulate water rights for profit.

The law of water rights was thus broadly egalitarian, in terms of the resource itself. Though it did not strive for absolute equality among users, it did aim to maximize the number of water-right holders and limited the extent of their individual water holdings. And while the egalitarian measures applied to water only, this resource's role as the limiting factor in much economic activity (for mining and farming in particular) meant that resulting distributions of wealth in general tended toward equality as well. This sort of keystone status is what made water law such a focus of popular attention in this period. Moreover, while on a formal level a rich farmer stood to gain as much from Colorado water law as did his poor neighbor, the law's favoring of the interests of the irrigator over those of the investor-owned corporation, and of the actual user over the speculator, gave the law an overall progressive cast.

In the overall scheme of water rights, temporal priority was but a secondary principle, though one with a distributive role as well. As outlined in Chapters 2 and 3, the distributive principle of equality was modified by that of sufficiency. The legal form this latter principle took was the rule of priority, meant to ensure that the generally egalitarian rules did not lead to a situation where rights were so small as to be worthless.

The importance of water for the economic and political independence of the yeoman farmer explains the attention given it by contemporary lawmakers. It also helps us relate the appropriation doctrine to modern accounts of distributive justice in property. A prominent group of progressive property scholars recently argued, for instance: "Because of the equal value of each human being, property laws should promote the ability of each person to obtain the material resources necessary for full social and political participation."[4] Similarly, Joseph Singer has argued that property law properly contains within it a distributive imperative that "everyone should have some."[5] This position was the view of the "radical Lockeans" discussed in Chapter 2, and of the creators of the appropriation doctrine in water law.

To the extent that an appeal to tradition makes for a normative argument (in property law in particular it seems that it often does), this work can thus be read as an argument in favor of the "everyone should have some" view of property in general, and of the right to water in particular. Furthermore, it can be seen as an argument for making distributive concerns a dominant consideration in the legal allocation of property rights, and not leaving the distributive work to the tax system, despite the supposed efficiency advantages of the latter.[6] Indeed, normative implications will be explored further toward the end of this chapter.

I turn now, though, to positive property theory—the theory of how and why property regimes develop as they do. This book has argued that the driving force behind the development of the appropriation doctrine was a desire to distribute a crucially important resource in accordance with contemporary norms of fairness. In order to solidify this argument, alternative theoretical explanations need to be examined as well. I turn now to the dominant set of such approaches, all associated in one way or another with the economic analysis of legal institutions.

The Appropriation Doctrine and Economic
Efficiency—the Demsetz Thesis

As outlined in Chapter 1, the prior appropriation doctrine has come to be strongly associated, by admirers and critics alike, with the idea of welfare-maximizing private property in natural resources. By clearly defining rights, allowing owners to exclude others from use, and allowing free transfers of these rights, assigning private-property rights in a resource facilitates its allocation to its most productive use. The rejection in the western United States of relatively unspecified common-property riparian rights in favor of the private-rights system of prior appropriation is thought to have been motivated by these efficiency considerations.

We have seen, however, that according to claims made by contemporaries, the adoption of the appropriation doctrine in Colorado water law was motivated by distributive-justice concerns, in particular by a desire to have this critical resource distributed as widely as possible. Achieving allocative efficiency through freely conveyable private-property rights was not a primary goal of the farmers, lawyers, and publicists who advocated, framed, and developed the rules that made up the Colorado Doctrine, or at least not one they made explicit. This much is clear from our examination of the early water law of Colorado in its context.

Now, it might be argued that intent aside, the law nevertheless inexorably evolved in the direction of efficiency, a thesis sometimes thought to be particularly applicable to areas of law, like the Colorado Doctrine, with a large judge-made component, or law developed in the nineteenth century.[7] Statements by contemporaries explaining developments in the law as based on abstract principles of distributive justice or fairness, so the argument might go, may reflect nothing more than self-serving rhetoric, naïveté, or a lack of understanding; what really counts are the legal rules themselves, especially as applied—the law in action.[8]

Proponents of the efficient private-property and wealth maximization theses for prior appropriation indeed have claimed to rely on the terms of the law itself, not on the various forms of historical evidence examined in this study. Nonetheless, even they have found it hard to explain many specifics of appropriation law, and so their account even of the law itself is incomplete and stylized, leaving out or downgrading in importance various inefficient or common-property-like aspects of the Colorado Doctrine. Constrained by the efficiency paradigm, these elements of the doctrine have been viewed as exceptions to the general rule, explained historically as foreign, external norms unfortunately grafted onto the pure appropriation doctrine. My argument is that these specific principles and norms, to be summarized shortly, are integral parts of the appropriation doctrine, so that understanding them properly may require something of a paradigm shift. Viewing the Colorado Doctrine through the lenses of the ideology that has been variously termed radical Lockean, Jeffersonian, agrarian, or populist reveals it to have been an organic whole, the components of which may not have allowed for a smoothly functioning system of private-property rights, but which did work together to further this set of beliefs on the proper distribution of the bounties of the public domain.

This study has focused throughout on the development of the Colorado Doctrine as understood by contemporaries, and on explaining the various rules that evolved as expressions of the agrarian ideology of wide distribution of property. Along the way, it has also tried to point out some of the ways in which the doctrine's rules impeded the development of a true system of marketable private-property rights or were otherwise efficiency-impairing, but this negative analysis was secondary to the primary goal of connecting the developments in the law in a coherent narrative and linking them with the distributive ideals at their roots. At this point let us look at the law from the other perspective, summarizing and clarifying some of the ways in which Colorado water law, as it developed to reflect these distributive goals, actively frustrated any efficiency gains that might have been hoped for from a system of nominally private rights. The legal norms we have examined were all reflections of the twin doctrinal pillars of Colorado appropriation law: the theory that water was public property, and therefore open to appropriation by all, and the principle of beneficial use, restricting the acquisition of water rights to actual users and limiting those rights in quantity to the amount actually used. The details of this latter doctrine in particular played havoc with the efficiency of the new system.

The first point to note about beneficial use is that it was (and is) inefficient per se, encouraging uneconomical use of water for the purpose of staking and holding on to claims.[9] The principle behind it, that speculation in water should be prohibited, is also at odds with efficiency goals, since prohibiting speculation in a resource prevents its being held for its most valuable use.[10] Some have tried to justify these rules as ensuring that the valuable water would not be wasted, but others have rightly pointed out that under a market system more productive users would simply be able to buy the water right from the original holders.[11]

Besides encouraging inefficient use, the use requirement had other serious efficiency-hampering effects. As discussed in Chapter 5, the use requirement as applied by Colorado courts practically nullified the utility of water-rights records. Since these records usually reflected the amount claimed, typically based on the amount diverted or canal capacity, while the true right (under the case law) was only the amount actually used, the records were next to useless.[12] This was a significant obstacle to the creation of a functioning market in water rights that could have moved water to its most valued uses. Worse, due to the anticommons created by interlocking property rights in return flows, efficient transfers of uses were made practically impossible. According to economic theory, high transaction costs, lessening the opportunities to realize efficiency gains from trade, should have militated against the creation of a system of individual appropriative rights,[13] but historically that was not the case—they went, rather, hand in hand with the development of the appropriation system. This picture is difficult to square with the Demsetzian story of the evolution of private-property rights, but not with the radical Lockean view of private property, in which wide distribution, not facilitation of higher productivity, was the goal.

The law's recognition of beneficial use as the measure of a water right, and the attendant weakening of the significance of water decrees, had yet another important consequence: it made enforcement of water rights difficult and expensive. Rights were not clearly delineated such that owners could exclude others with ease; litigation was usually required, and a water right holder who felt his right was being violated by a junior user had to prove in court not only that his right was superior on paper, but that he needed and had been using his right, or at least that portion of it he wished to protect, on a more or less continuous basis.[14] The costly enforcement of rights was another significant drag on efficient allocation; on the Demsetzian view yet another factor that should have discouraged the adoption of private-property rights in this resource.[15] The fact that the use requirement was part and parcel of the appropriation from its inception is thus another indication that broad distribution, not Demsetzian efficiency, was the goal of Colorado water law.

Of course, the need for expensive litigation to enforce water rights had negative distributive consequences as well, since it gave large and well-capitalized organizations an advantage over the small farmer.[16] Significantly, it was this imbalance, not the drag on productivity, that was the force behind the constant pressure for reform in the enforcement of priorities, pressure that always came from Colorado's agrarian element, led by the Grange and other farmers' organizations. The true motivation behind the reforms is indicated also by the form they took: increased state involvement in administration of water rights, without clarification or strengthening of prior rights by tying them to canal capacity or the amount diverted.

It is important to emphasize that it is very difficult to explain these effects of the beneficial use rule in conventional efficiency terms. Some have suggested that the use requirement in the early mining camps was an efficient solution to the problem of notice, supplying it without the need for a complicated recordation system,[17] but as shown in Chapter 2, most mining camps had a system for recording claims. The costs of highly unspecified and constantly fluctuating rights created by the use requirement certainly outweighed by far any supposed savings in administrative costs. More damning, in any case, is the fact that after enactment of the 1879 Irrigation Act, the use requirement actually defeated the statutory scheme for notice, as discussed in Chapter 5.[18] It is hard to see how these inefficiencies created by the use requirement can be explained as anything other than what the contemporary historical evidence demonstrates the doctrine to have been: a check on speculative holdings in water, bought at the expense of a considerable drag on wealth maximization. Historically speaking, efficiency was not a primary goal of prior appropriation; the goal was limiting appropriations in order to maximize the number of appropriators.[19] The details of the doctrine as well as contemporary explanations reflect this history.

Other Economic Explanations for the Colorado Doctrine's Norms of Wide Distribution

Given that the Colorado appropriation doctrine was consistent with wide distribution of the resource, while interfering with an efficient market in water rights, can this distributive program be nevertheless reconciled with the idea of economic factors explaining the development of the law?

The answer, of course, may depend partly on the definition of efficiency. If an efficient allocation is simply one that maximizes social welfare, and distributive concerns are incorporated in the relevant welfare function, then it is possible for an arrangement with widely distributed property rights to be more efficient than another producing wealth that is greater in the aggregate but more concentrated.[20] Applying this approach to the case of water rights, it could be argued that adoption of the Colorado Doctrine was welfare-enhancing, assuming that the utility function (in general, or possibly for water in particular) was such that any efficiency losses attributable to the factors discussed above were more than offset by the welfare gains due to a wider distribution of water rights. This type of argument seems to me unanswerable as well as unobjectionable; if efficiency must be brought into the picture, the theme of this study, that the development of the Colorado Doctrine is best explained by a certain distributive ideology, may be restated as claiming that the development of the Colorado Doctrine is best explained by a social welfare function that privileges that distributive ideology. But the social welfare function approach also seems less than entirely helpful, since it essentially means that any distribution can be explained as efficient by appropriately manipulating the social welfare function. Indeed, most economic analyses of property rights have never really taken this approach seriously, having typically confined their analysis of property regimes to their effects on productivity.[21] In any case, arguing that the shape of the social welfare function is such that increased welfare due to broad distribution outweighs the welfare losses caused by the same institutions designed to achieve that broad distribution is essentially the same thing as arguing that distribution, not allocative efficiency, is what matters in the evolution of property rights; it basically concedes the point.

A different approach is the argument that the distributive norms evident in Colorado water law advanced efficiency goals (narrowly conceived)—that is, they were themselves wealth-maximizing, as Richard Zerbe and Leigh Anderson have claimed for the miners' laws of the California Gold Rush. In matching claim sizes to the amount that could be worked by an individual miner, so they suggest, contemporary ideas of producerist "fairness," adopted due to their salience as "focal points" for the miners, may have reflected or at least coincided with efficiency considerations;[22] we may add that the same analysis would apply to the appropriation doctrine's use requirement. In light of our discussion of the sufficiency principle, this explanation seems at least partially correct: establishing claim sizes based on the amount a miner could work, along with tying water rights to the amount needed for actual use, and then ranking these rights by the priority rule, ensured that rights did not fall below a certain utility threshold, the point of insufficiency, which could have been the case under a rule of strict equality.

But it is clear that tying the measurement of water rights to use, in addition to establishing an efficient minimum for the size of a property right when twinned with priority, had another effect (and function) as well: establishing a maximum for the amount that might be claimed, thereby preserving for as many users as possible the opportunity to benefit from the resource. This limitation of property claims was plainly productivity-hampering. While it is true that beyond some point on the quantity axis, the marginal utility from larger water rights would likely diminish, so that it would be more efficient for water exceeding that quantity to be used by another user, such would be the case for water rights as they were used, not for their initial distribution. In a situation of cost-free transfers of water rights, their initial distribution would raise purely distributive issues; the holder of an inefficiently large claim would sell excess water to a user who valued it more. Nor is the Coasian rejoinder—that the high transaction costs associated with water transfers required the initial distribution of entitlements to reflect an efficient allocation[23]—apposite in this case, as these transaction costs were themselves largely the result of the use doctrine and the related restrictions on corporate ownership of water. It would have been more efficient to have no use requirement whatsoever, allowing the initial appropriators (or riparian owners) to take as much as they could, and letting them sell or rent their rights to the most efficient users in a low-transaction-cost environment. Furthermore, the establishment of a minimum size that Zerbe and Anderson identify as efficient was only made necessary in the first place by the partial accommodation of the equality ideal inherent in the limitation of water right sizes; had early claimants been allowed to claim water based on their diverted amount, ditch capacity, or other generous measure, as desired by the capitalists operating in the West, there would have been no need to ensure a minimum claim size.

Thus, while Zerbe and Anderson are right in pointing to the salience in mid-nineteenth-century America of the types of rules we have been discussing as a factor in their adoption, the conclusion that these rules sacrificed efficiency for wide distribution in the case of prior appropriation seems unavoidable. However, these researchers' analysis of the costs associated with the creation of a new system of property rights focuses attention on another avenue of exploration: how various interests and commitments, viewed as transaction costs, may have caused the appropriation doctrine to evolve as it did. Even if the norms of prior appropriation themselves would have been inefficient in a theoretical world with no such costs, attention to the incentives and interests of the actors involved in its adoption may help explain the form these rules took in the real world.[24] Indeed, Gary Libecap has applied the public-choice model to explain transitions in property regimes in the western United States in our period, though not the case of water rights.[25]

The most prominent school of thought associated with this way of thinking is public-choice theory. As Stuart Banner notes, considering the transaction costs involved in transitions between property regimes may lead to the conclusion that such transitions are not always efficiency-enhancing. According to this "darker" story, "societies reallocate property rights when some exogenous political realignment enables a powerful group to grab a larger share of the pie."[26] The appropriation doctrine, with its clear winners (small farmers) and losers (speculators, corporations, outside capitalists), seems at first a prime exemplar of the interest-group sort of redistributive story. Seen through the lens of public choice, the adoption of the Colorado Doctrine, with its restrictions on speculation and corporate ownership, seems to have been the result of one interest group, the small-scale irrigators, reworking the law to suit their own interests, to the detriment of society's aggregate wealth.

There are several problems with the classic public-choice under-standing of the adoption of prior appropriation in the West, however. The first set of problems has to do with the characteristics of interest-group dynamics posited by public-choice theorists. Perhaps the most basic premise of interest-group theory, first advanced by Mancur Olson, is that large groups have a more difficult time in organizing to provide collective goods than do smaller groups; this tendency toward subopti-mality is further reinforced when members of the group place relatively similar values on the collective good in question.[27] This model is difficult to square with the victories of the agrarian forces in the Colorado contro-versies over water rights, since the farmer groups were composed of rela-tively large numbers of individuals, arguing for a relatively equal distribution of water rights, while the large canal companies were rela-tively few in number, the highly variable project size of which gave them relatively unequal valuations of the water they wanted to control. Moreover, the farmers were what Olson would characterize as a "latent" group: the failure of any one farmer to help in fighting for the collective good (prior appropriation) would have no significant effect on the campaign as a whole, thus giving each no incentive to do so.[28] The success of the farmers was yet more surprising given that they were arguing against significant vested interests, specifically the speculators and corporations who stood to profit from the continued application of riparian law.[29] Also working against the adoption of prior appropriation was the absence of a factor that Libecap identifies as having encouraged agreement on mining rights: large expected aggregate gains in welfare from the new system.[30] Water rights were already specified under the riparian system and, as we have seen, appropriation law did not really establish a system of secure or easily transferable rights. It seems, thus, that the direction of change in property rights predicted by public choice was at odds with the direction of change in practice; instead of favoring the concentrated and powerful corporate interests, the transition to the appropriation doctrine favored the diffuse and hard-to-organize farmers of Colorado.

Similarly, the victory of the agrarian interests in the battle over how water rights would be delineated was not the result predicted by economic theory. Henry Smith has argued that groups that advocate uses that are easier to measure can more readily organize in the political process and push through their proposals.[31] Yet, as described in the preceding chapter, smallholding farmers defeated corporate interests in this matter, with the Colorado Supreme Court consistently ruling that only hard-to-measure actual use, rather than easily metered diversion, was the true measure of a water right. The distributive imperative of basing property rights on actual use turned out to be more powerful than the countervailing institutional costs described by Smith.

Another set of problems with a public-choice explanation for the adoption of prior appropriation involves the nature of the rules of water law themselves. Colorado's bona fide settlers at any given time were winners with respect to some developments in water law, securing restrictions on the ability of land speculators and out-of-state investors to gain control of the state's water and earn economic rents from its owner-ship. Yet they were at the same time losers in another respect, since the beneficial use requirement sharply limited their own appropriations and ability to profit from large appropriations from the public domain. While preserving the right to appropriate for as many settlers as possible did benefit another group, future settlers who would need water for their farms, Colorado "political entrepreneurs" at any given time could expect to gain little from this inchoate group. Any political returns the agrarian lawmakers (broadly defined) could expect from future settlers would almost certainly be outweighed by the returns they could gain from enriching settlers and corporations already on the scene.[32] In other words, even were we to assemble a plausible story about the economic factors that allowed the state's small-scale irrigators to prevail over their opponents in this battle, we would be hard-pressed to explain their adoption of the Colorado Doctrine in terms of interest-group politics.[33] The victorious interest group in Colorado water law, the agrarian party, enacted rules that worked to some extent against its own financial self-interest.

The final problem with the public-choice theory as an explanation for the adoption of the Colorado Doctrine has to do with the utility of the theory itself, as it has been defined by its proponents. For this school of thought, as for most economics-centered approaches, the criterion by which success in transitions among property regimes is measured is economic productivity alone,[34] while in contrast, institutions demonstrating public-choice failure are those benefiting a special-interest minority at the expense of overall productivity.[35] The case of the Colorado Doctrine is hard to shoehorn into these categories. Increased productivity does not seem to have been its result, but then neither was that its intent—so was it really a failure? Moreover, the beneficiaries of this inefficient system of property rights were not a narrow class of special interests, but a broad sector of the population; it is the corporations whose interests were harmed who would be better classified as a special-interest minority. The transition to prior appropriation thus seems to fit neither category proposed by mainstream public-choice analysis.

Fortunately, some economic models of property-rights transitions are more nuanced than that of the public-choice Gradgrinds who inveigh against the consideration of anything but "rational" self-interest as an explanation for institutional change.[36] Douglass North, for instance, has acknowledged the role of subjective mental constructs, including ideological conviction, in influencing the range and "costs" of available alternatives, thereby determining the path of institutional change. His analysis of nineteenth-century agrarian protest movements in general is consistent with our depiction of the adoption of appropriation law: Perceived sources of the farmers' misfortune, he writes, "consisted of immediately observed grievances filtered through ongoing intellectual currents and ideologies of the actors. . . . We cannot make sense out of the protest movements and policy prescriptions of the period without understanding those intellectual currents. Nor can we make sense out of the direction of change in the polity and the economy that resulted from those movements without an understanding of them. Whatever the real underlying sources of the farmers' plight that produced discontent in the late nineteenth century, it was the farmers' perceptions that mattered and resulted in changing the political and economic institutional framework."[37]

Elsewhere, North identifies two functions of ideology relevant to our subject. First, ideology may lead political decision makers to act counter to organized interest-group pressure.[38] This seems to have been the case in Colorado, where courts and legislatures shaped the law of water rights in a way at odds with the interests of the highly influential capitalists of the state. Second, ideology can explain the actions of groups themselves in pressing for policies that seem to harm the interests of their members (when ideology is excluded from consideration).[39] Here, too, the persistence of the farmers' groups in fighting for limits on appropriations through a strict interpretation of the use requirement, even though they themselves probably would have benefited from a more liberal approach, seems to exemplify ideology at work. Specifically, we may profitably understand the prevailing distributional norms of radical Lockeanism as having influenced or even determined the paths available for the development of Colorado water law; this set of ideals lowered the "contracting costs" for alternatives seen as just, alternatives that otherwise would have been expensive to adopt. At the same time it raised the costs of other alternatives that may have been more consistent with interest-group pressure or wealth-maximization criteria, but at odds with the distributional ethic.[40]

Whether or not viewed through the lens of economic incentives, this study certainly supports the claim that distributional ideology played the dominant role in shaping the water law of nineteenth-century Colorado. It thus joins Joshua Getzler's analysis of earlier, English water law in rejecting economic development or efficiency as the moving force behind at least some historical developments in the law.[41] While Getzler, however, is able to explain legal evolution purely in terms of internal, doctrinal influences,[42] no doubt an accurate portrayal of the common law of the Westminster courts, the present study has taken a broader view of the legal conceptualism at work. The norms that came to be expressed in the appropriation doctrine were not necessarily viewed as deriving from precedents in the strict, legal sense of the word, nor were they necessarily taken from water law, or even law in general. They were, rather, openly recognized as expressions of the Jeffersonian and Jacksonian world view, one that valued the broad distribution of property, an ideal evident already in the law of the land, particularly in the laws of miners and the public domain. Judges and legislators were simply giving these ideological ideals further expression in the specific rules of water law they worked out.

Practical Implications

Whether the appropriation doctrine lived up to its promise as an egalitarian doctrine in practice is an issue beyond the historical scope of this project. Similarly, an extended exploration of the practical implications of the early history of western water law is best left for future normative, policy-oriented research. Yet it bears noting that the story of the early years of Colorado water law is of continuing relevance today, particularly when claims regarding desirable policies are supported by appeals to what is supposed to be the true essence of the Colorado Doctrine. Whatever Colorado water law has become, its origins as a radical, anti-monopoly law can serve an instructive and inspirational role in current debates related to the allocation of water, and to some extent over other property controversies as well. The following points are thus offered as tentative sketches of directions in which arguments might be made in the spirit of the history of the Colorado Doctrine of water law.

The Current Water-Privatization Debate

One of the most contentious issues of natural-resources policy today is the privatization of water supplies and water-delivery systems. Around the world, the increasing prominence of multinational corporations in the provision of water services has attracted attention, and often opposition.[43] Among the many factors driving business involvement in a field that has traditionally been the preserve of governments is the private sector's superior ability to mobilize capital.[44] This is an attractive feature to governments with little spare cash facing burgeoning needs for investments in infrastructure.

While the context in which water-corporation law developed over a century ago in the Rocky Mountain West was obviously different in many ways from that of today's water-corporation controversies, the similarities—demand for capital investment in water infrastructure, the accompanying rush of large corporations to fill this need, and vehement public opposition—are striking. In both cases, capitalists undertook massive investments in the acquisition and development of water infra- structure. In the late nineteenth century, the investment capital for proj- ects in frontier areas (the arid West) came primarily from wealthy, economically developed regions (the eastern United States and Europe); today, much of the opposition to privatization has arisen in the context of similar takeovers of water supplies in areas of relative underdevelopment (the global South) by companies based and funded in the developed world (the North). Then, as now, wealthy foreign actors' control of this elemental resource, as well as its effect on local users, aroused intense opposition.

Given these parallels, the law as developed in the western United States holds lessons for today's situation, and may point the way to legal doctrines that provide appropriate encouragement for investment in infrastructure and supply while at the same time guaranteeing access to all sectors of the population. Just as regulation of water corporations in Colorado was based by courts on doctrines of property law, limiting the power of today's water conglomerates may ultimately be effected by a turn to property law, rather than the human rights approach taken by many advocates of local users.[45]

For instance, while many have objected to the creation of private prop- erty in water per se, seeing it as necessarily negating public ownership, Chapters 3 and 4 of this book have shown that the recognition of private rights in what had been considered hitherto a public resource is not necessarily antithetical to retaining its public nature. If carried out in the proper way, privatization may effectively advance the value of broad distribution of water among its actual users, and prevent its monopoliza- tion by the wealthy or well-connected. The link the appropriation doctrine made between private rights and actual use was the critical factor in keeping water under broad public control in Colorado. Other legal strategies may yield similar results.

Similarly, the Colorado experience demonstrates that recognition of corporate ownership need not be synonymous with subordination of consumers' interests to that of the companies charged with developing or controlling water resources, as some have argued.[46] Legal recognition of public ownership of water sources may provide a basis for enforcing public and consumer rights, even when legislation has presumed to grant the water to an investor-owned corporation.[47]

One major point of contention in modern water-privatization controversies concerns radical increases in prices sometimes imposed by corporations that have taken over water-supply systems.[48] The Colorado precedent shows that recognition of the public nature of water can provide a theoretical basis not only for imposition of price controls, but also for other legal measures designed to prevent water companies from extracting excessive economic rents from water sales. Colorado courts of the late nineteenth century saw clearly that while investors funding the development of water systems had a legitimate claim to a reasonable return on their investment, profits beyond this level properly belonged to users—the true owners of the water.

Another injustice decried by critics of modern water privatization is the practice of forcing users to pay multinational companies for water from sources from which they had been drawing water before the company took over.[49] As argued in Chapters 2 and 3, the primary motivation behind the adoption of the appropriation doctrine in the West was the desire to prevent similar ousting of early uses by riparian landowners. Chapter 4 showed that the threat posed specifically by corporations granted water rights by the government was dealt with in similar fashion—judicial invocation of the use requirement to invalidate legislative grants and preserve the prior rights of those who developed the water resources on their own. The principle of prior use may be a valuable tool today, too, in protecting traditional and local uses of water from expropriation by well-connected corporations.[50]

Whether policymakers, jurists, and other actors involved in today's water-privatization controversy choose to adopt concrete doctrinal innovations of Colorado law in the Gilded Age or not, they may in any case draw inspiration from the judges and legislators of the Rocky Mountain frontier who succeeded in creating a body of law that dealt creatively with the social and economic challenges posed by the similar controversy of those days.

Property Rights in Natural and Other Resources

Historical insight into the way the appropriation doctrine's creators viewed property regimes has implications also for the place of distributive-justice concerns in our theories of property rights in natural resources in general. The literature on the historical origins and development of property in natural resources is dominated by economic models, whether of the Panglossian sort, according to which we necessarily live in the most efficient of all possible natural-resource regimes (or at least we used to, until government tampering got in the way), or the jaded view focusing on the deleterious influence of interest groups on the creation of property rights.[51] In contrast, deferential references to Locke in property law casebooks aside, little work seems to have been done on attempting to relate the theoretical discussions of the very large literature on distributive justice in property rights to actual historical norms for distribution of those rights.[52] As I hope this book has shown, this is unfortunate, because our understanding of various historical instances of property law regimes may be enriched by paying attention to motivating concerns of distributive justice. It seems that some may have the impression that distributive justice consists of nothing more than theoretically thin notions like "fairness" and simplistic norms like "allocate the right to the poorer party"; yet, as the Colorado water-law experience demonstrates, norms such as equality and sufficiency have, from a historical standpoint, guided lawmakers, and are robust enough to serve as criteria for normative critique of existing law.

This lack of attention to distributive justice in the property-theory literature may be attributable, at least in part, to what seems to be the view that issues regarding the initial distribution of property rights are of little or no contemporary importance in a modern, developed society. It is notable, for instance, that Demsetz's article on the economics of the creation of private property analyzes an archaic historical episode,[53] and that a prominent philosophical defense of current distributional inequalities treats the initial distribution of property as practically a one-time event, with attention focused on subsequent dispositions of rights.[54] Attention tends to focus, instead, on the workings of the system of property rights already in being. It seems that most would agree with Locke that "in the beginning all the world was America,"[55] but assume that with America now safely settled, situations of initial distribution of rights are of minor importance, reserved for intellectual property and exotic settings like outer space and the deep-sea floor.

This assumption regarding the contemporary rarity of situations involving an initial distribution of property rights is, however, both mistaken and pernicious. The truth is that initial distributions are of continuing and vital relevance. Perhaps the most obvious example concerns public lands, where the continued vast extent of the public domain in the United States, and conflicts over its disposition and use, leave distributive questions with as important a role to play as ever. In these areas, our America is still very much Locke's America.

In other societies, too, redistributions of property still occur, for a variety of reasons. For example, in its attempts to rectify the unjust distributions of the apartheid regime, South Africa has embarked upon a program of distributing land and water to blacks. The goal is clearly distributive justice, yet the form that has been taken in some cases, allocation of water to tribal groups, may be problematic. Common property can lead to injustice when the mechanisms for distribution within the owner group allow or encourage unjust distribution; this may be the case for the tribal authorities, where local chiefs control the allocation of water, often to the detriment of particular individuals, especially women.[56] An insistence by the government on redistribution directly to black citizens as private property, rather than to tribal groups as a sort of common property, might be preferable from a distributive justice point of view.

Perhaps less obvious, but even more significant for our everyday well-being, are new rights formed when society realizes the value of a resource previously unrecognized, or one previously thought to be abundant but now seen as scarce. These resources, which heretofore may have been understood poorly, if at all, and rights in them crudely delineated and assigned, typically more by inattention than design, rise to newfound prominence with changes in our understanding of the world and our increasing pressure on it.

In the environmental realm, distributional concerns have been raised about the private-property mechanisms being implemented to cost-effectively allocate the burdens of climate-change-related pollution control.[57] While common property may indeed be most consonant with distributive ideals in most environmental contexts, the functional distributive analysis proposed here suggests that in some situations the real problem may be not too much private property, but too little. Most climate change–mitigation schemes call for allocating tradable greenhouse-gas allowances among states, whether on the basis of historical emissions[58] or of relative population size.[59] In effect, both approaches would initially create a national-level commons in each country, with the attendant potential for exploitation by the country's elites, and concentration of the benefits of the allowances (whether through use or sale to businesses) in their hands. An alternative approach, more sensitive to distributive justice on the individual level and the comedic possibilities of private rights and even the anticommons, might allocate allowances directly to citizens of every country. While this scheme might create an anticommons, with rights hopelessly scattered, unused, among billions of people, it might be right to sacrifice wealth maximization for a fairer distribution of the costs and benefits of climate change and its mitigation.[60]

Intellectual property is another context in which distribution is an important but underemphasized factor. While current debates over the balance between intellectual property and the public domain tend to revolve around the question of whether excessive regard for private rights fosters or destroys value,[61] the distributive approach, with its focus on the distributive aspects of property institutions, places the emphasis on the issue of who benefits and loses from any allocation of a given resource. On this view, we may find that in some contexts, the institution of private rights, distributed widely, may be fairer.[62] While distributional considerations may sometimes encourage downplaying the private-property aspects of some goods, like life-saving drug designs, in order to make them more widely available, strengthening intellectual-property rights at the expense of the public domain may be preferable in other situations. For instance, as Chander and Sunder suggest, recognizing the property rights of people in developing nations in culturally or scientifically valuable aspects of their surroundings may be more desirable—from a distributional point of view—than freeing these assets for the public domain.[63] Distributing intellectual property in this way might be inefficient—the cost of assembling the property rights held by native individuals and groups could be very expensive—but at least the benefits would likely accrue to the people of the developing countries, rather than to western economic interests. Here is another context where it might be appropriate, in some situations, to sacrifice efficiency for distributive goals. These goals might include not only the traditional distributive consideration of improving the lot of less well-off countries, but also the ensuring of a broad distribution of intellectual property resources without undue concentration in a few hands, so that all countries might participate in the knowledge economy and its benefits.

More generally, expanding upon the observation that commons regimes have often been inhospitable to the relatively powerless,[64] private-property rights may be used to ensure that members of disadvantaged groups are ensured a bare minimum of access to the benefits of cultural and technological progress;[65] in other contexts, meanwhile, it is preservation of the commons that ensures that the benefits of a resource are not overly concentrated in the hands of a powerful few.

The issue of electromagnetic spectrum allocation provides another example of the ambiguity of private property's distributional valence. As described in Thomas Streeter's history of spectrum regulation in 1920s America,[66] the idea of public ownership of the airwaves, managed in the public interest, effectively gave control of this resource to the corporate networks, while squeezing out nonprofit, independent, and amateur broadcasters. Public ownership was plausibly seen as advancing social welfare (encouraging the improved technology and broadcast range that giants like NBC and CBS could provide) but worked to concentrate ownership in the hands of a powerful few. An alternative property regime, based on private rights freely available to all, might have been more chaotic and could have slowed some technical advances (though this is debatable), but it would have distributed the benefits of access to the new technology differently, encouraging small, independent broadcasters.[67] (Whether the benefits to listeners would have been distributed more widely under such a scheme seems to me impossible to answer.)

Another example involves privatization of public housing. While it seems that such privatization may actually have negative welfare effects, for instance in the realm of maintenance,[68] it has nevertheless been advocated as a means of achieving a broader distribution of private property, and the accompanying empowerment, to disadvantaged sectors.[69]

Private Property, Public Property, Commons, and Anticommons

Early commentators recognized that Colorado water law's revolutionary aspect did not lie in its instituting a system of private property in place of common property.[70] In fact, the appropriation doctrine was viewed as stemming from the view of water as the common property of the people. One lawyer went so far as to state that "it is declared by the constitution and enforced by repeated decisions that the water is the common property of the people of the State, and that therefore it is incapable of private appropriation."[71]

The doctrine's novelty was rather in its breaking the concentration of water wealth in the hands of the few and spreading that wealth among as many users as possible. As one Colorado water lawyer wrote in the *Yale Law Journal*, "The Colorado doctrine of riparian rights [that is, surface water rights] may be summed up in the statement that riparian proprietors, as such, have no rights; that is to say, they have no usufruct of the waters flowing in the natural streams, not enjoyed by others whose estates are non-riparian."[72] Similarly, and in contrast to the modern view of prior appropriation as a paradigm of private-property rights,[73] nineteenth- and early twentieth-century writers identified prior appropriation as an instance of the law's *denial* of private-property claims.[74] Clesson Kinney's treatise on water law emphasized the themes of equality, necessity, and prevention of monopoly in its discussion of the "physical cause of the doctrine of appropriation":

> Thus it happens that when the water reaches the valleys in the arid region on its way to the ocean, instead of being precipitated nearly equally upon the earth, as is the case in what is known as the "humid region" or "rain belt," it is gathered in natural channels, which only touch a very small proportion of the land within the arid region. Under a strict construction of the rules of the common law . . . a very few riparian owners would control all of the water in that part of the country to the exclusion of all others. Nature clearly designed, in spite of the facts set forth above as to the inequality of precipitation, that the rain should still be permitted to shed its blessings on all, and that a nonriparian land owner should not be prevented from securing his just proportion of the water, simply because of the topographical features of the country thereabouts, which are

entirely beyond his control. The water which he should receive drains from its storage source in the mountains into streams which flow only by his neighbor's land, who, as an incident of his ownership of the soil adjoining the stream, controls all of its waters, although the same may be far in excess of what he and all other riparian owners may need.[75]

It should thus not be surprising that courts in several states held statutes attempting Colorado-style abolition of riparian rights to be unconstitutional takings of property.[76]

Nonetheless, the form that the anti-monopoly, anti-private-property institution took, the appropriative water right, was itself a variant of private property. Squaring this circle was made possible by the fact that a little more than a century ago some private-property rights, particularly those held for use, were viewed not as antithetical to "public ownership," but as a logical expression or consequence of it. For many nineteenth-century Americans, the real dichotomy in their conceptualization of property types was the divide between widely held property, whether private or public, on the one hand, and concentrated property, whether held by wealthy individuals or their corporate creatures, on the other. Lockean principles of justice demanded that resources originating in the public domain be distributed as widely as possible, with equal opportunity for all to appropriate what each needed. Whether this ideal was implemented through pure private-property rights or by public supervision was less important than keeping this public property out of the hands of the dreaded speculators and monopolists. Thus were the ideas of anti-charter Jacksonians of the antebellum period carried over to the pro-government ideals of the Progressive movement.

This seemingly paradoxical connection between the private appropriative rights of the Colorado Doctrine and the principle of common (public) ownership diverges strikingly from conventional assumptions. Property regimes, in their ideal forms, are often viewed as lying along a bipolar continuum, with private property on one end and common property on the other. These two poles tend to be seen as corresponding with distributional patterns, concentration of wealth and the right to exclude on the one hand and egalitarian distribution and inclusion on the other.[77] But the view of Colorado's appropriation doctrine presented in this book calls into question the validity of the private-property-inequality/ commons-equality antithesis. Common property, of course, has a prominent exclusionary aspect: while ensuring access to all the owners, it simultaneously excludes those outside the privileged group. The adoption of the appropriation doctrine, and the contemporary criticisms leveled at riparian law, demonstrate that in the context of nineteenth-century Colorado, this exclusionary feature of the riparian-rights commons[78] was viewed as dominating its inclusive and egalitarian side, leading to a sort of polarity reversal: The common-property regime of riparian law was rejected as too exclusionary and tending to the concentration of the resource in the hands of an undeserving few, and replaced by a regime of private rights, designed to ensure distribution of water rights to as wide a population as possible. The use of private-property rights to achieve distributive goals highlights the idea that the law's adoption of private property, or any other property regime, may have been used to effect a variety of distributive and allocative goals beyond the ones usually associated with each type.

Alongside exclusion, common property can facilitate distributive injustice in another manner—by unfair distribution of the resource among the common owners. The laws of common ownership, cooperatives, condominiums, and corporations all attempt to deal with this problem, whether through substantive protections for members of the community of owners or by the creation of institutions and procedural safeguards to protect their interests. As discussed in Chapters 4 and 5, Colorado water law, led by farmers' groups and a supportive judicial branch, took another tack. While allowing for cooperative and corporate ditch-building, property rights in water always remained in the hands of the actual user, at the same time that the state retained the ultimate property interest. Attempts by capitalist investors to appropriate the economic surpluses created by irrigated agriculture, whether by charging high prices for water rights, diluting their value by prorating, attaching conditions to their sale, and the like, were repeatedly foiled by the state legislature and supreme court. Contract and corporate law were subordinated to the property rights of irrigators in water—rights that could not be held or controlled by speculators or non-users, no matter how hard they tried. In fact, as discussed in Chapter 4, property held by a corporation was viewed not as true private property, but as something less deserving of legal protection.[79] Though the relevant statutes made no distinction between the title to water registered under the name of an individual user and that registered in the name of a diverting corporation, Colorado's courts forged a new body of law based on distinguishing ownership of water by individuals and user-owned corporate bodies from control by investor-owned companies, giving different legal effects to what was, on paper, one type of property.

I have so far argued that the early history of Colorado's appropriation doctrine undercuts the usual identification of private property with exclusion and concentration, and that of common property with inclusion and equality. Now I would argue further that the history of the Colorado Doctrine confirms a more general observation regarding the forms of property. The dominant typology leads to the framing of many issues, from intellectual property to environmental regulation, in terms of a private/public/commons distinction: critics often see either too much or too little of private, public, common, or anticommon property. The early history of appropriation law, on the other hand, shows that a clearer picture of the real issues regarding control of resources may be gained by avoiding a focus on these conceptual categories, or on the supposed distinctions between them, and instead paying closer attention to who effectively controls and benefits from the resource in question—in other words, how the resource is distributed. What is often truly at stake is not the type of property at hand according to abstract categories, but the identity and type of the parties given rights to the resource, especially when dealing with a resource, like water in the arid West, that is effectively the key to other resources or power.

Thus the lawmakers—legislators, judges, lawyers, and farmers—who shaped Colorado water law in its early years slid easily between the idiom of private property, held up as a bulwark against oppression by greedy corporations, and that of public property, from which they derived the requirement that only actual users could be true owners and beneficiaries of the state's water—and no tension between the two was felt. Similarly, when distributive goals required emphasizing the inviolability of private rights, as when the no-injury rule (discussed in Chapter 5) was used to prevent transfer and concentration of water rights, this was the path taken. Yet, when those goals pointed to radically limiting private rights in other ways, such as through the use requirement, the same lawmakers found no difficulty in doing so. Water was seen as both private and public, both categories that were aimed at preserving control of the crucial resource among the people, and keeping it out of the hands of speculators and monopolists.

A lesson to be learned is that the advantages of every form of property, whether commons, private, public, or anticommons, cannot be assessed a priori, but should be measured in terms of actual distributive consequences in every concrete context. What is needed is a paradigm shift, in which property regimes will be classified not along the governance axis (commons, private, anticommons, and so on), but first and foremost along the distributive one. How broadly distributed or concentrated a given resource is may well be a more significant parameter than the form of its allocation, both for understanding the evolution of the property institution and for evaluating its desirability.

NOTES

Chapter 1: Introduction

1. Coffin v. Left Hand Ditch Co., 6 Colo. 443, 447 (Colo. 1882).

2. See Joseph L. Sax et al., Legal Control of Water Resources 27–37 (4th ed. 2006).

3. Colorado was the first state to do away entirely with riparian rights, applying the doctrine of appropriation to all surface water in the state, including that found on private land—hence "pure appropriation." The Pacific coast states and those on the semi-arid eastern fringe of the prior appropriation region have retained some mixture of riparian and appropriative rights for surface water, while the law of the drier states lying in between these two groups followed the lead of the "Colorado Doctrine," abolishing riparian rights completely. See Sax et al., supra note 2, at 326–51; John T. Ganoe, *The Beginnings of Irrigation in the United States,* 25 Miss. Valley Hist. Rev. 59, 65–70 (1938).

4. For *Coffin*'s influence on the adoption of the appropriation doctrine by other jurisdictions, see 1 Report of the Special Comm. of the U.S. Sen. on the Irrigation and Reclamation of Arid Lands, Sen. Rep. 928, 51st Cong., 1st Sess. 74 (1890); Tom I. Romero, II, *Uncertain Waters and Contested Lands: Excavating the Layers of Colorado's Legal Past,* 73 U. Colo. L. Rev. 521, 540 (2002). For its continuing status as a leading case, see, for example, Barlow Burke, Natural Resources Cases and Materials 280 (1998); Dean Lueck, *First Possession,* in 2 New Palgrave Dictionary of Economics and the Law 132, 133–36 (1998); Sax et al., supra note 2, at 335.

5. James Willard Hurst, Law and the Conditions of Freedom in the Nineteenth-Century United States 6 (1956); see also Donald J. Pisani, *Promotion and Regulation: Constitutionalism and the American Economy*, 74 J. Am. Hist. 740, 750 (1987).

6. See, for example, Richard A. Posner, *A Theory of Negligence*, 1 J. Leg. Stud. 29 (1972); George L. Priest, *The Common Law Process and the Selection of Efficient Rules*, 6 J. Leg. Stud. 65 (1977).

7. For justice in morality plays, see J. Wilson McCutchan, *Justice and Equity in the English Morality Play*, 19 J. Hist. Ideas 405 (1958).

8. See, for example, Robert C. Ellickson, *Property in Land*, 102 Yale L. J. 1315 (1993); Clifford Holderness, *A Legal Foundation for Exchange*, 14 J. Legal Stud. 321 (1985); Richard A. Posner, Economic Analysis of Law 32–33 (6th ed. 2003).

9. Garrett Hardin, *The Tragedy of the Commons*, 162 Science 1243 (1968).

10. Harold Demsetz, *Toward a Theory of Property Rights*, 57 Am. Econ. Rev. (papers & proc.) 347 (1967). See also Terry L. Anderson & P. J. Hill, *The Evolution of Property Rights: A Study of the American West*, 18 J. L. & Econ. 163 (1975); Gary D. Libecap, *Economic Variables and the Development of the Law: The Case of Western Mineral Rights*, 38 J. Econ. Hist. 338 (1978).

11. See, for example, Terry L. Anderson & Donald R. Leal, Free Market Environmentalism (rev. ed. 2001); Abraham Bell & Gideon Parchomovsky, *Of Property and Antiproperty*, 120 Mich. L. Rev. 1 (2003); Dean Lueck, *The Rule of First Possession and the Design of the Law*, 38 J. L. & Econ. 393 (1995).

12. Stuart Banner, *Transitions Between Property Regimes*, 31 J. Leg. Stud. S359 (2002); Saul Levmore, *Two Stories About the Evolution of Property Rights*, 31 J. Leg. Stud. S421 (2002); Gary D. Libecap, Contracting for Property Rights (1989).

13. The classic work is Elinor Ostrom, Governing the Commons: The Evolution of Institutions for Collective Action (1990).

14. Carol Rose, *The Comedy of the Commons: Commerce, Custom and Inherently Public Property*, 53 U. Chi. L. Rev. 711 (1986). See also Carol Rose, *Energy and Efficiency in the Realignment of Common-Law Water Rights*, in Property and Persuasion 163 (1994); Henry E. Smith, *Exclusion Versus Governance: Two Strategies for Delineating Property Rights*, 31 J. Leg. Stud. S453 (2002). In the intellectual-property context, see, for example, Yochai Benkler, *Coase's Penguin, or, Linux and the Nature of the Firm*, 112 Yale L. J. 369 (2002); James Boyle, *The Second Enclosure Movement and the Construction of the Public Domain*, 66 Law & Contemp. Probs. 33 (2003); Michael A. Heller & Rebecca S. Eisenberg, *Can Patents Deter Innovation? The Anticommons in Biomedical Research*, 280 Science 698 (1998).

15. The leading article is Michael Heller, *The Tragedy of the Anticommons: Property in the Transition from Marx to Markets*, 111 Harv. L. Rev. 621 (1998). See also James M. Buchanan & Yong J. Yoon, *Symmetric Tragedies: Commons and Anticommons*, 43 J. L. & Econ. 1 (2000).

16. See, for example, Steven Shavell, Foundations of Economic Analysis of Law 654–55 (2004).

17. Libecap, supra note 12.

18. Robert C. Allen, *The Efficiency and Distributional Consequences of Eighteenth Century Enclosures*, 92 Econ. J. 937 (1982); Morton J. Horwitz, The Transformation of American Law, 1780–1860 (1977).

19. A notable exception, though limited to the intellectual-property context, is Anupam Chander & Madhavi Sunder, *The Romance of the Public Domain*, 92 Cal. L. Rev. 1331 (2004); distributive justice has also long been recognized as a central factor in takings scholarship; see Frank I. Michelman, *Property, Utility, and Fairness: Comments on the Ethical Foundations of "Just Compensation" Law*, 80 Harv. L. Rev. 1165 (1967); Hanoch Dagan, *Takings and Distributive Justice*, 85 Va. L. Rev. 741 (1999). A few studies have noted the importance of "fairness" in the establishment of property rights, but primarily as a "focal point" facilitating privatization for efficiency goals, see Andrea G. McDowell, *From Commons to Claims: Property Rights in the California Gold Rush*, 14 Yale J. L. & Human. 1 (2002), and Richard O. Zerbe Jr. & Leigh Anderson, *Culture and Fairness in the Development of Institutions in the California Gold Fields*, 61 J. Econ. Hist. 114 (2001).

20. But see Lon. L. Fuller, *Irrigation and Tyranny*, 17 Stan. L. Rev. 1021, 1037–42 (1965) (distributive justice the central issue of irrigation law).

21. See Dale D. Goble, *Prior Appropriation and the Property Clause: A Dialogue of Accommodation*, 71 Or. L. Rev. 381, 382 (1992) (water plays key role in founding myth of West); Charles F. Wilkinson, *In Memoriam: Prior Appropriation, 1848–1991*, 21 Envtl. L., pt. 3, v, v (1991) (story of prior appropriation's birth "has been told so often that it has become part of the bedrock of western history").

22. Wilkinson, id. at viii, has it thus in his personification of Prior Appropriation and the General Mining Law: "Prior and the General knew every bar from Columbia to the Klondike and from Virginia City to Cripple Creek and they caroused and drank and whored and fought in them all. They were men's men—broad-shouldered, barrel-chested, and square-jawed. Prior, who not only read Mark Twain but knew him, was fond of summing it all up by quoting Twain's comment upon his first visit to Nevada in the 1860s: 'This is no place for a God-fearing Methodist and I did not long remain one.'"

See also Joseph W. Dellapenna, *Adapting Riparian Rights to the Twenty-first Century*, 106 W. Va. L. Rev. 539, 567–68 (2004); Goble, supra note 21, at 381–82; Norris Hundley, Jr., Water and the West 67 (1975); Patricia Nelson Limerick, The Legacy of Conquest 66–67 (1987); J. Byron McCormick, *The Adequacy of the Prior Appropriation Doctrine Today*, in Water Resources and the Law 33, 34 (1958); A. Dan Tarlock, *Prior Appropriation: Rule, Principle, or Rhetoric?*, 76 N. Dak. L. Rev. 881, 890 (2000).

23. 6 Colo. 443. For an overview of the origins of the prior appropriation doctrine in miners' practice and its adoption by the law, see 1 Samuel C. Wiel, Water Rights in the Western States 65–117 (3rd ed. 1911); Robert G. Dunbar, Forging New Rights in Western Waters 59–85 (1983) [hereinafter Dunbar, New Rights]; U.S. v. Gerlach Live Stock Co., 339 U.S. 725, 745–48 (1950). The view that the law of prior appropriation was a necessary response to the aridity of the West is associated most strongly with Walter Prescott Webb, The Great Plains 431–52 (1931). See also Gordon M. Bakken, *The English Common Law in*

NOTES TO PAGE 6

the Rocky Mountain West, 11 Ariz. & the West 109, 121–28 (1969); Yoram Barzel, Economic Analysis of Property Rights 118–19 (2nd ed. 1997); Robert G. Dunbar, *The Adaptability of Water Law to the Aridity of the West,* 24 J. of the West 57, 57 (1985) [hereinafter Dunbar, *Adaptability*]. The element of secure title as encouraging commoditization and economic expansion is developed in Gordon Morris Bakken, The Development of Law on the Rocky Mountain Frontier 71–72 (1983) [hereinafter Bakken, Development of Law]; Norris Hundley, Jr., *The Great American Desert Transformed: Aridity, Exploitation, and Imperialism in the Making of the Modern American West,* in Water and Arid Lands of the Western United States 21, 34 (Mohammed T. El-Ashry & Diana C. Gibbons eds. 1988); see also Horwitz, supra note 18, at 33, 43 (emphasizing the dimension of monopoly in the stimulation of development by the recognition of priority as the basis for property rights). A useful bibliographic essay is Peter L. Reich, *Studies in Western Water Law: Historiographical Trends,* 9 W. Leg. Hist. 1 (1996).

24. See, for example, Terry L. Anderson & Donald R. Leal, Free Market Environmentalism 33–35 (rev. ed. 2001); Water Rights: Scarce Resource Allocation, Bureaucracy, and the Environment passim (Terry L. Anderson ed. 1983), described by a reviewer as "a hymn of praise to the doctrine of prior appropriation and to the ideal of water rights as exclusively private property," Paul Herrington, in *Book Notes,* 94 Econ. J. 1013, 1043 (1984), particularly Alfred G. Cuzán, *Appropriators versus Expropriators: The Political Economy of Water in the West,* in id. 13, 19; Dunbar, *Adaptability,* supra note 23, at 64; Jack Hirshleifer et al., Water Supply 232 (rev. ed. 1969); Lueck, supra note 11, at 427–30; J. W. Milliman, *Water Law and Private Decision-making: A Critique,* 2 J. L. & Econ. 41 (1959); Timothy D. Tregarthen, *The Market for Property Rights in Water,* in Water Needs for the Future 139, 142–43 (Ved P. Nanda ed. 1977).

25. Terry L. Anderson & P. J. Hill, *The Evolution of Property Rights: A Study of the American West,* 18 J. L. & Econ. 163, 176–78 (1975); see also Dunbar, New Rights, supra note 23, at 60. Cf. Gary D. Libecap, *Economic Variables and the Development of the Law: The Case of Western Mineral Rights,* 38 J. Econ. Hist. 338 (1978) (Demsetzian explanation of increased specificity of property rights in minerals in West).

26. See, for example, Terry L. Anderson & Pamela Snyder, Water Markets: Priming the Invisible Pump 33–34 (1997); Hirshleifer et al., supra note 24, at 233; Timothy D. Tregarthen, *Water in Colorado: Fear and Loathing of the Marketplace,* in Water Rights 119, supra note 24, at 119.

27. See Sarah F. Bates et al., Searching Out the Headwaters: Change and Rediscovery in Western Water Policy 136–137 (1993); Mark Fiege, Irrigated Eden: The Making of an Agricultural Landscape in the American West (1999); Robert Glennon, *Bottling a Birthright?,* in Whose Water Is It? 9, 15 (Bernadette MacDonald & Douglas Jehl eds. 2003); William Lilley III & Lewis L. Gould, *The Western Irrigation Movement, 1878–1902: A Reappraisal,* in The American West: A Reorientation 57, 63 (Gene M. Gressley ed. 1966); Donald J. Pisani, *Enterprise and Equity: A Critique of Western Water Law in the Nineteenth Century,* 18 W. Hist. Q. 15, 19 (1987); Marc Reisner & Sarah Bates, Overtapped Oasis 62–65 (1990);

Vandana Shiva, Water Wars: Privatization, Pollution and Profit 20–23 (2002); Frank J. Trelease, *Alternatives to Appropriation Law*, in Water Needs for the Future 59, supra note 24, at 59–60; Donald Worster, Rivers of Empire 88–92 (1985). Interestingly, Theodore Steinberg's influential account of riparian law in industrializing New England, Nature Incorporated: Industrialization and the Waters of New England 85–89 (1991), stresses the destruction, alienation, and commodification brought about by riparian law. This negative characterization of riparian rights tends to be ignored by those finding the same faults in the appropriation doctrine.

28. Eric T. Freyfogle, The Land We Share 101–03, 124 (2003).

29. Donald J. Pisani, *Promotion and Regulation: Constitutionalism and the American Economy*, 74 J. Am. Hist. 740, 750 (1987).

30. See, for example, Stefania Barca, Enclosing Water: Nature and Political Economy in a Mediterranean Valley, 1796–1916 95–116 (2010); Shiva, supra note 27; Erik Swyngedouw, *Dispossessing H₂O: The Contested Terrain of Water Privatization*, 16 Capitalism Nature Socialism 81 (2005); Paul Trawick, *The Moral Economy of Water: Equity and Antiquity in the Andean Commons*, 103 Am. Anthropologist (n.s.) 361 (2001).

31. See, for example, Dunbar, New Rights, supra note 23; Bakken, Development of Law, supra note 23; Hundley, supra note 23; Donald J. Pisani, *Natural Resources and Economic Liberty in American History*, in The State and Freedom of Contract 236, 245 (Harry N. Scheiber ed. 1998); Pisani, supra note 29, at 750. But see Gregory J. Hobbs, Jr., *Colorado Water Law: An Historical Overview*, 1 U. Denv. L. Rev. 1 (1997) (noting anti-speculation aspects of Colorado water law); Sam S. Kepfield, *Great Plains Legal Culture and Irrigation Development: The Minitare (Mutual) Irrigation Ditch Company, 1887–1896*, 19:4 Envtl. Hist. Rev. 49, 51 (1995) (Colorado laws aimed against corporations); Donald J. Pisani, *"I am resolved not to interfere, but permit all to work freely": The Gold Rush and American Resource Law*, in A Golden State: Mining and Economic Development in Gold Rush California 123, 125 (James J. Rawls & Richard J. Orsi eds. 1999) (prior appropriation encouraged equal access as well as monopoly).

32. On the inefficiency of these rules, see Terry L. Anderson & P. J. Hill, *The Race for Property Rights*, 33 J. L. & Econ. 177 (1990); Lueck, supra note 4, at 133–36; Tregarthen, supra note 26, at 123–24, 132–33; Stephen F. Williams, *The Requirement of Beneficial Use as a Cause of Waste in Water Resource Development*, 23 Natural Resources J. 7 (1983). For their supposed origins outside of the pure appropriation rule, see, for example, Mohamed T. El-Ashry & Diana C. Gibbons, *The West in Profile*, in Water and Arid Lands of the Western United States 1, supra note 23, at 4; Bates et al., supra note 27, at 140; Anderson & Snyder, supra note 26, at 34, 79.

33. See Frank J. Trelease, *Government Ownership and Trusteeship of Water*, 45 Cal. L. Rev. 638, 642 (1957). It also fails to explain the diversity of water rights regimes in arid environments outside the western United States; see, for example, D. A. Caponera, Water Laws in Moslem Countries (1973); Fuller, supra note 20, at 1039; Arthur Maass & Raymond L. Anderson, . . . and the Desert Shall Rejoice (1978).

34. See, for example, Anderson & Snyder, supra note 26, at 53–56, 61.

Chapter 2: The Sources of the Colorado Appropriation Doctrine

1. Ovando J. Hollister, The Mines of Colorado 75–76 (Springfield, Mass.: Samuel Bowles & Co. 1867).

2. The code adopted in Jackson Diggings, May 9, 1859, in id. 70, consisting of three sections, is the only code on record with an earlier date, and appears to have had little influence.

3. Robert G. Dunbar, Forging New Rights in Western Waters 74 (1983).

4. Resolutions of June 8, 1859 [hereinafter Gregory Dist. Resolutions 1859], in Laws and Regulations of the Miners of the Gregory Diggings District (Denver, n.d.), Yale Collection of Western Americana, Beinecke Rare Book and Manuscript Library [hereinafter Yale Collection]; reprinted in Hollister, supra note 1, at 78.

5. The language appears in substantially the same form in, for example, Miners' Laws of Nevada Dist.: Jefferson Territory, 1860, Nov. 10, 1860 [hereinafter Nevada Dist. Act], § 7, Nevada Mining Dist. Records, 1860–1861, Yale Collection. For variant forms, see infra note 7 and accompanying text.

6. Gregory Dist. Resolutions 1859, supra note 4. In Hollister, supra note 1, at 78, the text is slightly different: "when two parties wish to use water on the same stream or ravine for quartz-washing, it shall be equally divided between them." Quartz mining (i.e., mining of gold-bearing quartz veins) involved the use of water to power quartz-crushing machinery to extract the gold.

7. An Act Defining Claims and Regulating the Title Thereto § 10, in Laws of Gregory District, Enacted February 18 & 20, 1860 at 3 (Denver City, Wm. N. Byers & Co. 1860), Yale Collection, reprinted in United States Mining Laws and Regulations Thereunder, and State and Territorial Mining Laws 360 (14 Tenth Census of the United States, Clarence King ed., Washington, D.C.: G.P.O. 1885) [hereinafter United States Mining Laws]. This language appears in the codes of other districts, as well; for example Griffith Mining Dist. laws, Mar. 9, 1861 ch. 18, § 11, Id., at 381.

8. See Ralph W. Aigler, *The Operation of the Recording Acts*, 22 Mich. L. Rev. 405, 406 (1924); William E. Colby, *The Freedom of the Miner and Its Influence on Water Law*, in Legal Essays in Tribute to Orrin Kip McMurray 67, 70 (Max Radin & A. M. Kidd eds. 1935).

9. This theme has been highlighted in the California context by Andrea G. McDowell, *From Commons to Claims: Property Rights in the California Gold Rush*, 14 Yale J. L. & Human. 1, 34–39 (2002). See also Richard O. Zerbe Jr. & Leigh Anderson, *Culture and Fairness in the Development of Institutions in the California Gold Fields*, 61 J. Econ. Hist. 114, 128 (2001).

10. Gregory Dist. Resolutions 1859 § 4, supra note 4; Donald Wayne Hensel, A History of the Colorado Constitution in the Nineteenth Century 10 (unpublished Ph.D. thesis, U. Colo. 1957).

11. Gregory Dist. Resolutions 1859 § 2, supra note 4; Russell District Laws of June 18, 1859 [hereinafter: Russell Dist. Laws 1859], rule 1, in Early Records of Gilpin County, Colorado, 1859–1861, 48 (Thomas Maitland Marshall ed. 1920). A few codes, however,

did attempt to limit accumulation of claims through agents, by requiring good faith and fair compensation. See, for example, Russell Dist. Resolutions of July 28, 1860 § 61, in United States Mining Laws, supra note 7, at 392. At least one did limit the number of claims that a person could purchase to two. Wisconsin District, Laws Enacted Feb. 13, 1860, Art. 5, in Marshall, 147.

12. See, for example, Gregory Dist. Resolutions 1859 § 5, supra note 4 (work required within ten days of claim); Russell District Laws of June 18, 1859, rule 5, supra note 11, at 49 (work required within six days); Downeyville Dist. Laws, July 29, 1859, art. 6, in United States Mining Laws, supra note 7, at 352 (at least two weeks of work required, plus one day in ten if claim unrecorded).

13. Cf. Zerbe & Anderson, supra note 9, at 128 (California mining-claim sizes limited to amount one man could work).

14. The diverse treatment of water rights in the miners' laws is a point made in the California context by Donald J. Pisani, To Reclaim a Divided West 12, 20 (1992); Donald J. Pisani, *"I am resolved not to interfere, but permit all to work freely": The Gold Rush and American Resource Law*, in A Golden State: Mining and Economic Development in Gold Rush California 123, 136–38 (James J. Rawls & Richard J. Orsi eds. 1999). For the standard account, see, for example, Dunbar, supra note 3.

Out of the ninety-one codes examined, eleven codes made some reference to priority in connection with water rights (see, for example, Russell Dist. Laws 1859 rule 3, supra note 12, at 48); one, without using the word, established a system for registering water claims, with the preference for earlier appropriations implied (Report of Committee on Credentials, Erie Mining Dist., Apr. 21, 1861 [hereinafter: Erie Dist. Laws] §§ 2–8, in United States Mining Laws, supra note 7, at 407); and another thirteen established priority as a principle for resolving conflicting claims in general, without specific mention of water, as in § 8 of the Gregory Dist. Resolutions 1859, supra text accompanying note 4.

Out of the twelve codes that explicitly declared that water should be divided proportionately between the users, six numbered among the group also mentioning priority in connection with water (see, for example, Gregory Dist. Act 1860 §§ 16, 17, supra note 7, at 4) and another three were of the group mentioning priority only in regard to claims in general (see, for example, Gregory Dist. Resolutions 1859 § 9, supra note 4). In addition to these twelve, another eight codes mandated that water users return their water to the stream or prohibited obstruction of flow, in effect instituting sharing among diverters of water through a no-consumption rule (see, for example, Eureka Mining Dist. Laws, Aug. 17, 1873, art. 8, in United States Mining Laws, supra note 7, at 478); another possibly instituted a system of rotation among water claims (Griffith Mining Dist. Laws, Jan. 12, 1861, § 7, in United States Mining Laws, supra note 7, at 376).

15. For an example of an explicit limitation, see Gregory Dist. Act 1860 § 4, supra note 7, at 3. For implicit limitations, see McDowell, supra note 9, at 34.

16. See, for example, Griffith Mining Dist. Laws, Mar. 9, 1861, chap. 17, § 1, in United States Mining Laws, supra note 7, at 381 (limiting water rights to mining claims adjacent to

the stream); Ohio Mining Dist. Laws, April 12, 1860 § 22, in United States Mining Laws, supra note 7, at 365 (priority to riparians); Constitution & By-Laws of Carpenter's Dist., American Gulch, Utah Terr., June 16, 1860, art. 25, in United States Mining Laws, supra note 7 [hereinafter Carpenter's Dist. Laws] at 371 (forbidding interference with natural flow); Laws of Bay State Mining Dist., amdt. of Dec. 29, 1860, § 23, in United States Mining Laws, supra note 7, at 347 (ditch easements for non-riparians); Gregory Dist. Act 1860 § 18, supra note 7, at 4 (right of non-riparians to "bring water into the mines").

17. Russell Dist. Laws 1859 rule 3, 11, at 48 (limit of "one sluice or tom head"); Carpenter's Dist. Laws, art. 19, supra note 16, at 371 (limit of "one usual sluice head" per claim); Erie Dist. Laws, supra note 14 (water claim limited to 12 "miners' inches" flow for twelve hours per day). The quotes are from Resolutions of Gold Hill Mountain Dist. No. 1, July 30th 1859, res. 2, in United States Mining Laws, supra note 7, at 348; Griffith Mining Dist. Laws, ch. 17, § 1, supra note 7, at 381; Wisconsin Mining Dist. Laws, Dec. 13, 1860, art. 10, in United States Mining Laws, supra note 7, at 417.

All told, thirty-four codes from thirty-two districts had length restrictions on water claims. A further three codes limited water mill claims by area; see, for example, Revised Laws of S. Boulder Dist., Mar. 30, 1861, ch. 7, § 2, in id., at 442 (water claim limited to 300 square feet).

18. Sixteen codes gave each claimant a measure of head on the stream, one of them offering an alternative length limit as well (Laws as Amended Aug 25, 1860, Bull Run Independent Mining Dist., art. 3, in United States Mining Laws, supra note 7, at 394). The notion of hydraulic "head" is a measurement of the relationship of velocity, pressure, and elevation in a fluid, and is constant along a streamline (assuming no friction). See George M. Hornberger et al., Elements of Physical Hydrology (1998). In the miners' laws "head" seems to stand for "fall" of the water (in technical terms, a change in elevation head), so that, for example, "a sufficient distance along any stream to give a head twenty feet" would mean a sufficient distance along the stream to give an elevation differential of 20 feet. Since hydraulic head is a constant, a drop in elevation will entail an increase in velocity or pressure (or both), which increase could be used to turn a water wheel. This book's use of the term "head" conforms to the colloquial usage of the miners.

The quotes are from Gold Hill Mining Dist., Bill passed Nov. 5, 1859 [hereinafter: Gold Hill Dist. Laws], art. 3, in United States Mining Laws, supra note 7, at 348; Constitution and By Laws, Sugar Loaf Mining Dist., Organized and Established Nov. 9, 1860, art. 7, in United States Mining Laws, supra note 7, at 409; Laws of Clear Creek Mining Dist., May 7, 1864 § 5, in United States Mining Laws, supra note 7, at 466, also in Laws of Granite Dist., May 7, 1864 § 5, in id., at 466; Laws of Central Dist., Sep. 4, 1860, § 2 (manuscript), Denver Public Library Western History Collection.

19. Harry G. Frankfurt, *Equality as a Moral Ideal,* in The Importance of What We Care About 134 (1988); Joseph Raz, The Morality of Freedom, 217–44 (1986). For recent discussions of the sufficiency principle, see Yitzhak Benbaji, *Sufficiency or Priority?,* 14 Eur. J. Phil. 327 (2006); Paula Casal, *Why Sufficiency Is Not Enough,* 117 Ethics 296 (2007).

For the guiding principle of equality of opportunity in western law, see John Phillip Reid, *The Layers of Western Legal History*, in Law for the Elephant, Law for the Beaver 23, 33 (John McLaren et al. eds. 1992); McDowell, supra note 9, at 57.

20. Regarding the unfairness of insufficiently large claim sizes, see Zerbe & Anderson, supra note 9, at 130; Restatement (Second) of Torts, § 850A, Comment j (making this point with regard to riparian doctrine).

21. On the population of the gulch, see Hollister, supra note 1, at 63, 76; Carl Abbott et al., Colorado: A History of the Centennial State 59 (3rd ed. 1994). Percy Stanley Fritz, Colorado: The Centennial State 128 (1941), relates claim sizes to the best judgment of the miners as to the amount of the resource that could be worked by one person. The quote is from Frank Fossett, Colorado: Its Gold and Silver Mines, Farms and Stock Ranges, and Health and Pleasure Resorts 122–123 (New York: C. G. Crawford, 1879). Cf. Edith James, Claims' Law and Miners' Courts of the Montana Gold Camps, 1862–1870, 85 (unpublished M.A. dissertation, U. Chicago, 1949).

22. Nevada Dist. Act § 8, supra note 5. The assumption behind the "one half" rule seems to have been that at any point along the stream there would be one claim holder on each bank; each could divert up to a half of the water and would have to return it to the stream after use (or after others on his side of the stream had used it too) so that the next set of claim holders downstream would have an opportunity to use the water.

23. Laws and Regulations of Arkansas River Mining Dist., Dec. 10, 1864 § 13, in United States Mining Laws, supra note 7, at 472; By-Laws of California Mining Dist. California Gulch, Arkansas River, Jan. 22, 1866 art. 6, in id., at 369.

24. The connection between non-consumptive uses and common-property-like regimes of equality and correlative rights has been made by Carol Rose, *Energy and Efficiency in the Realignment of Common-Law Water Rights*, in Property and Persuasion 163 (1994).

25. Gregory Dist. Act 1860, supra note 7, at 4. As noted earlier, supra note 14, many codes invoking the priority principle did so alongside provisions for equal sharing (six of the twelve codes awarding water rights by priority also mandated sharing). Why specifically temporal priority should have been chosen as the mediating principle in case of insufficient water for all will be explored in the next chapter.

26. Jennison v. Kirk, 98 U.S. 453, 457 (1878) (emphasis added).

27. See Downeyville Dist. Laws, supra note 12, at 352, cited by Dunbar, supra note 3 and accompanying text.

28. See, for example, An Act Defining Claims and Regulating the Title Thereto, Nov. 3, 1860 §§ 2, 9, Laws of Lincoln Dist. 2 (Denver, News Print. Co. 1860), Yale Collection (reprinted in United States Mining Laws, supra note 7, at 436) (water claim not to exceed 250 feet, oldest claimant to have priority of right to use of water when insufficient for general use). Of the twelve codes with priority rules for water claims (see supra note 14), ten set a maximum length and two limited the size of water claims by flow. Of the thirteen codes lacking priority preferences for water claims but with general rules of priority (id.), two had no specific water-claim rules, six set a maximum length for water claims,

and three established a maximum area. The remaining two put no absolute limit on water claim sizes, but required sharing in case of insufficient water.

29. Laws of Montgomery Mining District, Organized Aug. 22, 1861, art. 13, Denver Public Library manuscript collection.

30. By-Laws for the Government of Central Mining District, Nov. 21, 1859 [hereinafter Central Mining District By-Laws], art. 9, Laws and Regulations of the Central Mining District (Denver, n.d.), Yale Collection, Fig. 4. The quoted text is at the top of the middle column. Art. 10 of the bylaws (also in Fig. 4) added the requirement that water claims be improved to the amount of $100. All told, seventeen codes imposed some sort of use or improvement requirement on water claims specifically, while four provided that recorded water claims would be held as real estate or vested rights, probably intending to negate any work requirement for water claims. Of codes with water-claim rules not establishing water-claim-specific work requirements, twenty-one had general work requirements presumably applying to water claims, while nine provided that claims in general were to be considered real estate or vested rights.

31. For the claim that the use requirement was an efficient tool for publicizing rights, see Terry L. Anderson & Pamela Snyder, Water Markets: Priming the Invisible Pump 80 (1997). Cf. also Carol M. Rose, *Possession as the Origin of Property*, 52 U. Chic. L Rev. 73, 82 (1985). For recording procedure, see, for example, Nevada Dist. Act § 30, supra note 5, which states simply that the recorder was to record all claims in his book. See generally Percy Stanley Fritz, *The Constitutions and Laws of Early Mining Districts in Boulder County, Colorado*, 21 Univ. Colo. Stud. 127, 132 (1934); James Grafton Rogers, *The Beginnings of Law in Colorado*, 36 Dicta 111, 116 (1959). For mandatory recordation of water claims, see, for example, Gold Hill Dist. Laws, art. 2, supra note 18, at 348. For a minimum work requirement, along with recordation, see, for example, Downeyville Dist. Laws, art. 6, supra note 12, at 352.

32. Absentee ownership was also sharply curtailed in many district laws by allowing service of lawsuits by posting on the defendant's claim and allowing very short periods for answer, in effect divesting all absentees of ownership; Richard Hogan, Class and Community in Frontier Colorado 51 (1990). See, for example, Gregory Dist. Act 1860 § 1, supra note 7, at 2 (three days to answer). The influence of this ideology was evident, as well, in the mechanic's lien, a feature of several mining district codes, which was created to favor productive labor at the expense of what were seen as parasitic lenders; see Lawrence M. Friedman, A History of American Law 243–245 (2nd ed. 1985); William Trimble, *The Social Philosophy of the Loco-Foco Democracy*, 26 Am. J. Sociology 705, 712 (1921). For an example, see Laws of Iowa Mining Dist., Nov. 17, 1860, § 32, in United States Mining Laws, supra note 7, at 416.

33. For the idea that the riparian-rights doctrine reflected an ideal of equality, see, for example, Dunbar, supra note 3, at 60; Vandana Shiva, Water Wars: Privatization, Pollution and Profit 20–21 (2002).

34. 4 Ill. at 495.

35. See, for example, Nevada Dist. Act § 8, supra note 5; Constitution and By Laws of Long Island Mining Dist., July 27, 1861, in United States Mining Laws, supra note 7, at 458. Ironically, the Illinois District law cited by Dunbar as a source for the prior appropriation doctrine, supra text at note 3, likely belonged to this category of preference for riparian users: "Each miner having the use of water on his or their claims shall have the priority of right," Illinois Mining Dist. Laws, Sep. 26, 1859, art. 11, in United States Mining Laws, supra note 7, at 355.

36. See, for example, Gregory Dist. Act 1860 § 19, supra note 7, at 4.

37. See, for example, Laws of Bay State Mining Dist. § 23, supra note 16 (right of way for miners); Central Mining District By-Laws Art. 11, supra note 30 (right of way for water companies).

38. "Agrarian" is used in this book in the term's classical sense, referring to land policies redistributive in nature, particularly in the direction of wider distribution; see Paul K. Conkin, Prophets of Prosperity 224–25 (1980).

39. On the "actual settler," see Henry Tatter, The Preferential Treatment of the Actual Settler in the Primary Disposition of the Vacant Lands in the United States to 1841 (unpublished Ph.D. dissertation, Northwestern Univ., 1933); Daniel Feller, The Public Lands in Jacksonian Politics 29 (1984); for examples, see Rep. Van Allen, Ann. Cong., 4th Cong., 1st Sess. 865 (1796); A Bill to arrest monopolies of the public lands, and purchases thereof, for speculation, and substitute sales to actual settlers only, June 15, 1836, S. 295, 24 Cong. 1 Sess.; Sen. Walker, Cong. Globe, 24th Cong., 2d Sess. 420 (1837); Rep. Cable, Cong. Globe, 32nd Cong., 1st Sess. App. 298 (1852); Rep. Smith, Cong. Globe, 33rd Cong., 1st Sess. App. 208 (1854); Henry George, Our Land and Land Policy 69 (1999) (1871); George Henry Evans, *Working Man's Advocate*, Mar. 16, 1844, in Fred A. Shannon, American Farmers' Movements 132 (1957); George W. Julian, *Our Land Policy*, 43 Atlantic Monthly 325, 327 (1879); Edward T. Peters, *Evils of Our Public Land Policy*, 25 Century 599, 600 (1883).

For the "actual miner," see John Evans, *Governor's Message*, Rocky Mtn. News, Jul. 24, 1862, p. 1.

40. See Thomas Jefferson, Notes on the State of Virginia 164 (William Peden ed. 1954) (1787); Theodore Sedgwick, Public and Private Economy, Part I 43 (New York: Harper & Bros., 1836); Rep. Payne, Cong. Globe, 29th Cong., 1st Sess. App. 806 (1846); George, supra note 39, at 59; Julian, supra note 39, at 336. See also Douglas G. Adair, The Intellectual Origins of Jeffersonian Democracy 160–61 (Mark E. Yellin ed. 2000); Gregory S. Alexander, Commodity & Propriety 1–34 (1997); Lance Banning, The Jeffersonian Persuasion 204 (1978); Chester E. Eisinger, *The Influence of Natural Rights and Physiocratic Doctrines on American Agrarian Thought During the Revolutionary Period*, 21 Agr. Hist. 13 (1947); Nathan Fine, Labor and Farm Parties in the United States 1828–1928, at 21 (1961); A. Whitney Griswold, *The Agrarian Democracy of Thomas Jefferson*, 40 Am. Pol. Sci. Rev. 657, 672 (1946); Stanley N. Katz, *Thomas Jefferson and the Right to Property in Revolutionary America*, 19 J. L. & Econ. 467 (1976); Leo Marx, The Machine in the Garden: Technology and the

Pastoral Ideal in America 124–30 (1964); John Opie, The Law of the Land 28–29 (1987); Carol M. Rose, *Property as the Keystone Right?*, 71 Notre Dame L. Rev. 329, 340–48 (1996); William B. Scott, In Pursuit of Happiness 41–54, 58–59 (1977); John L. Thomas, Alternative America 1–5 (1983).

41. See Paul W. Gates, History of Public Land Law Development 454–55 (1968); Gene M. Gressley, West by East: The American West in the Gilded Age 6 (1972); W. Kirkland, *The West, Paradise of the Poor*, 15 U.S. Dem. Rev. 182 (1844); Roy M. Robbins, Our Landed Heritage 92–116 (2d ed. 1976); Henry Nash Smith, Virgin Land: The American West as Symbol and Myth 140–43, 170 (1950); Rush Welter, The Mind of America, 1820–1860, at 299–304 (1975); Richard White, It's Your Misfortune and None of My Own: A New History of the American West 620 (1991); Mary E. Young, *Congress Looks West: Liberal Ideology and Public Land Policy in the Nineteenth Century*, in The Frontier in American Development 74 (David M. Ellis ed. 1969).

42. Richard Hofstadter, The Age of Reform: From Bryan to F.D.R. 27–28 (5th ed. 1963). See John Taylor, An Inquiry in to the Principles and Policy of the Government of the United States 124 (W. Stark ed. 1950) (1814); Sedgwick, supra note 40, at 133, 148–51; John Pickering, The Working Man's Political Economy 46–50 (Cincinnati: Thomas Varney 1847); Horace Greeley, Hints toward Reforms 18 (New York: Harper & Bros. 1850). See generally Smith, supra note 41, at 169–70; Scott, supra note 40, at 54–55; Stephen A. Siegel, *Understanding the Nineteenth Century Contract Clause: The Role of the Property-Privilege Distinction and "Takings" Clause Jurisprudence*, 60 S. Cal. L. Rev. 1, 57–66 (1986); Robert C. McMath, Jr., American Populism: A Social History 1877–1898, at 51 (1993); James L. Huston, *The American Revolutionaries, the Political Economy of Aristocracy, and the American Concept of the Distribution of Wealth, 1765–1900*, 98 Am. Hist. Rev. 1079, 1080–83, 1095–96 (1993); Tony A. Freyer, Producers versus Capitalists 3–40 (1994); Michael Kazin, The Populist Persuasion 13–14 (1995).

43. John Locke, The Second Treatise of Government §§ 27 & 31, at 17, 19 (Thomas P. Peardon ed. 1952) (1690). See Eisinger, supra note 40, at 14; A. Whitney Griswold, Farming and Democracy 39–40 (1948); Scott, supra note 40, at 15–21, 65–68; Richard J. Ellis, *Radical Lockeanism in American Political Culture*, 45 W. Pol. Q. 825, 827 (1992).

44. See, for example, Langton Byllesby, Observations on the Sources and Effects of Unequal Wealth 41–42 (New York: Russell & Russell 1961) (1826); Thomas Jefferson, Draft Constitution for Virginia, in II Works of Thomas Jefferson 179 (Paul Leicester Ford ed. 1904) (1776); George, supra note 39; Evans, supra note 39; Greeley, supra note 42, at 18–23, 312–15. See generally John R. Commons, *Horace Greeley and the Working Class Origins of the Republican Party*, 24 Pol. Sci. Q. 468 (1909); Conkin, supra note 38, at 222–55; Eisinger, supra note 40, at 18–19; Smith, supra note 41, at 170; Paul W. Gates, The Jeffersonian Dream 100–105 (1996); Irving Mark, *The Homestead Ideal and Conservation of the Public Domain*, 22 Am. J. Econ. & Soc. 263 (1963); Richard White, *Contested Terrain: The Business of Land in the American West*, in Land in the American West: Private Claims and the Common Good 190, 198–99 (William G. Robbins & James C. Foster eds. 2000); Helene Sara Zahler, Eastern Workingmen and National Land Policy, 1829–1862, at 29–35 (1941).

45. See, for example, Sedgwick, supra note 40, at 15, 25; F. Byrdsall, The History of the Loco-Foco or Equal Rights Party (New York: Burt Franklin 1842); Julian, supra note 39, at 336. See also Chester McArthur Destler, *Western Radicalism, 1865–1901: Concepts and Origins,* 31 Miss. Valley Hist. Rev. 335 (1944); Arthur P. Dudden, *Men Against Monopoly: The Prelude to Trust-Busting,* 18 J. Hist. Ideas 587 (1957); Gates, supra note 41, at 454; Edith James, Claims' Law and Miners' Courts of the Montana Gold Camps, 1862–1870, 40 (unpublished M.A. dissertation, U. Chicago, 1949); Robert W. Larson, Populism in the Mountain West 13 (1986); Lawrence Frederick Kohl, The Politics of Individualism 31 (1989); Kazin, supra note 42, at 31–33; James L. Huston, Securing the Fruits of Labor 40–42 (1998). For the origins of anti-monopoly ideology, see Arthur P. Dudden, Antimonopolism, 1865–1890: The Historical Background and Intellectual Origins of the Antitrust Movement in the United States 4–49 (Ph.D. diss. U. Mich. 1950); Charles R. Geisst, Monopolies in America 11–13 (2000); William J. Novak, The People's Welfare 94–101 (1996); Steven L. Piott, The Anti-Monopoly Persuasion 5–6 (1985). The quote is from Thomas McIntyre Cooley, *Limits to State Control of Private Business,* 1 Princeton Rev. 233, 257 (1878).

46. See W. Scott Morgan, History of the Wheel and Alliance 677 (St. Louis: C. B. Woodward 1891); Zahler, supra note 44, at 190–91; Destler, supra note 45, at 361–62; Smith, supra note 41, at 170; Kohl, supra note 45, at 193.

47. See Zahler, supra note 44, at 33–35; Ellis, supra note 43, at 840–41; McMath, supra note 42, at 52–53; Huston, supra note 45, at 208. James Fenimore Cooper gave voice to this attitude in the following exchange between a trapper and a squatter, The Prairie 64 (1827), quoted in The Golden Age of American Law 453 (Charles M. Haar ed. 1965):

> "He who ventures far into the prairie, must abide by the ways of its owners."
>
> "Owners!" echoed the squatter, "I am as rightful an owner of the land I stand on, as any governor of the States! Can you tell me, stranger, where the law or the reason is to be found, which says that one man shall have a section, or a town, or perhaps a county to his use, and another have to beg for earth to make his grave in? This is not nature, and I deny that it is law. That is, your legal law."
>
> "I cannot say that you are wrong," returned the trapper.

48. Andrew Jackson, Veto Message, July 10, 1832, 2 Messages and Papers of the Presidents 576, 590 (James D. Richardson ed. 1968). For anti-charter and anti-corporate-privilege ideology, see Louis Hartz, Economic Policy and Democratic Thought: Pennsylvania, 1776–1860, 69–72 (1948); James Willard Hurst, The Legitimacy of the Business Corporation in the Law of the United States, 1780–1970, 30–39 (1970); Lawrence Frederick Kohl, The Politics of Individualism 27 (1989).

49. See Destler, supra note 45, at 356; Worth Robert Miller, *The Republican Tradition,* in American Populism 209, 210–11 (William F. Holmes ed. 1994).

50. See, for example, Nathaniel Chipman, Sketches of the Principles of Government 172–78 (Rutland, Vt.: J. Lyon 1793). See also William Trimble, *The Social Philosophy of the Loco-Foco Democracy,* 26 Am. J. Sociology 705 (1921); McMath, supra note 42, at 52.

51. See Ellis, supra note 43.

52. See Hartz, supra note 48, at 69, 139–40, 172, 299; Scott, supra note 40, at 122–24; Turpin v. Lockett, 10 Va. 113, 156 (1804) (Tucker, J., dissenting, arguing that property of corporation not private property, could be taken by state). Cf. Young, supra note 41, at 108–09 (land reformers came to argue for government monopoly against private monopolies).

Of course corporations eventually appropriated the mantles of private property and individualism for themselves. See Hartz, id., 173–74; Thurman W. Arnold, The Folklore of Capitalism 185–206 (rev. ed. 1962); Alan Trachtenberg, The Incorporation of America 5 (1982).

53. See Homestead Act of 1862 §§ 1, 2, 5 & 6, 37 Cong. Ch. 75, 12 Stat. 392–93.

54. Preemption Act of 1841 §§10, 11 & 13, 27 Cong. Ch. 16, 5 Stat. 455–56.

55. Sen. Young, Cong. Globe, 26th Cong., 2d Sess. App. 99 (1841); see also Sen. Hubbard, Cong. Globe, 26th Cong., 2d Sess. App. 41 (1841); Julian, supra note 39, at 327; John Ashworth, *The Jacksonian as Leveller,* 14 J. Am. Stud. 407, 416 (1980).

56. See Jacob Ferris, States and Territories of the Great West 270, 319 (New York: Miller, Orton & Mulligan 1856); Jesse Macy, Institutional Beginnings in a Western State 11–12 (Baltimore: Johns Hopkins University, 1884); Constitution and Records of the Claim Association of Johnson County, Iowa 17 (Benjamin F. Shambaugh ed.; Iowa City: St. Hist. Soc. of Iowa 1894). Benj. F. Shambaugh, *Frontier Land Clubs or Claim Associations,* 1900 Ann. Rep. Am. Hist. Assn., Vol. 1, at 69; Everett Dick, *Some Aspects of Private Use of Public Lands,* 9 J. of the West 24 (1970); Tatter, supra note 39, at 273–303.

57. Hill v. Smith, 1 Morris 70 (Iowa 1840).

58. Dubuque Mining Regulations of June 17, 1830, Art. 1, in Macy, supra note 56, at 6. These regulations followed precedents from Galena, Illinois. Id. at 6; Tatter, supra note 39, at 290.

The pedigree of the typical mining district rules actually dated back to Spanish Civil Law and even medieval Germany and England, a fact recognized by early scholars of western mining law, but overlooked by some local boosters, as well as later scholars possibly influenced by the Turner school's emphasis on the local origins of American institutions. Cf. Gregory Yale, Legal Titles to Mining Claims and Water Rights in California 58, 66, 71 (San Francisco: A. Roman & Co. 1867); Henry George, Progress and Poverty 384–86 (1905) (1880); Charles Howard Shinn, Land Laws of Mining Districts 6–8 (Baltimore: N. Murray 1884); Charles Howard Shinn, Mining Camps: A Study in American Frontier Government 8, 20–30 (New York, Alfred A. Knopf 1948) (1885) [hereinafter Shinn, Mining Camps]; Arthur S. Aiton, *The First American Mining Code,* 23 Mich. L. Rev. 105 (1924) (all tracing the origins of mining camp law to early precedents) with Sen. Stewart, Cong. Globe, 39th Cong., 1st Sess. 3226 (1866); John R. Umbeck, A Theory of Property Rights (1981); Richard O. Zerbe Jr. & Leigh Anderson, *Culture and Fairness in the Development of Institutions in the California Gold Fields,* 61 J. Econ. Hist. 114 (2001) (treating miners' laws as spontaneous creations).

59. Cong. Globe, 39th Cong., 1st Sess. 3226 (1866), reprinted in 70 (3 Wall.) U.S. 777 (1867). The remarks of the senator are said by the reporter, John William Wallace, to have

attracted general notice. Sparrow v. Strong, 70 U.S. 97, 100 n.5 (1865). On the influence of the California miners' codes, see Rodman Wilson Paul, Mining Frontiers of the Far West, 1848–1880, at 42, 169 (rev. ed. 2001). For a contrary position to that taken here, claiming that the egalitarian and anti-capitalist norms of the California mines were opposed to standard American views on property, see McDowell, supra note 9, at 7.

60. Jennison v. Kirk, 98 U.S. 453, 457 (1878).

61. John Wesley Powell, Report on the Lands of the Arid Region of the United States 41 (Wallace Stegner ed. 1962) (1878).

62. George, supra note 58, at 384. See also Shinn, Mining Camps, supra note 58, at 223–24.

63. Ansel Watrous, History of Larimer County Colorado 46 (1911); Joseph Lyman Kingsbury, The Development of Colorado Territory 1858–1865, at 121–22 (unpublished Ph.D. dissertation, U. Chicago 1922); Alvin T. Steinel, History of Agriculture in Colorado 39–42 (1926); Marjorie E. Large, Appropriation to Private Use of Land and Water in the St. Vrain Valley Before the Founding of the Chicago-Colorado Colony (unpublished M.A. thesis, U. Colo. 1932); *The Middle Park Claim Club, 1861,* 10 Colo. Mag. 189, 191 (1933); George L. Anderson, *The El Paso Claim Club, 1859–1862,* 13 Colo. Mag. 41 (1936); George L. Anderson, *The Canon City or Arkansas Valley Claim Club, 1860–1862,* 16 Colo. Mag. 201, 203 (1939) [hereinafter Anderson, *Canon City*]. The revisionist view advanced by Allan G. Bogue, *The Iowa Claim Clubs: Symbol and Substance,* 45 Miss. Vall. Hist. Rev. 231 (1958) (arguing that Iowa claim clubs were themselves used to facilitate speculation by settlers) is of limited import here, as the speculation he refers to was of a minor sort, used by settlers to raise money for the eventual purchase of their lands. In any case, the limited evidence available suggests that speculation may not have been a major factor in Colorado claim clubs. See Anderson, *Canon City,* supra, at 207 (transactions recorded for only 30 of 260 recorded claims, with average price of $1.25 per acre).

On the origins of Colorado settlers in the Mississippi Valley, see Howard Roberts Lamar, The Far Southwest, 1846–1912, at 185 (rev. ed. 2000); Paul, supra note 59, at 39.

64. *Chief Justice Hall,* (Denver) Weekly Commonwealth, Aug. 20, 1863, p. 2. See An Act Concerning Actions by Persons Holding Lots, Lands or mining claims, except as against the United States, 1861 Colo. Sess. Laws 249; An Act Declaratory of the Rights of Occupants of the Public Domain except as against the United States, 1861 Colo. Sess. Laws 168.

At least sixteen extant mining codes allowed farm or ranch claims of 160 acres (for example, Gregory Dist. Act 1860 §2, in Laws of Gregory District, supra note 7, at 2) and one limited such claims to 100 acres (Fairfield Mining Dist. Laws, July 2, 1860, §2, in Marshall, supra note 11, at 198).

65. Middle Park Claim Club Laws, May 23, 1861 §6, in *The Middle Park Claim Club,* supra note 63, at 191 (water claim not to exceed 12 feet fall).

66. Two leading histories of Colorado seem to take this tack; Fritz, supra note 21, at 130–47; Carl Ubbelohde, A Colorado History 90–92 (1965). See also Gary D. Libecap,

Contracting for Property Rights 33–36 (1989) (ideology regarding federal lands influenced adoption of miners' rules); Reid, supra note 19, at 43–44 (emphasizing continuity between miners' rules and eastern norms); Robert W. Swenson, *Legal Aspects of Mineral Resources Exploitation,* in Gates 699, supra note 41, at 709 (priority principle of mining laws related to preemption principle).

For the view that the water law originated in the mines, see, for example, John Norton Pomeroy, Treatise on the Law of Water Rights 18–20 (Henry Campbell Black ed.; St. Paul, Minn.: West Pub. Co., 1893). The most famous proponent of the aridity view is Walter Prescott Webb, The Great Plains 442–44 (1931); Walter Prescott Webb, The Great Frontier 254–59 (2nd ed. 1964). For the western law as a natural outgrowth of Hispanic law, see 1 Wells A. Hutchins, Water Rights Laws in the Nineteen Western States 159–62 (1971); Tom I. Romero, II, *Uncertain Waters and Contested Lands: Excavating the Layers of Colorado's Legal Past,* 73 U. Colo. L. Rev. 521, 535–36 (2002).

67. George W. Haight, *Riparian Rights,* 5 Overland Monthly 561, 566 (1885).

68. Appellant's Br. 8, Combs v. Agric. Ditch Co. (No. 2360) (Colo. St. Archives) (1889).

Chapter 3: Early Colorado Water Law and *Coffin v. Left Hand Ditch Co.*

1. Carl Abbott et al., Colorado: A History of the Centennial State 63–66 (3rd ed. 1994).

2. Act Concerning Irrigation §§ 1–3, Dec. 7, 1859, Provisional Laws and Joint Resolutions Passed at the First and Called Sessions of the General Assembly of Jefferson Territory 214 (1860).

3. An Act to Protect and Regulate the Irrigation of Lands, 1861 Colo. Sess. Laws 67 [hereinafter 1861 Irrigation Act], codified at 1877 Colo. Gen. Laws § 1372 et seq.; 1883 Colo. Gen. Stats. § 1714 et seq.

4. 1861 Colo. Sess. Laws at 67.

5. It has also been suggested that the law was intended to encourage development of stream-valley lands before the technically more difficult to irrigate uplands; Gregory A. Hicks & Devon G. Peña, *Community Acequias in Colorado's Rio Culebra Watershed: A Customary Commons in the Domain of Prior Appropriation,* 74 U. Colo. L. Rev. 387, 423 (2003).

6. 1861 Colo. Sess. Laws at 67–69.

7. See 1861 Irrigation Act §§ 5–7, 1861 Colo. Sess. Laws at 68.

8. 1861 Irrigation Act, 1861 Colo. Sess. Laws at 68 (superseded by An Act To regulate the use of Water for Irrigation and providing for settling the Priority of Right thereto, etc. § 18, 1879 Colo. Sess. Laws 99).

9. For the standard as adopted from riparian law, see Dale D. Goble, *Making the West Safe for the Prior Appropriation Doctrine,* in Law in the Western United States 153, 155 (Gordon Morris Bakken ed. 2000). At least one western judge construed the section as requiring equal distribution, Thorp v. Freed, 1 Mont. 651, 668–69 (1872) (Wade, C. J., concurring) (construing § 4 of Montana's irrigation statute of Jan. 11, 1865, copied from Colorado's 1861 Irrigation Act).

Hicks & Peña, supra note 5, at 421–22, argue for Hispanic origins. In the traditional *acequias* of Mexico and some portions of Spain, water was apportioned by giving each irrigator turns at taking water from the main ditch, the frequency of which turns varying with the amount of water available for all; see Thomas F. Glick, Irrigation and Society in Medieval Valencia 207–08 (1970); Arthur Maass & Raymond L. Anderson, . . . and the Desert Shall Rejoice 11–52 (1978).

10. 1861 Irrigation Act § 4, 1861 Colo. Sess. Laws 68.

11. See infra text at notes 69–76.

12. An Act Defining rights and liabilities of miners and millmen in certain cases § 2, 1870 Colo. Sess. Laws 81.

13. See Richard Moss Alston, Commercial Irrigation Enterprise, the Fear of Water Monopoly, and the Genesis of Market Distortion in the Nineteenth Century American West 74–106 (1978).

14. An Act to Enable Road, Ditch, Manufacturing and Other Companies to Become Bodies Corporate § 13, 1862 Colo. Sess. Laws 48 [hereinafter 1862 General Incorporation Act].

15. Appellants' Br. 12, Coffin v. Left Hand Ditch Co. (No. 865) (Colo. St. Archives) (1882). *Coffin v. Left Hand Ditch Co.*, 6 Colo. 443, 450–52 (1882).

For the position (which I now believe to be mistaken) that the 1862 law gave priority to riparian owners, see Goble, supra note 9, at 155; David B. Schorr, *Appropriation as Agrarianism: Distributive Justice in the Creation of Property Rights*, 32 Ecology L. Q. 3, 37–38 (2005).

16. An Act to Amend "An Act to Enable Road, Ditch, Manufacturing and Other Companies to Become Bodies Corporate" § 32, 1864 Colo. Sess. Laws 58; An Act to Provide for the Formation of Corporations § 85, 1877 Colo. Gen. Laws § 275 (passed March 14, 1877).

17. For examples with superior rights to riparians, see, for example, An Act to Incorporate the Blue River and Buffalo Flats Ditch Company § 17, 1861 Colo. Sess. Laws 443 (mining); An Act to Incorporate the South Platte and Fontaine qui Bouille Irrigating and Ditch Company § 12, 1862 Colo. Sess. Laws 134 (irrigation). For the "paying quantities" limitation, see, for example, An Act to Incorporate the Snowy Range Ditch Co. § 9, 1862 Colo. Sess. Laws 145.

18. An Act Concerning Lode Claims § 2, 1861 Colo. Sess. Laws 166; 1868 Rev. Stat. Colo. ch. 62, § 2.

19. For price controls, see, for example, An Act to Incorporate the South Platte and Fontaine qui Bouille Irrigating and Ditch Company § 7, 1862 Colo. Sess. Laws 133 (maximum price of $3/acre for farmers, $1/inch for undershot or turbine mill wheels, and $3/inch for overshot wheels). For investing local government with price control authority, see An Act to Incorporate the Boulder and Weld County Ditch Company § 4, 1866 Colo. Sess. Laws 126; 1862 General Incorporation Act § 14, 1862 Colo. Sess. Laws at 48.

20. See 1862 General Incorporation Act § 14. For chartered corporations, see, for example, An Act to Incorporate the Blue River and Buffalo Flats Ditch Company § 16, 1861 Colo. Sess. Laws at 443.

21. See An Act to exempt Irrigating Ditches from Taxation, 1872 Colo. Sess. Laws 143.

22. An Act To prevent the Waste of Water during the Irrigating Season §§ 1–2, 1876 Colo. Sess. Laws 78 (now at Colo. Rev. Stat. § 37–84–108 (2009)). The law applying only to certain counties was An Act To amend Chapter forty-five (45) of the Revised Statutes of Colorado, 1872 Colo. Sess. Laws 144.

23. Fine not less than $100. Id. § 3, at 78. This sum has not been updated. Colo. Rev. Stat. § 37–84–109 (2009).

24. 1861 Irrigation Act § 1, 1861 Colo. Sess. Laws 67.

25. 4 Ill. 491, 495 (1842), quoted in Chapter 2, under "The Real Demise of Riparian Rights."

26. Contra, for example, Jack Hirshleifer et al., Water Supply 238 (rev. ed. 1969) (criticizing anti-waste rule as pointless when no third-party effects).

27. All sections remain in force today, unamended. Colo. Const. art. 16, §§ 5–8.

28. See Curt Arthur Poulton, A Historical Geographic Approach to the Study of the Institutionalization of the Doctrine of Prior Appropriation: The Emergence of Appropriative Water Rights in Colorado Springs, Colorado 21–26 (unpublished Ph.D. dissertation, U. Minn., 1989).

29. Territorial legislation had left open the question of ownership of water, dealing only with the right to its use. See 1861 Irrigation Act § 1, 1861 Colo. Sess. Laws 67, quoted supra at note 4. Avoidance of the ownership issue seems to have been due to deference to the federal government, which was the owner of most riparian lands in Colorado (and hence, at common law, owner of the water rights as well) and had veto power over territorial legislation. However, with the enactment of a federal law recognizing as valid water rights acquired on federal lands in accordance with local customs and laws, An Act granting the Right of Way to Ditch and Canal Owners over the Public Lands, and for other Purposes § 9, ch. 262, 14 Stat. 251, 253 (1866) [hereinafter Mineral Lands Act], paramount federal title to water on federal lands no longer needed to be recognized. The only American precedent for such a declaration of public ownership was an Arizona territorial statute. See Frank J. Trelease, *Government Ownership and Trusteeship of Water,* 45 Cal. L. Rev. 638, 641 (1957).

30. Colo. Const. art. 16, § 5.

31. 1 Report of the Special Committee of the U.S. Senate on the Irrigation and Reclamation of Arid Lands, Sen. Rep. 928, 51st Cong., 1st Sess. 74 (1890).

32. "All rivers, creeks and streams, running water, in the territory of Colorado, are hereby declared public," § 1 of bill proposed by Farmers' Union, in *Irrigation,* Rocky Mtn. News, Jan. 9, 1874, at 2; "The water in each and every natural stream within this territory is hereby declared to be public property," § 2 of C.B. 28, in *Two Irrigation Bills,* Rocky Mtn. News, Jan. 20, 1874, at 2. See also Elwood Mead, Irrigation Institutions 144 (1903).

33. Alvin Marsh, in Denver Daily Trib., Feb. 19, 1876.

34. Victor Elliott & H. N. Haynes, Appellant's Br. 10–11, Cache La Poudre Reservoir Co. v. Water Supply & Storage Co. (No. 3638) (Colo. St. Archives) (1896) (italics in original). Elliott was a Colorado judge and lawyer, involved in many of the leading water cases of the day. As district judge, he adjudicated the all-important general adjudication for Water District No. 3 (the Cache La Poudre River) (see Decree in the Matter of Priorities of Water Rights in Water District No. 3, Entered by the Hon. Victor Elliott, Judge of the Second Judicial District, April 11th, 1882 (Fort Collins, Colo.: Evening Courier Printing House, 1882) (a page of which is reproduced in Fig. 15, p.120), as well as other water-law suits (see, for example, Union Colony of Colo. v. Elliott, 5 Colo. 371 (1880); Farmers' Highline Canal & Reservoir Co. v. *Southworth*, 21 P. 1028 (Colo. 1889)). As supreme court judge, see, for example, *Southworth*, id.; Platte Water Co. v. N. Colo. Irrigation Co., 21 P. 711 (Colo. 1889); Combs v. Agricultural Ditch Co., 28 P 966 (Colo. 1892). As counsel, in addition to the instant case, see, for example, Bruening v. Dorr, 47 P. 290 (Colo. 1896); Water Supply & Storage Co. v. Larimer & Weld Irrigation Co., 51 P. 496 (Colo. 1897); Broadmoor Dairy & Live-Stock Co. v. Brookside Water & Improvement Co., 52 P. 792 (Colo. 1898).

Haynes was court-appointed referee for the 1882 general adjudication of water rights in Water District No. 3 over which Elliott presided as district judge. Appellee's Br. 15, Cache La Poudre Reservoir Co. v. Water Supply & Storage Co., supra this note.

35. See Embrey v. Owen, 6 Exch. 353, 155 Eng. Rep. 579 (1851); 1 Samuel C. Wiel, Water Rights in the Western States 753–54 (3rd ed. 1911). The state supreme court later ruled that water had been *publici juris* in Colorado even before the adoption of the state constitution. Derry v. Ross, 5 Colo. 295, 301 (1880). For *publici juris* in American law, see Harry N. Scheiber, *The Road to* Munn: *Eminent Domain and the Concept of Public Purpose in the State Courts,* in Law in American History 329–402 (Donald Fleming & Bernard Bailyn eds. 1971).

36. 1 Wiel, supra note 35, at 197; City of Denver v. Bayer, 2 P. 6, 7 (Colo. 1883); Wheeler v. N. Colo. Irrigation Co., 17 P. 487, 489–90 (Colo. 1888); Ft. Morgan Land & Canal Co. v. S. Platte Ditch Co., 30 P. 1032, 1033 (1892); Suffolk Gold Mining & Milling Co. v. San Miguel Consol. Mining & Milling Co., 48 P. 828, 830 (Colo. App. 1897); Stockman v. Leddy, 129 P. 220, 222 (Colo. 1912).

37. *The Grangers,* Rocky Mtn. News, Dec. 18, 1875, at 4. The Grange was part of a larger post–Civil War agrarian movement, often referred to as "the Granger movement," whose goals included strengthening the independence of yeoman farmers and combating the power of the corporations. See generally Solon Justus Buck, The Granger Movement (1913); Carl C. Taylor, The Farmers' Movement, 1620–1920, at 139 (1953).

38. R. T. Ely, Economics of Irrigation, unpublished manuscript, in Henry C. Taylor & Anne Dewees Taylor, The Story of Agricultural Economics in the United States, 1840–1932, at 833 (1952) (1905); see also Samuel C. Wiel, *Public Control of Irrigation,* 10 Colum. L. Rev. 506, 511–15 (1910); Trelease, supra note 29, at 640–41.

39. Trelease, supra note 29, at 646. See also Michael C. Blumm et al., *Renouncing the Public Trust Doctrine: An Assessment of the Validity of Idaho House Bill 794*, 24 Ecology L. Q. 461, 502–03 (1997). See generally Joseph L. Sax, *The Public Trust Doctrine in Natural Resource Law: Effective Judicial Intervention*, 68 Mich. L. Rev. 471 (1970).

40. *Constitutional Convention*, Denver Daily Times, Feb. 18, 1876, at 4; Proceedings of the Constitutional Convention Held in Denver, December 20, 1875, at 44 (1907). By contemporary account, Bromwell was styled the "Orthodox Blackstone of the convention," *Our Constitution Makers, Who and What They Are*, Denver Trib. Supp., Feb. 14, 1876. For his anti-corporate activity in the Illinois convention, see Debates and Proceedings of the Constitutional Convention of the State of Illinois 84, 330–31, 418, 487 (Springfield, Mass.: E. L. Merritt 1870). See also Colin B. Goodykoontz, *Some Controversial Questions Before the Colorado Constitutional Convention of 1876*, 17 Colo. Mag. 1, 11 (1940).

41. *Constitutional Convention*, supra note 40, at 4; Denver Daily Trib., Feb. 19, 1876; *The Grangers*, Rocky Mtn. News, Dec. 17, 1875, at 4. See Platte Water Co. v. N. Colorado Irrigation Co., 21 P. 711 (Colo. 1889), in which a grant to a water company of exclusive rights in a section of a river was held beyond the power of the legislature.

42. Colo. Const. art. 16, § 6.

43. Denver Daily Trib., Feb. 19, 1876.

44. Harvey Huston, The Right of Appropriation and the Colorado System of Laws in Regard to Irrigation 41 (Denver, Chain & Hardy 1893) (italics in original).

45. Colo. Const. art. 16, § 6. See R. H. Hess, *Arid-Land Water Rights in the United States*, 16 Colum. L. Rev. 480, 488–89 (1916).

46. Denver Daily Trib., Feb. 24, 1876.

47. Quoted supra at note 42.

48. See G. G. Anderson, *Some Aspects of Irrigation Development in Colorado*, 1 Transactions of the Denver Society of Civil Engineers & Architects 52, 54–55 (1890). For the former view, see, for example, Eric T. Freyfogle, *Water Rights and the Common Wealth*, 26 Envtl. L. 27 (1996) (advocating using doctrine to ban ecologically harmful uses); Eric T. Freyfogle, The Land We Share 231–33 (2003); Timothy D. Tregarthen, *Water in Colorado: Fear and Loathing of the Marketplace*, in Water Rights: Scarce Resource Allocation, Bureaucracy, and the Environment 119, 123–24 (Terry L. Anderson ed. 1983) (criticizing the doctrine for not letting the market determine which uses are desirable).

49. It also effectively provided a floor for the size of a water right, since a diversion of less than the amount necessary for beneficial use would not ripen into a water right. My thanks to Prof. Carol Rose for this insight. For legislative giveaways, see Platte Water Co. v. N. Colorado Irrigation Co., 21 P. 711 (Colo. 1889).

50. John Norton Pomeroy *Riparian Rights—The West Coast Doctrine* (Part 13), 2 W. Coast Rep. 297, 300 (1884); see also id. (Part 7), 1 W. Coast Rep. 641, 646 (1884); John E. Ethell, *Irrigation—the Continually Growing Importance of the Conservation and the Equitable Distribution and Use of Water in the Arid and Semi-Arid States and Territories*, 74 Cent. L. J. 244 (1912); Richard J. Hinton, *Water Laws, Past and Future*, Irrigation Age, Nov. 1, 1891, at 269; Elwood Mead,

Rise and Future of Irrigation in the United States, 1899 Yearbook of the U.S.D.A. 591, 607 (1900); 1 Wiel supra note 35, at 313; Gordon R Miller, *Shaping California Water Law, 1781 to 1928,* 55 S. Cal. Q 9, 15 (1973).

51. S. W. Carpenter, The Law of Water for Irrigation in Colorado 23-34 (Denver: W. H. Lawrence & Co., 1886).

52. Freyfogle, The Land We Share, supra note 48, at 101-03, discussed in Chapter 1.

53. See, for example, Burnham v. Freeman, 19 P. 761 (Colo. 1888); Greer v. Heiser, 26 P. 770 (Colo. 1891); Combs v. Agric. Ditch Co., 28 P 966, 968 (Colo. 1892); Nichols v. McIntosh, 34 P. 278 (Colo. 1893). The specter of monopolization of water by the first settlers was raised by Montana's chief justice in Thorp v. Freed, 1 Mont. 651, 676-78, 686 (1872) (Wade, C. J. concurring).

54. See 3 Henry Philip Farnham, The Law of Waters and Water Rights 2063, 2076 (1904).

55. Contra, for example, Terry L. Anderson & Pamela Snyder, Water Markets: Priming the Invisible Pump (1997).

56. John E. Field, Irrigation from Big Thompson River 56 (U.S.D.A. Office of Experiment Stations Bulletin No. 188, 1902).

57. 1 Wiel, supra note 35, at 169-70; 1 Report of the Special Comm., supra note 31, at 74.

58. The salience of this one element of water law in historical consciousness may have its roots in two related causes. One is the lawyer's imperative to describe property rights in terms of their jural-opposite duties, a conceptual framework that highlights the legal relationships between and among appropriators rather than the conditions of initial appropriation from the public domain. The other, related, source of the phenomenon is the fact that lawmaking and litigation have naturally focused on the same issue: the relative rights of the appropriators from a given stream. A justified focus for practicing lawyers, however, may become a myopic handicap to understanding the origins of the doctrine.

59. For prior appropriation as a rule of capture, see, for example, Dean Lueck, *The Rule of First Possession and the Design of the Law,* 38 J. L. & Econ. 393, 427-430 (1995).

60. Richard A. Epstein, *Possession as the Root of Title,* 13 Ga. L. Rev. 1221, 1234 (1979); see also Lawrence Berger, *An Analysis of the Doctrine that "First in Time is First in Right,"* 64 Neb. L. Rev. 349, 372 (1985). Similarly, both the riparian and the prior appropriation doctrines may be fairly characterized as giving equal rights to users of water, the former the right to use the water itself, and the latter the right to acquire a right of use. See James Gordley, *The Origin of Riparian Rights,* in Themes in Comparative Law 107 (Peter Birks & Arianna Pretto eds. 2002). A related issue is whether the reasonable-use doctrine as applied by American courts in practice uses priority as the prime criterion for determining the reasonableness of uses. See Restatement (Second) of Torts, § 850A(h) and Comment k.

61. See 1 Wiel, supra note 35, at 255. See also Hammond v. Rose, 19 P. 466 (Colo. 1888) (rejecting similar rule for Colorado).

62. T. K. Dow, A Tour in America 113 (Melbourne: The Australasian, 1884). Freyfogle, The Land We Share, supra note 48, at 101–03.

63. John Wesley Powell, Report on the Lands of the Arid Region of the United States 33 (Wallace Stegner ed. 1962) (1878); John Wesley Powell, *Address at North Dakota Constitutional Convention, Aug. 5, 1889*, 36 N. Dak. Hist. 373, 375 (1969). See also J. W. Powell, *Institutions for Arid Lands*, 40 Century Mag. 111, 112 (1890); Paul W. Gates, History of Public Land Law Development 467 (1968); William Lilley III & Lewis L. Gould, *The Western Irrigation Movement, 1878–1902: A Reappraisal*, in The American West: A Reorientation 57, 61 (Gene M. Gressley ed. 1966); Walter Prescott Webb, The Great Plains 451 (1931); Stowell v. Johnson, 26 P. 290 (Utah 1891).

64. Testimony of Henry H. Metcalf, in Report of the Public Lands Commission 297, H. Ex. Doc. No. 46, 46th Cong. 2d Sess. (1880), cited in Ernest Staples Osgood, Day of the Cattleman 184 (1929). See also John T. Ganoe, *The Desert Land Act in Operation, 1877–1891*, 11 Agric. History 142 (1937); A. A. Hayes, Jr., *The Cattle Ranchers of Colorado*, 59 Harpers Monthly 877, 883, 886 (Issue 354, November 1879); Richard Hogan, Class and Community in Frontier Colorado 175 (1990); Mead, supra note 32, at 35–38; Veeder B. Paine, *Our Public Land Policy*, 71 Harpers New Monthly Mag. 741, 742 (Issue 425, October 1885); Ora Brooks Peake, The Colorado Range Cattle Industry 65 (1937).

65. Elliott West, The Contested Plains 249 (1998).

66. George W. Haight, *Riparian Rights*, 5 Overland Monthly 561, 568–69 (1885) (on riparian law in California); see also M. M. Estee, Address to Cal. St. Agric. Society, Sep. 1874, in Ezra S. Carr, Patrons of Husbandry on the Pacific Coast 319, 324 (San Francisco: A. L. Bancroft 1875); C. E. Grunsky, *Water Appropriations from Kings River*, in Report of Irrigation Investigations in California 259, 273 (U.S.D.A. Office of Experiment Stations Bulletin No. 100, 1901); Elwood Mead, *The Agricultural Situation in California*, in Report of Irrigation Investigations in California, id., at 17, 49; William E. Smythe, *The Irrigation Problems of Honey Lake Basin, Cal.*, in Report of Irrigation Investigations in California, id., at 71, 106–07. In modern times, only resource economist Mason Gaffney seems to have understood this point. See Mason Gaffney, *Economic Aspects of Water Resource Policy*, 28 Am. J. Econ. & Soc. 131, 139 (1969).

67. William E. Smythe, *The Struggle for Water in the West*, 86 Atlantic Monthly 646, 647 (Issue 517, Nov. 1900).

68. State Sen. Steck, quoted in *Anti-Royalty*, Rocky Mtn. News, Mar. 3, 1887, at 6.

69. Philip A. Danielson, *Water Administration in Colorado—Higher-ority or Priority*, 30 Rocky Mtn. L. Rev. 293, 298 (1958).

70. Perkins v. Dow, 1 Root 535 (Conn. Super. 1793); Weston v. Alden, 8 Mass. 136 (1811).

71. Evans v. Merriweather, 4 Ill. 491, 495 (1842), discussed in Chapter 2, "The Real Demise of Riparian Rights." See also, for example, Wadsworth v. Tillotson, 15 Conn. 366 (1843). For the majority view, see Joseph K. Angell, Treatise on the Law of Watercourses 208–10 (Boston: Little, Brown & Co., 7th ed. 1877).

72. Thorp v. Freed, 1 Mont. 651, 654–55 (1872) (rejecting lower court's position in favor of upstream users). Colorado courts were rejecting similar claims as late as 1896. See Strickler v. City of Colorado Springs, 26 P. 313, 315 (Colo. 1891) (diversion from tributary junior to earlier appropriation from main stream), rejecting argument made in Plaintiff in Error's Br. 1–4, Strickler v. City of Colorado Springs (Colo. St. Archives) (1890); McClellan v. Hurdle, 33 P. 280, 282 (Colo. Ct. App. 1893) (appropriation of subterranean water junior to prior right of diverter from surface, otherwise upstream owners' location would trump temporal priority); Bruening v. Dorr, 47 P. 290 (Colo. 1896) (right of owner of land on which stream rises inferior to prior appropriations from stream).

73. 1861 Irrigation Act § 4, 1861 Colo. Sess. Laws 68, quoted supra at note 10.

74. J. C. Ulrich, Irrigation in the Rocky Mountain States 43 (U.S.D.A. Office of Experiment Stations Bulletin No. 73, 1899). See also id., at 44; Elwood Mead, *The Growth of Property Rights in Water*, 6 Int'l. Q. 1, 4 (1902); Frederick Haynes Newell, Irrigation in the United States 333 (New York: Crowell & Co., 1902); Alvin T. Steinel, History of Agriculture in Colorado 198 (1926); Joseph O. Van Hook, *Development of Irrigation in the Arkansas Valley*, 10 Colo. Mag. 3, 7 (1933); Elinor Ostrom, Crafting Institutions for Self-Governing Irrigation Systems 6 (1992); Michael Holleran, Anderson Ditch: A History and Guide 12–13 (2000).

75. An Act Concerning Irrigation § 2, supra note 2, at 214 (emphasis added).

76. David Boyd, A History: Greeley and the Union Colony of Colorado 120 (Greeley, Colo.: Greeley Tribune Press, 1890). See also *The Blossoming Desert*, Rocky Mtn. News, Aug. 17, 1873, at 2; David Boyd, Irrigation near Greeley, Colorado 61 (U.S. Geological Survey Water Supply and Irrigation Paper no. 9, 1897) (conflicts on Boulder and St. Vrain Creeks); *Gleanings*, Rocky Mtn. News, Oct. 23, 1868, at 4 (conflict on Fontaine River); *Irrigation and Herding Laws*, Rocky Mtn. News, Dec. 28, 1871, at 2 (same); E. S. Nettleton, Report of the State Engineer to the Governor of Colorado for the Years 1883 and 1884, at 83–84 (Denver, Times Co. 1885); Van Hook, supra note 74, at 7.

77. Boyd, A History, supra note 76, at 120–21; Boyd, Irrigation near Greeley, supra note 76, at 61; David Boyd, *Appendix*, in Nettleton, supra note 76, at 116.

78. See Platte Water Co. v. N. Colorado Irrigation Co., 21 P. 711 (Colo. 1889) (1860 charter of Capitol Hydraulic Co. by Kansas Territory legislature granting exclusive rights to South Platte water in Denver area ruled ineffectual beyond what had been appropriated by actual use), discussed further in Chapter 4. For another example of this type of legislative grant, see Charter of the Consolidated Ditch Co. from General Assembly of Territory of Jefferson, Nov. 28, 1859, Minutes of the Consolidated Ditch Co. Board of Directors, Consolidated Ditch Co. collection, Archives, Univ. of Colo. at Boulder Libraries.

79. *The Water Question*, Greeley Trib., Feb. 2, 1876, at 2. Cf. Restatement (Second) of Torts, § 850A, Comment j (regarding common-law reasonable use, "the courts will not carry the requirement of sharing to an extreme if the share of each riparian would be reduced to a quantity that is sufficient for none").

80. William H. Grafflin, Rocky Mtn. News, Feb. 2, 1881, at 4.

81. Armstrong v. Larimer County Ditch Co., 27 P. 235, 237 (Colo. Ct. App. 1891). See also Drake v. Earhart, 23 P. 541 (Idaho 1890); Ulrich, supra note 74, at 43; Mead, supra note 32, at 63–65.

82. See Schilling v. Rominger, 4 Colo. 100 (1878) (the first judicial statement of the priority rule in Colorado, upholding the rights of the earlier settler against the threat of dilution by newcomers to the area); Webb, supra note 63, at 439–40. Cf. Robert G. Dunbar, *The Search for a Stable Water Right in Montana*, 28 Agr. Hist. 138, 139 (1954). The point about the riparian system has been made by Theodore E. Lauer, *The Riparian Right as Property*, in Water Resources and the Law 133, 161–163 (1958); Arthur Maass & Raymond L. Anderson, . . . and the Desert Shall Rejoice (1978). In the humid environments of England and the eastern United States, this did not create significant inequalities, since surface water was both widely dispersed and not typically needed for farming.

83. Cf. Berger, supra note 60, at 350 (distinguishing between application of temporal priority between first occupant and society and its application between first occupant and subsequent claimants).

84. This line of reasoning is evident in the opinion of Knowles J. in Thorp v. Freed, 1 Mont. 651 (1872), construing the Montana irrigation statute that had been copied from the Colorado Irrigation Act of 1861, supra note 4: "If it is claimed that this statute does not recognize the doctrine of 'prior in time, prior in right,' the answer to this is, that when the law gives a man the right to divert water from a stream to irrigate his land to the full extent of the soil thereof, and in pursuance of this law he goes and digs a ditch, or constructs machinery for the purpose of taking water from a stream for this purpose at great expense, the principles of equity come in and say that no other man can come in and divert this water away from him. That he is prior in time in availing himself of the benefits of such a statute, and his rights are prior to any subsequent appropriator." Id. at 657.

85. Oppenlander v. Left Hand Ditch Co., 31 P. 854, 856 (Colo. 1892); see also Charles E. Gast, *The Colorado Doctrine of Riparian Rights, and Some Unsettled Questions*, 8 Yale L. J. 71, 71–72 (1898).

86. The quote is from Colo. Const. art. 16, § 6. Though this provision was later interpreted as applying only to "such use as the riparian owner has at common law to take water for himself, his family or his stock, and the like," with large canals for municipalities required to acquire the water of an inferior use by condemnation and compensation (Montrose Canal Co. v. Loutsenhizer Ditch Co., 48 P. 532, 534 (Colo. 1896); D. B. Kinkaid, Kinkaid on Irrigation Law of Colorado 59 (1912); see also An Act in Relation to Municipal Corporations §14(73), 1877 General Laws Colo. 874, 890 [compensation required for condemnation of water rights by municipality]), it is clear that the framers intended to subordinate the rule of priority to the needs of domestic users. Frank J. Trelease, *Preferences to the Use of Water*, 27 Rocky Mtn. L. Rev. 133, 134, 145 (1955). This also seems to have been the practice for some time at least with regard to municipal supplies needed for classic domestic uses, as indicated by the argument of counsel for a water

corporation in *Platte Water Co. v. N. Colo. Irrigation Co.*, 21 P. 711 (Colo. 1889): "whenever there is a scarcity of water for domestic purposes, the use of water from [appellant's] ditch as to irrigation must cease, the same as in any other company's ditch." Appellee's Br. 13, Platte Water Co. v. N. Colo. Irrigation Co. (No. 1360) (Colo. St. Archives) (1885). By 1894, though, the state engineer was advising water officials not to give domestic uses priority over earlier irrigation rights unless under court order, apparently due to unreasonably large claims being made for domestic use, Irrigation Laws and Instructions to Superintendents and Water Commissioner Colorado 11–12 (Denver: Smith-Brooks Printing Co., 1894).

87. *Colorado Legislature*, Colo. Springs Gazette, Jan. 10, 1874, at 6.

88. See, for example, *The Independent Convention*, Colo. Farmer, Aug. 28, 1890, at 6; *Sons of the Soil*, Rocky Mtn. News, Jan. 13, 1881, at 3; Journal of Proceedings of the Fourteenth Annual Session of the Colorado State Grange 17–18 (Golden, Colo.: Golden Globe Print, 1888); Proceedings of the Second Annual Session of the Farmers' State Alliance and Industrial Union of Colorado, Nov. 25–26, 1890, 10–11; Proceedings of Colorado State Grange, Seventeenth Annual Session 48 (Golden, Colo.: Globe Print, 1891). See also Leonard Peter Fox, Origins and Early Development of Populism in Colorado, chap. 4 (unpublished Ph.D. thesis, U. Penn. 1916); Wayne E. Fuller, A History of the Grange in Colorado 104–05, 111 (unpublished M.A. thesis, U. Denver 1949).

89. See, for example, Robert G. Dunbar, *The Adaptability of Water Law to the Aridity of the West*, 24 J. of the West 57, 60 (1985); James N. Corbridge Jr. & Teresa A. Rice, Vranesh's Colorado Water Law 7 (rev. ed. 1999). Sections 5 and 6 are quoted above at notes 30 & 42.

90. Colo. Const. art. 16, § 7.

91. The connection between these two constitutional provisions was noted in an annotation to John Norton Pomeroy, Treatise on the Law of Riparian Rights 160 n.1 (Henry Campbell Black ed.; St. Paul, Minn.: West Pub. Co. 1887). At least one modern legal historian has tentatively recognized the anti-monopoly function of the ditch easement. Harry N. Scheiber, *Property Law, Expropriation, and Resource Allocation by Government: The United States, 1789–1910*, 33 J. Econ. Hist. 232, 247–48 (1973).

92. 25 Hubert Howe Bancroft, The Works of Hubert Howe Bancroft 643 (San Francisco: The History Co. 1890).

93. This ditch easement, originally considered an easement of necessity arising automatically and not requiring compensation (see Yunker v. Nichols, 1 Colo. 551 (1872)), was eventually held to require condemnation and compensation, in keeping with the law of eminent domain, Stewart v. Stevens, 15 P. 786 (Colo. 1887). In any case, it was considered "a most material incumbrance [*sic*] upon all riparian owners, and hinderance [*sic*] to their enjoyment and free use of their own property," John Norton Pomeroy, Treatise on the Law of Water Rights 222 (Henry Campbell Black ed.; St. Paul, Minn.: West Pub. Co. 1893).

94. See Goodykoontz, supra note 40, at 12–13; Buck, supra note 37, at 198. For the Grange's demand, see *The Grangers*, Rocky Mtn. News, Dec. 18, 1875, at 4. The constitutional provision allowing for the revocation of charters was Colo. Const. art. 15, § 3.

95. Colo. Const. art. 16, § 8.

96. Colo. Const. art. 10, § 3. For the statutory exemption, see An Act to exempt Irrigating Ditches from Taxation, 1872 Colo. Sess. Laws 143, discussed supra text accompanying note 21. See also Murray v. Bd. of County Comm'rs, 65 P. 26, 27 (Colo. 1901).

97. 1 Colo. 551.

98. Wilbur F. Stone, *Colorado's Judiciary Department,* in 1 Jerome C. Smiley, Semi-centennial History of the State of Colorado 649, 653 (1913); John D. W. Guice, *Moses Hallett, Chief Justice,* 47 Colo. Mag. 136, 137–38 (1970).

99. 1861 Irrigation Act §§ 2–3, 1861 Colo. Sess. Laws 67, quoted supra at note 6.

100. 1 Colo. at 555. For counsel's argument, see Justice Belford's statement regarding an attack on the constitutionality of the statute, id. at 566.

101. 4 Ill. 491, 495 (1842), quoted supra in Chap. 2, "The Real Demise of Riparian Rights." Though *Evans* was not cited in Colorado case law on water rights, the connection between this case and the appropriation doctrine seems to have been recognized by contemporaries. See Appellee's Br. 3, Schilling v. Rominger (No. 475) (Colo. St. Archives) (1877).

102. *Yunker,* 1 Colo. at 553–55 (citations omitted).

103. Id. at 569 (citing Snyder v. Warford, 11 Mo. 513, 516 (1848) (way of necessity constitutional, citing Jefferson on this point)).

104. Id. at 566–69.

105. Id. at 570.

106. 1 Wiel, supra note 35, at 252–53.

107. Coffin v. Left Hand Ditch Co., 6 Colo. 443 (1882).

108. Statement of Jos. C. Helm, 3 Report of the Special Comm., supra note 31, at 328. For commentators, see, for example, Samuel C. Wiel, *Public Policy in Western Water Decisions,* 1 Cal. L. Rev. 11, 21–22 (1912); Ralph Henry Hess, *The Colorado Water Right,* 16 Colum. L. Rev. 649, 649–52 (1916). See also Stowell v. Johnson, 26 P. 290, 291 (Utah 1891).

109. 4 Colo. 103 (1878).

110. 5 Colo. 589 (1881). See also Mason v. Cotton, 4 F. 792 (C.C.D. Colo. 1880) (applying riparian law to dispute between mills). Note that the opinion in *Mason,* a federal case, was authored by Hallett J., the chief justice of the state supreme court in *Yunker,* 1 Colo. 551 (1872), discussed above.

111. See Carol Rose, *Energy and Efficiency in the Realignment of Common-Law Water Rights,* in Property and Persuasion 163 (1994).

112. See, for example, Bealey v. Shaw, 102 Eng. Rep. 1266 (K.B. 1805); Hatch v. Dwight, 17 Mass. 289 (1821); Rose, supra note 111, at 173–79.

113. Appellant's Br., Crisman v. Heiderer (No. 657) (Colo. St. Archives) (1880).

114. *Crisman,* 5 Colo. at 596. "Sic utero tuo ut alienum non loedas" translates as "so use your own as not to injure another's property."

115. The territorial statute is 1861 Irrigation Act § 3, 1861 Colo. Sess. Laws 67, quoted supra at note 6. For the miners' codes, see supra Chapter 2.

116. *Crisman,* 5 Colo. at 597.

117. Contra, for example, Anderson & Snyder, supra note 55.

118. See supra Chapter 2, under "The Real Demise of Riparian Rights" (miners' codes applying riparian-law rules in cases not covered by code), this chapter supra at note 12 (territorial statute applying riparian-law rules for liability from return flow).

119. 6 Colo. 443 (1882).

120. Id. at 446. "Usufructuary" means the right to enjoy or use something.

121. Tregarthen, supra note 48, at 122.

122. Angell, supra note 71, at 7–8 (italics in original). See also id. at 97 (property in water usufructuary); 3 Blackstone's Commentaries ch. 25 (St. George Tucker ed.; Philadelphia: William Young Birch 1803); 3 James Kent, Commentaries on American Law 355 (New York: O. Halsted 1828) (riparian right incident to ownership of land); John M. Gould, Treatise on the Law of Waters 360 (Chicago, Callaghan & Co. 1883) (riparian right "parcel of the land").

123. 1861 Irrigation Act § 1, 1861 Colo. Sess. Laws 67, quoted supra at note 4. See Abstract R. 3–4, 8–9, Coffin v. Left Hand Ditch Co. (No. 885) (Colo. St. Archives) (1882).

124. Appellants' Br. 17–18, Coffin v. Left Hand Ditch Co. (No. 885) (Colo. St. Archives) (1882); 6 Colo. at 444, 449.

125. Appellants' Br. 9–13. For the statutes, see supra at notes 4, 14.

126. 1 Wiel, supra note 35, at 139–43; see, for example, Irwin v. Philips, 5 Cal. 140 (1855).

127. An Act granting the Right of Way to Ditch and Canal Owners over the Public Lands, and for other Purposes (Mineral Lands Act) § 9, 14 Stat. 251, 253.

128. Vansickle v. Haines, 7 Nev. 249 (1872) (overruled Jones v. Adams, 6 P. 442 (Nev. 1885)); Union Mill & Mining Co. v. Ferris, 24 F. Cas. 594 (C.C.D. Nev. 1872). Cf. Gibson v. Chouteau, 80 U.S. 92 (1872) (possessor of land for over ten years ousted in favor of patentee from federal government).

129. Pomeroy, supra note 93, at 50.

130. 1 Wiel, supra note 35, at 94–96. The California Supreme Court had gone even further in favor of land speculators, holding the rights of owners of riparian land patented in 1872 superior to those of non-riparians who had been diverting water since 1856. See Pope v. Kinman, 54 Cal. 3 (1879). The import of this decision has been missed by modern commentators. See Eric T. Freyfogle, Lux v. Haggin *and the Common Law Burdens of Modern Water Law,* 57 U. Colo. L. Rev. 485, 503 (1986); Mark T. Kanazawa, *Efficiency in Western Water Law: The Development of the California Doctrine, 1850–1911,* 27 J. Legal Stud. 159, 169 (1998).

131. Samuel C. Wiel, *The Water Law of the Public Domain,* 43 Am. L. Rev. 481, 490–93 (1909).

132. Abstract R. 13–15; Appellants' Br. 9, 13, 16–19, 23–24. This argument, based on *Vansickle,* supra note 128, was advanced as well by the appellant in *Hammond v. Rose,* 19 P. 466 (Colo. 1888). Appellant's Br., Hammond v. Rose (No. 1345) (Colo. St. Archive) (1885). The connection between *Coffin* and the Nevada cases was recognized by Wiel, supra note 131, at 490–94.

133. *Coffin*, 6 Colo. at 449–50.

134. 1 Wiel, supra note 35, at 141.

135. Minutes for Oct. 19, 1863, Carnegie Branch Library for Local History, Boulder, Colo. It is unclear that under state law the Board of County Commissioners had authority to attach conditions to the incorporation of the company or the building of the ditch, as the 1862 General Incorporation Act, supra note 14, seems to have given the county commissioners no role in incorporation.

For the issue of the claimed agreement, see Abstract R. 9–11, 22–24; Appellants' Br. 5; *Coffin*, 6 Colo. at 445.

136. The earliest Left Hand Ditch Company records on file at the Colorado State Archives date to 1866, see Colorado Water Company Incorporations 1861–1914, Index J–Z, at http://www.colorado.gov/dpa/doit/archives/digital/water.htm.

137. 1862 General Incorporation Act § 13, 1862 Colo. Sess. Laws 48, quoted supra at note 14. See *Coffin*, 6 Colo. at 450–52.

138. 6 Colo. 530, 532 (1883) (italics in original).

139. In the instant case, the court found that Guiraud's appropriations "were not greater in quantity than was reasonably necessary" for irrigating his own lands, and so concluded that its qualifications of the priority principle were not relevant. *Thomas*, 6 Colo. at 532–33.

Chapter 4: The Regulation of Colorado Water Corporations

1. Wheeler v. N. Colo. Irrigation Co., 17 P. 487, 489 (Colo. 1888) (emphasis in original).

2. J. C. Ulrich, Irrigation in the Rocky Mountain States 22 (U.S.D.A. Office of Experiment Stations Bulletin No. 73, 1899). Such unincorporated associations or partnerships were still referred to as "companies." See Clesson S. Kinney, A Treatise on the Law of Irrigation 2616–33 (2d ed. 1912).

3. Appellee Eaton's Br. 2, Wyatt v. Larimer & Weld Irrigation Co. (Colo. Ct. App.) (in file of Supreme Court case No. 3117) (Colo. St. Archives) (1892).

4. Paul Sibley Barnett, Colorado Business Corporations, 1859–1900, at 145 (unpublished Ph.D. dissertation, U. Illinois 1966) (putting the beginning of the dominance of large corporations somewhere between 1887 and 1890); John E. Field, *Development of Irrigation,* in 1 History of Colorado 491, 492 (Wilbur Fiske Stone ed. 1918); Leonard P. Fox, *State Regulation of the Canal Corporation in Colorado,* 16 Mich. L. Rev. 158, 159 (1917) [hereinafter *State Regulation*]. E. S. Nettleton, Third Biennial Report of the State Engineer of the State of Colorado 216–17 (1887).

5. See, for example, William W. Cook, The Corporation Problem 118 (New York: G. P. Putnam's Sons 1893) ("'The Corporation Problem' in its entirety has become one of the great social questions of the age.").

6. John Franklin Graff, Graybeard's Colorado 41 (Philadelphia: J. B. Lippincott & Co. 1882). Graff, whose book was based on his letters published in the *Philadelphia Press* in 1881–82, added further: "With what corporations have done, and are now doing, and

promise to do, it is a great Commonwealth, destined to become the home of millions of happy, prosperous, and contented people. Whatever may be the ultimate outcome of this corporate power in the State, no one here questions its present value and importance. . . . Its first roads and ditches were the work of companies, and among the most prosperous Colorado corporations now are those formed (some of them with large capital) to irrigate the arable portions of the State."

Id. at 41. See also *The Wright Law,* Irrigation Age, Feb. 1, 1892, at 442 (praising corporate-led development of irrigation facilities).

7. William E. Smythe, *The Struggle for Water in the West,* 86 Atlantic Monthly 646, 648 (1900).

8. *The Unemployed and the Public Lands,* Irrigation Age, June 1894, at 229. See also the testimony of Levi Booth, in 3 Report of the Special Committee of the U.S. Senate on the Irrigation and Reclamation of Arid Lands 345, S. Rep. No. 928, 51st Cong. (1st Sess. 1890); Levi Booth, in Proceedings of Colorado State Grange, Sixteenth Annual Session 14 (Denver, Colo. Farmer Publishing Co. 1890) [hereinafter 16th Proceedings Colorado Grange]; William E. Smythe, *Ways and Means in Arid America,* 51 Century Mag. 742, 752 (1896).

9. Donald E. Worster, *Irrigation and Democracy in California: The Early Promise,* 28 Pac. Historian 30, 30 (1984); see, for example, Elwood Mead, *Letter of Submittal,* in Ulrich, supra note 2, at 5–6; Elwood Mead, *Rise and Future of Irrigation in the United States,* 1899 Yearbook of the U.S.D.A. 591, 597, 609–10 (1899); William E. Smythe, *The Irrigation Idea and Its Coming Congress,* 8 Rev. of Reviews 394, 399–403 (1893); Smythe, *Ways and Means,* supra note 8, at 758; Thomas F. Walsh, The Humanitarian Aspect of National Irrigation (1902); *Obstacles to the Movement,* Irrigation Age, June 1894, at 299. See also Paul S. Taylor, *Reclamation: The Rise and Fall of an American Idea,* 7:4 Am. West 27 (1970); Paul S. Taylor, *Water, Land, and People in the Great Valley—Is It True That What We Learn from History Is That We Learn Nothing from History?,* 5:2 Am. West 24, 68 (1968).

10. W. E. Smythe, *Speech to Opening Session,* in Official Proceedings of the Third National Irrigation Congress 9 (Denver: n.p. 1894).

11. See, for example, J. S. Greene, Acquirement of Water Rights in the Arkansas Valley in Colorado 67 (U.S.D.A. Office of Experiment Stations Bulletin No. 140, 1903); William Hammond Hall, *Irrigation in California,* 1 Nat'l. Geographic Mag. 277, 289 (1889); 1 Richard J Hinton, Irrigation in the United States: Progress Report for 1890, at 16–19, Sen. Exec. Doc. No. 53 (1891); Richard J. Hinton, *The Irrigation Year,* Irrigation Age, Feb. 1, 1892, at 395, 397; William E. Smythe, The Conquest of Arid America 43–45 (rev. ed. 1905); *The Republic of Irrigation,* Irrigation Age, May 1894, at 187; *Advantages and Benefits of Farming by Irrigation,* 23 Manufacturer & Builder 204 (1891); *Irrigation and Farmers' Movements,* Irrigation Age, Feb. 15, 1892, at 482; see also Martin E. Carlson, *William E. Smythe: Irrigation Crusader,* 7 J. of the West 41 (1968); Donald E. Green, Land of the Underground Rain 25 (1973); Richard White, It's Your Misfortune and None of My Own 403 (1991); Worster, supra note 9, at 32.

12. See, for example, William E. Smythe, *The New Plymouth*, Irrigation Age, Mar. 1895, at 76; Smythe, *Ways and Means*, supra note 8, at 752; see also Lawrence B. Lee, *William Ellsworth Smythe and the Irrigation Movement: A Reconsideration*, 41 Pac. Hist. Rev. 289, 309 (1972); James Earl Sherow, Watering the Valley: Development Along the High Plains Arkansas River, 1870–1950, at 11, 18, 21 (1990).

13. *The Irrigating Convention*, Rocky Mtn. News, Dec. 7, 1878, at 2. See also, for example, Edmund G. Ross, *Future of the Arid West*, 161 N. Am. Rev. 438, 445 (1895).

14. Alfred Deakin, Royal Commission on Water Supply First Progress Report: Irrigation in Western America 46 (Melbourne: John Ferres, 1885). Extracts of Deakin's report were reprinted as an appendix to Richard J. Hinton, Irrigation in the United States 219, Sen. Misc. Doc. No. 15, at 197, 219 (1887).

15. Levi Booth, Speech to the Meeting of the Colorado Grange, in *Sons of the Soil*, Rocky Mtn. News, Jan. 13, 1881, at 3. For the Grange, see supra Chapter 3, under "Public Property," in notes.

16. Mead, *Rise and Future of Irrigation in the United States*, supra note 9, at 593 (describing corporate development in California). For discussion of Mead as a leader of the irrigation movement, see Paul K. Conkin, *The Vision of Elwood Mead*, 34 Agr. Hist. 88 (1960); James R. Kluger, Turning on Water with a Shovel (1992).

17. Elwood Mead, The Ownership of Water 3 (Denver: Times Print Works 1887).

18. Smythe, supra note 7, at 649. For Smythe as a leader of the irrigation movement, see Carlson, supra note 11; Stanley Roland Davison, The Leadership of the Reclamation Movement, 1875–1902, at 139–59, 183–204 (unpublished Ph.D. thesis, U. Cal. Berkeley 1952); Green, supra note 11, at 21–22, 25; Lee, supra note 13, at 309–10.

19. See, for example, Rep. Grow, Mar. 30, 1852, Cong. Globe, 32d Cong., 1st Sess. App. 427 (1852). See generally Mary E. Young, *Congress Looks West: Liberal Ideology and Public Land Policy in the Nineteenth Century*, in The Frontier in American Development 74, 90–97 (David M. Ellis ed. 1969). The quote is from id., at 90–91.

20. Col. A. B. Smedley, speech to Iowa Grange, Sept. 17, 1873, in Jonathan Periam, The Groundswell (Cincinnati: E. Hannaford 1874); see also, for example, Journal of Proceedings of the Fourteenth Annual Session of the Colorado State Grange 18 (Golden, Golden Globe Print 1888) [hereinafter 14th Proceedings Colorado Grange] ("serfdom" of Colorado husbandmen); Appellant's Br. 8, Combs v. Agric. Ditch Co. (No. 2360) (Colo. St. Archives) (1889) (legal controls on water corporations barrier "between that struggling agriculturist and those who would take advantage of our climatic conditions to reduce him to serfdom"); Julian Ralph, *Colorado and Its Capital*, 86 Harper's 935, 945 (1893) ("water-barons").

21. Mead, supra note 17, at 6.

22. Field, supra note 4, at 492–95; Leonard Peter Fox, Origins and Early Development of Populism in Colorado, ch. 1, 25 (unpublished Ph.D. thesis, U. Penn. 1916) [hereinafter Populism in Colorado]; Kate Lee Kienast, *Oasis in the "Great American Desert,"* 1998:2 Colo. Heritage 20, 30. This company's activities began in response to the initiative of Jay Gould

and his Union Pacific railroad. See James E. Sherow, *Watering the Plains,* 1988:4 Colo. Heritage 2, 4.

23. See Roger V. Clements, *British-Controlled Enterprise in the West Between 1870 and 1900, and Some Agrarian Reactions,* 27 Agr. Hist. 132, 136 n.30 (1953) (quoting Rocky Mtn. News, Feb. 9, 1891).

24. See, for example, *A People's Voice,* Rocky Mtn. News, Mar. 8, 1887, at 6; Charles Harvey, *The Way of Ditches,* Colo. Farmer, Mar. 29, 1888, at 12; Mead, supra note 17, at 6.

25. Booth, supra note 15.

26. Clements, supra note 23, at 136; see also Douglas W. Nelson, *The Alien Land Law Movement of the Late Nineteenth Century,* 9 J. of the West 46, 47–50 (1970). In response to these sentiments, Colorado enacted a statutory ban on aliens acquiring significant agricultural or range-land holdings. An Act Preventing Non-Resident Aliens from Acquiring Real Estate in Colorado, 1887 Colo. Sess. Laws 24–26. However, the law was appealed after just a few years. Roger V. Clements, *British Investments and American Legislative Restrictions in the Trans-Mississippi West, 1880–1900,* 42 Miss. Valley Hist. Rev. 207, 223 (1955).

27. An additional form was a modified version of the sale of a water right, with title to the canal passing to the irrigators once a certain number of rights had been sold; see infra at notes 109–110.

28. Message of Gov. Waite to the Extra Session of the Ninth General Assembly, 1894 Colo. House J. 36, 42. For examples of contracts, see § VI, Water Contract, The Fort Morgan Land and Canal Company, in Contract Forms of Western Water Companies in The Eighteen Eighties and Eighteen Nineties, The Bancroft Library, U. Cal., Berkeley; contracts quoted at 3 Report of the Special Comm., supra note 8, at 297–303, 330–39; Abstract of Record, Golden Canal Co. v. Bright (No. 1560) (Colo. St. Archives) (1884). For a case with this situation, see *The Rights of Farmers and Ditch Owners,* Rocky Mtn. News, Mar. 24, 1874, at 4. See also Fox, *State Regulation,* supra note 4, at 173.

29. See, for example, *A Ray of Light,* Rocky Mtn. News, Nov. 3, 1881 (one-sided contract allowed Golden Canal Co. to take farmers' money in advance and then fail to supply water). For condemnations of the contracts, see Fox, Populism in Colorado, supra note 22, ch. 3, at 9; Fox, *State Regulation,* supra note 4, at 163; Greene, supra note 11, at 63–65; Elwood Mead, *Irrigation in the United States,* 54 Trans. Am. Soc'y Civ. Eng'rs., pt. C, 83, 94 (1905); F. H. Newell, Report on Agriculture by Irrigation in the Western Part of the United States at the Eleventh Census: 1890, at 94–95 (Washington, D.C.: G.P.O. 1894); R. P. Teele, *The Organization of Irrigation Companies,* 12 J. Pol. Econ. 161, 163 (1904); Ulrich, supra note 2, at 52.

30. C. C. Wright, *Irrigation on Popular Principles,* Irrigation Age, Feb. 1, 1892, at 446, 448 (quoting President Harrison).

31. Fox, Populism in Colorado, supra note 22, ch. 2, at 26. It seems this was done in bad faith, with the investors, too, victims of the promoters initiating the projects. See Teele, supra note 29, at 165. For overselling of rights and unrealistic paper appropriations by companies, usually going unfilled, see Kienast, supra note 22, at 30; Newell, supra note

29, at 91; James Earl Sherow, Discord in the "Valley of Content": Strife over Natural Resources in a Changing Environment on the Arkansas River Valley of the High Plains 91 (unpublished Ph.D. dissertation, U. Colo. Boulder, 1987); Sherow, supra note 22, at 5–7; Sherow, supra note 12, at 13, 24; Byron S. Wheeler, in 3 Report of the Special Comm., supra note 8, at 346.

32. Teele, supra note 29, at 165 (quoting Commander Booth-Tucker of the Salvation Army).

33. Elwood Mead, *Irrigation in Colorado,* Colo. Farmer, Feb. 2, 1888, at 3.

34. *Mr. Goudy and Water,* Rocky Mtn. News, Feb. 9, 1891, at 4.

35. Mead, supra note 16, at 600.

36. Teele, supra note 29, at 161.

37. Mead, supra note 16, at 595–96.

38. John Norton Pomeroy, Treatise on the Law of Water Rights 369 (Henry Campbell Black ed.; St. Paul, Minn.: West Pub. Co., rev. ed. 1893). For the citations to Colorado cases, see id., at 386–98; see also Joseph R. Long, A Treatise on the Law of Irrigation 494–95 (2d ed. 1916). For the origins of irrigation company regulation in Colorado, actually beginning as early as the first territorial legislature in 1861, see Chapter 3, "Territorial Legislation" and "Control of Corporations."

39. Kinney, supra note 2, at 2652; 2 Samuel C. Wiel, Water Rights in the Western States 1150–53 (3d ed. 1911).

40. The quotes are from Barnett, supra note 4, at 51; Fox, supra note 22, chap. 2, at 25. See also, for example, Barnett, supra note 4, at 51–52; Donald J. Pisani, *Promotion and Regulation: Constitutionalism and the American Economy,* 74 J. Am. Hist. 740, 750 (1987); William Lilley III & Lewis L. Gould, *The Western Irrigation Movement, 1878–1902: A Reappraisal,* in The American West: A Reorientation 57, 63 (Gene M. Gressley ed. 1966).

41. Wheeler v. N. Colo. Irrigation Co., 17 P. 487, 489 (Colo. 1888) (emphasis added).

42. Fox, supra note 4, at 171–72, writes that Colorado courts "have shown commendable zeal in dispensing even-handed justice to farmer and capitalist alike," but proceeds to enumerate substantive legal issues decided by the court, all of them in favor of the small farmer.

43. David Boyd, A History: Greeley and the Union Colony of Colorado 102 (Greeley: Greeley Tribune Press 1890).

44. See, for example, Wheeler, supra note 31, at 347; Mead, supra note 16, at 595; *Colorado Clamor,* Colo. Farmer, Mar. 22, 1888, at 4; 14th Proceedings Colorado Grange, supra note 20, at 18; 1 Report of the Special Comm., supra note 8, at 75. See also Fox, supra note 22, ch. 3, at 10; Wayne E. Fuller, A History of the Grange in Colorado 117 (unpublished M.A. thesis, U. Denver 1949); Alvin T. Steinel, History of Agriculture in Colorado 202 (1926).

45. See, for example, An Act to Incorporate the Blue River and Buffalo Flats Ditch Company § 8, 1861 Colo. Sess. Laws 441, 442 (50¢ per "inch" during day, 25¢ at night).

46. An Act to Enable Road, Ditch, Manufacturing and Other Companies to Become Bodies Corporate § 14, 1862 Colo. Sess. Laws 48 [hereinafter 1862 General Incorporation Act]. An 1864 amendment to the Incorporation Act required the rates to be fixed "by the county commissioners, or the tribunal transacting county business," An Act to Amend "An Act to Enable Road, Ditch, Manufacturing and Other Companies to Become Bodies Corporate" § 33, 1864 Colo. Sess. Laws 59, while the post-statehood codification struck the "tribunal" language and left only the commissioners with this power, An Act to Provide for the Formation of Corporations § 87, 1877 Colo. Gen. Laws 143, 172 [hereinafter 1877 General Incorporation Act]. There was most likely no actual distinction between these bodies.

47. See, for example, An Act to Incorporate the Boulder and Weld County Ditch Company § 4, 1866 Colo. Sess. Laws 126.

48. Colo. Const. art. 16, § 8.

49. 1862 General Incorporation Act § 14, 1862 Colo. Sess. Laws 48.

50. See, for example, An Act to Incorporate the Blue River and Buffalo Flats Ditch Company § 16, 1861 Colo. Sess. Laws 443.

51. Deakin, supra note 14, at 46.

52. The Irrigating Convention, supra note 13, at 2.

53. 1877 General Incorporation Act §§ 87 & 106, 1877 Colo. Gen. Laws 172, 179–80.

54. An Act To regulate the use of Water for Irrigation and providing for settling the Priority of Right thereto, etc. §§1–2, 1879 Colo. Sess. Laws 94–96 [hereinafter 1879 Irrigation Act].

55. Id. § 3, at 96–97.

56. Golden Canal Co. v. Bright, 6 P. 142 (Colo. 1884). The case was initiated by Bright, who tendered to the water company the rate set by the county commissioners, refusing to pay the charge demanded by the company and refusing to assent to its rules and regulations. Id., 142; Abstract of Record 20–21, Defendant in Error's Br. 1, 5–6, Golden Canal Co. v. Bright (No. 1560) (Colo. St. Archives) (1884).

57. *Golden Canal Co.*, 6 P. at 144–45.

58. Id. at 144; Colo. Const. art. 16, § 8, discussed in Chapter 3.

59. The water right was typically for the water necessary to irrigate an 80-acre tract, usually defined as not to exceed 1.44 cubic feet per second (c.f.s.), Fox, supra note 29, at 163. See, for example, § I, Water Contract, The Fort Morgan Land and Canal Company, supra note 28; Wright v. Platte Valley Irrigation Co., 61 P. 603 (Colo. 1900).

60. Or, as an eastern journalist put it, "The plan may be justly described as making the farmers pay down at the outset for the privilege of having water afterward by paying for it over again every year. Like cows who come home to be milked at night-fall, the settlers of Colorado must 'give down' each year or go dry." Ralph, supra note 20, at 945.

61. Charles B. Cramer, Irrigation Laws and Instructions to the Superintendents and Water Commissioners Colorado 31 (Denver: Smith-Brooks Printing Co. 1893).

62. See Ray Palmer Teele, Irrigation in the United States 99 (1915); contra Richard Moss Alston, Commercial Irrigation Enterprise, the Fear of Water Monopoly, and the Genesis of Market Distortion in the Nineteenth Century American West 108–09 (1978) (arguing that settlers could wait for the companies to default on interest payments before buying water rights, and thus capture the rents for themselves).

63. See *Ditch Debates*, Rocky Mtn. News, Feb. 22, 1885, at 4; Greene, supra note 11, at 61; Ansel Watrous, History of Larimer County Colorado 69 (1911). For some figures on increased values, see Clements, supra note 23, at 139. For a justification, in wealth-maximization terms, of the capture by infrastructure companies of increased land values due to their development, see the discussion of railroad companies in Richard A. Posner, Economic Analysis of Law 101–02 (1972).

64. See, for example, Colorado as an Agricultural State: The Progress of Irrigation 12 (Denver: Local Comm. of Arrangements for the National Irrigation Cong., 1894): "It is undoubtedly true that the highest interest of farmers is in the ownership of their own canals; but it is also a fact that the great canals, which have required millions of capital to construct, would never have been built if the sale of water rights had not been permitted."

65. See, for example, R. Q. Tenney, *The Water Problem*, Colo. Farmer, Feb. 4, 1891, at 2; Fuller, supra note 44, at 117, quoting Denver Republican Jan. 11, 1883.

66. See 25 Hubert Howe Bancroft, Works 643 (San Francisco: The History Co. 1890); Teele, supra note 62, at 99, 196. The quote is from Smythe, supra note 7, at 649.

67. *Anti-Royalty*, Rocky Mtn. News, Mar. 3, 1887, at 6, quoting Sen. Amos Steck, speech in Colo. Sen. Comm. on Agriculture and Irrigation.

68. Sherow, supra note 12, at 10, quoting C. F. Strong. Strong was a member of the Grange and of the Executive Committee of the Farmers' Protective Association. 14th Proceedings Colorado Grange, supra note 20, at 23.

69. Letter from Executive Comm. Farmers' Protective Ass'n, Rocky Mtn. News, Mar. 3, 1887, at 6.

70. Rocky Mtn. News, Mar. 2, 1887, at 4; see Field, supra note 4 at 492.

71. *Anti-Royalty*, supra note 67, quoting Sen. I. E. Barnum, speech in Colo. Sen. Comm. on Agriculture and Irrigation.

72. Clements, supra note 23, at 138.

73. *A People's Voice*, supra note 24, quoting G. G. Merrick.

74. Clements, supra note 23, at 138.

75. Sherow, supra note 12, at 10, quoting C. F. Strong.

76. Steck, supra note 67.

77. *Royalty v. Right*, Rocky Mtn. News, Feb. 28, 1887, at 2.

78. Rocky Mtn. News, Mar. 2, 1887, at 4.

79. Steck, supra note 67.

80. *A People's Voice*, supra note 24. See also Bancroft, supra note 66, at 643 (water companies "condescendingly sold the water which belonged to the people").

81. *The Wright Law,* supra note 6. For a version of this argument made by a Colorado legislator in the context of the royalty controversy, see Barnum, supra note 71.

82. A People's Voice, supra note 24.

83. An Act to Define, Prohibit, Punish, and Restrain Extortion and Other Abuses in the Management of Ditches, Canals, and Reservoirs, 1887 Colo. Sess. Laws 308. For a prosecution under the act, quashed on a technicality, see Schneider v. People, 71 P. 369 (Colo. 1903).

84. For Wheeler's background, see 14th Proceedings Colorado Grange, supra note 20, at 23; Wheeler, supra note 31, at 346–47. For the "English Company," see supra text accompanying note 22.

85. Argument of Appellant at 4, Wheeler v. N. Colo. Irrigation Co. (No. 1891) (on file with Colo. St. Archives); S. W. Carpenter, The Law of Water for Irrigation in Colorado 103 (Denver: W. H. Lawrence & Co. 1886).

86. Wheeler v. N. Colo. Irrigation Co., 17 P. 487, 493 (Colo. 1888). See 1877 General Incorporation Act § 87, codified as 1883 Colo. Gen. Stats. § 311; supra text accompanying notes 49–53.

87. Id. at 489–90 (citing Colo. Const. art. 16, §§ 5, 6, discussed in Chapter 3).

88. Long, supra note 38, at 495.

89. *Wheeler,* 17 P. at 490. See Colo. Const. art. 16, § 8, discussed in Chapter 3.

90. *The Granger Cases,* 94 U.S. 113 (1887); Vincent v. Chicago & Alton R.R. Co., 49 Ill. 33 (1868) (holding that railroad cannot discriminate in charges for service mandated by statute); Chi. & Nw. Rwy. Co. v. People, 56 Ill. 365 (1870) (finding the railroad a common carrier thus cannot discriminate).

91. Price v. Riverside Land & Irrigating Co., 56 Cal. 431 (1880).

92. 1 Wiel, supra note 39, at 432; *Price,* 56 Cal. at 433.

93. *The Granger Cases,* 94 U.S. at 126 (quoting Matthew Hale, *De Portibus Maris,* in 1 Francis Hargrave, a Collection of Tracts Relative to the Law of England from Manuscripts 78 (1787); *Price,* 56 Cal. at 433.

94. J. S. Greene, *Concerning Rights in the Water of the Natural Streams of Colorado,* 1892 Ann. Am. Soc'y Irrigation Eng'rs 137, 140 (emphasis and ellipses in original). See also 2 Wiel, supra note 39, at 1149–53, 1161–63, 1224, 1235. Though the public-property argument and the public service arguments are usually viewed as distinct, Harry N. Scheiber, *The Road to Munn: Eminent Domain and the Concept of Public Purpose in the State Courts,* in Law in American History 329 (Donald Fleming & Bernard Bailyn eds. 1971) argues convincingly for property-law origins of the "affected with public interest" doctrine.

95. Wheeler v. N. Colo. Irrigation Co., 17 P. 487, 491–92 (Colo. 1888).

96. Id. at 492.

97. *Mr. Goudy and Water,* supra note 34. See also Steinel, supra note 44, at 208.

98. *Western Ignorance,* quoted in Colo. Farmer, Sep. 4, 1890, at 8.

99. Mead, supra note 33.

100. Robert G. Dunbar, *History of Agriculture,* in 2 Colorado and Its People 121, 128 (LeRoy R. Hafen ed. 1948).

101. S. Boulder & Rock Creek Ditch Co. v. Marfell, 25 P. 504, 505 (Colo. 1890).

102. Id. at 505.

103. See J. Warner Mills, Mills' Irrigation Manual 195–96 (1907); Teele, supra note 62, at 196.

104. Appellant's Br., Combs v. Agric. Ditch Co., supra note 20, at 7; Combs v. Agric. Ditch Co., 28 P. 966 (Colo. 1892). For *Wheeler,* see preceding section.

105. Combs v. Agric. Ditch Co., 28 P. at 967.

106. Id. at 968.

107. Id., citing Wheeler v. N. Colo. Irrigation Co., 17 P. 487, 491 (Colo. 1888), quoted supra at note 95.

108. *Combs,* 28 P. at 967, 969; Oppenlander v. Left Hand Ditch Co., 31 P. 854, 855 (Colo. 1892); Long, supra note 38, at 524.

109. For examples of this type of contract, see, for example, Murray v. Bd. of Comm'rs of Montrose County, 65 P. 26 (Colo. 1901); Butterfield v. O'Neill, 72 P. 807 (Colo. Ct. App. 1903).

110. Mills, supra note 103, at 196.

111. Pomeroy, supra note 38, at 392.

112. 1879 Irrigation Act § 4, 1879 Colo. Sess. Laws 97.

113. For fairness, see Donald J. Pisani, To Reclaim a Divided West: Water, Law and Public Policy, 1848–1902, at 58 (1992). For loss-spreading, see Greene, supra note 11, at 61; Willis H. Ellis, *Water Transfer Problems: Law,* in Water Research 233, 236 n.6 (Allen V. Kneese & Stephen C. Smith eds. 1965); Richard A. Epstein, *Common Carriers,* in 1 New Palgrave Dictionary of Economics and the Law 301, 303 (Peter Newman ed. 1998); Mason Gaffney, *Economic Aspects of Water Resource Policy,* 28 Am. J. Econ. & Sociology 131, 132 (1969); A. Dan Tarlock, *Prior Appropriation: Rule, Principle, or Rhetoric?,* 76 N. Dak. L. Rev. 881 (2000).

114. 16th Proceedings Colorado Grange, supra note 8, at 57–59. See also Fox, supra note 29, at 169; *Alliance Demands,* Rocky Mtn. News, Nov. 27, 1890, at 2 (Farmers' Alliance favors law securing priority of water).

115. See, for example, G. G. Anderson, *Some Aspects of Irrigation,* 1 Trans. Denver Soc'y Civ. Engrs & Architects 52, 58 (1890); Mark Fiege, Irrigated Eden 26–27 (1999); John E. Field, Irrigation from Big Thompson River 51 (U.S.D.A. Office of Experiment Stations Bulletin No. 118, 1902); J. S. Greene, Fourth Biennial Report of the State Engineer to the Governor of Colorado, pt. I, 99–100 (1889); Richard J. Hinton, A Report on Irrigation and the Cultivation of the Soil Thereby 141 (Washington, D.C.: G.P.O. 1892); B. S. La Grange, in 3 Report of the Special Comm., supra note 8, at 407; Frederick Haynes Newell, Irrigation in the United States 112, 292–94, 332 (New York: Crowell & Co. 1902); Teele, supra note 62, at 190–91.

116. H.B. 22 § 11, A Bill for An Act Entitled An Act Concerning Irrigation, Colorado State Archives (1879). Though this bill served as the basis of the 1879 Irrigation Act, in this, as in many other substantive matters, the law as passed diverged sharply from the original bill. See Chapter 5, "Water Decrees."

117. Golden Canal Co. v. Bright, 6 P. 142, (Colo. 1884); 1879 Irrigation Act § 3; discussed supra notes 55–57. The prorating rule was attacked in Defendant in Error's Br. 6, Golden Canal Co. v. Bright (No. 1560) (Colo. St. Archives).

118. *Farmers in Session,* Rocky Mtn. News, Jan. 7, 1887, at 6.

119. Id.; *Fancy Farmers,* Rocky Mtn. News, Jan. 14, 1885, at 4; *Love and Logic,* Colo. Farmer, Feb. 2, 1888, at 1; *Colorado Clamor,* supra note 44, at 4; 14th Proceedings Colorado Grange, supra note 20, at 23; 16th Proceedings Colorado Grange, supra note 8, at 7; Fuller, supra note 44, at 42–43. Southworth later had his position in the non-partisan Grange revoked for excessive "politicking" and being too close to the Populist Party, Wayne E. Fuller, *The Grange in Colorado,* 36 Colo. Mag. 254, 260–61 (1959). He was associated with the Populist governor Waite, serving as deputy state engineer in his administration. *The Populists Fighting,* New York Times, July 20, 1896, p. 1; Southworth to R. Q. Tenney, May 5, 1893, R. Q. Tenney Papers, Colorado State University Archives.

120. Appellee's Br. 8, Farmers' Highline Canal & Reservoir Co. v. Southworth (No. 2182) (Colo. St. Archives) (1888).

121. On Elliott, see Chapter 3, under "Public Property," in notes.

122. Appellee's Br. 6, supra note 120. See the discussions of the sufficiency principle in Chapter 2 and in Chapter 3, "Priority."

123. Interestingly enough, Justice Elliott, sitting in judgment on the appeal, joined Justice Hayt in voting to overturn for error (in not accepting the company's demurrer to Southworth's complaint) his own lower-court decision. Farmers' Highline Canal & Reservoir Co. v. Southworth, 21 P. 1028, 1029, 1033 (Colo. 1889).

124. Wheeler v. N. Colo. Irrigation Co., 17 P. 487 (Colo. 1888).

125. *Southworth,* 21 P. at 1028, 1030–32.

126. See Epstein, supra note 113, at 303.

127. See supra at notes 87–94.

128. *Southworth,* 21 P. at 1032.

129. See Coffin v. Left Hand Ditch Co., 6 Colo. 443 (1882), discussed in Chapter 3.

130. *Southworth,* 21 P. at 1034; Appellants' Br. 5, Farmers' Highline Canal & Reservoir Co. v. Southworth (No. 2182) (Colo. St. Archives) (1888). On the rule of "relation back," or "relating back," according to which an appropriation was considered to date from the day on which work on the diversion began, see Sieber v. Frink, 2 P. 901 (Colo. 1884); Taughenbaugh v. Clark, 40 P. 153 (Colo. Ct. App. 1895); 1 Wiel, supra note 39, at 423–27.

131. See Charles E. Gast, *The Colorado Doctrine of Riparian Rights, and Some Unsettled Questions,* 8 Yale L. J. 71, 78–79 (1898).

132. *Southworth,* 21 P. at 1037; see also Wyatt v. Larimer & Weld Irrigation Co., 33 P. 144 (Colo. 1893), discussed infra in text accompanying notes 133–141 (enjoining sale of water rights beyond estimated capacity to furnish water); Blakely v. Ft. Lyon Canal Co., 73 P. 249 (Colo. 1903).

133. 33 P. 144 (Colo. 1893).

134. Sam S. Kepfield, *Great Plains Legal Culture and Irrigation Development: The Minitare (Mutual) Irrigation Ditch Company, 1887–1896*, 19:4 Envtl. Hist. Rev. 49, 51 (1995) describes Eaton as belonging to a class of "empire-builders" equal to Hill, Vanderbilt, and Cooke in the East, adding, "Irrigation for them was a means of financial self-aggrandizement, the perfect embodiment of America's entrepreneurial ethic brought west."

135. *Wyatt*, 33 P. at 144–46 (1893); David Boyd, Irrigation Near Greeley, Colorado 37–38 (Water Supply and Irrigation Papers of the U.S.G.S. No. 9, 1897).

136. *Wyatt*, 33 P. at 147, citing, inter alia, Wheeler v. N. Colo. Irrigation Co., 17 P. 487 (Colo. 1888), discussed supra in text accompanying notes 84–96; Farmers' Highline Canal & Reservoir Co. v. Southworth, 21 P. 1028 (Colo. 1889), discussed supra in text accompanying notes 123–32; Combs v. Agricultural Ditch Co., 28 P. 966 (Colo. 1892), discussed supra in text accompanying notes 105–8. For the Court of Appeals decision, see Wyatt v. Larimer & Weld Irrigation Co., 29 P. 906, 908–13 (Colo. Ct. App. 1892).

137. See Greene, supra note 11, at 64; Herbert M. Wilson, *American Irrigation Engineering*, 13 Ann. Report U.S. Geological Survey, H. Exec. Doc. No. 1, pt. 3, at 101, 149 (1892).

138. Complaint of Wyatt et al. (1891), Abstract of Record, Appellants' Br. 10 (1892), Wyatt v. Larimer & Weld Irrigation Co. (Colo. Ct. App.) (in file of Supreme Court case No. 3117) (Colo. St. Archives); 33 P. at 148.

139. *Wyatt*, 33 P. at 149, citing *Southworth*, 21 P. 1037.

140. See supra at note 132. The reason for the court's (and appellants') adoption of Helm's minority opinion from *Southworth* is uncertain. The majority opinion in that case, which found prorating among rights of different priorities unconstitutional, would have rendered the Wyatt appellants immune to the effects of the proposed Eaton deal, avoiding the factually difficult question of whether the canal's outstanding water rights had exhausted its capacity to furnish water. The reason for the appellant's adoption of Helm's approach (see supra note 138), and not that of the majority in *Southworth*, is probably that the original irrigators were interested in prorating among themselves, and wished only to enjoin dilution of their rights by prorating with new stockholders. It is also possible that the facts of *Wyatt* were thought to be distinguishable, as the appellants had contractually agreed to prorating and had acquiesced in it, whereas in *Southworth* the company was apparently relying on the force of the prorating statute alone. See Larimer & Weld Irrigation Co. v. Wyatt, 48 P. 528, 532 (Colo. 1897); cf. O'Neill v. Ft. Lyon Canal Co., 90 P. 849, 852 (Colo. 1907) (prorating allowed when authorized by contract). The majority rule in *Southworth*, according to which the prorating statute did not apply to consumers with different priority dates supplied by the same canal, was followed in several subsequent cases, including the two just mentioned. See also Farmers' Independent Ditch Co. v. Agricultural Ditch Co., 45 P. 444, 447 (Colo. 1896); Brown v. Farmers' High Line Canal & Reservoir Co., 56 P. 183 (Colo. 1899); Farmers' High Line Canal & Reservoir Co. v. White, 75 P. 415 (Colo. 1903); 1 Wiel, supra note 39, at 328 n.6.

141. Statutory language to similar effect was proposed in the 1890s. J. S. Greene, *Concerning Rights in the Water of the Natural Streams of Colorado*, 1892 Annual Am. Soc'y

Irrigation Eng'rs 137, 144; see also Blakely v. Ft. Lyon Canal Co., 73 P. 249 (Colo. 1903) (invalidating water rights issued after estimated capacity of canal had been reached). Contra Pisani, supra note 113, at 58 ("Later settlers were left to bear water shortages alone because the courts required Colorado ditch companies to serve customers according to the strict priority of individual rights, even though the earliest users often wasted water and claimed far more than they actually used").

142. Barnett, supra note 4, at 9.

143. Id., at 45–46, 106 (twenty-seven corporations created; nine water companies).

144. John Evans, *Governor's Message,* Rocky Mtn. News, July 19, 1862, at 2.

145. 1862 General Incorporation Act, 1862 Colo. Sess. Laws 44, 48; Barnett, supra note 4, at 48.

146. See Charter of the Consolidated Ditch Co. from General Assembly of Territory of Jefferson, Nov. 28, 1859, Minutes of the Consolidated Ditch Co. Board of Directors, Consolidated Ditch Co. collection, Archives, Univ. of Colo. at Boulder Libraries. See also An Act to incorporate the Consolidated Ditch Company, Oct. 11, 1861, printed in Colorado Republican and Rocky Mountain Herald, Oct. 26, 1861, p. 2. On the origins of the company, see Jerome C. Smiley, History of Denver 288 (Denver: Times-Sun Publishing Co., 1901).

147. *Platte Water Co.,* 21 P. 711 (Colo. 1889). An Act granting the Right of Way to Ditch and Canal Owners over the Public Lands, and for other Purposes [hereinafter Mineral Lands Act], 14 Stat. 251.

148. 21 P. at 712–13, citing Mineral Lands Act § 9, 14 Stat. at 253.

149. Yunker v. Nichols, 1 Colo. 551 (1872), discussed in Chapter 3; Coffin v. Left Hand Ditch Co., 6 Colo. 443 (1882), discussed in Chapter 3; Wheeler v. N. Colo. Irrigation Co., 17 P. 487, 489–90 (Colo. 1887), quoted supra text accompanying note 87.

150. *Platte Water Co.,* 21 P. at 713.

151. An Act Relating to Irrigating Ditches and the Manner of Their Construction, 1881 Colo. Sess. Laws 164.

152. San Luis Land, Canal & Improvement Co. v. Kenilworth Canal Co., 32 P. 860, 862 (Colo. Ct. App. 1893).

153. See Ralph, supra note 20.

154. *The Irrigation Industry of Colorado,* Irrigation Age, July 1893, at 58, 59.

155. J. W. Powell, *Institutions for the Arid Lands,* 40 Century Mag., 1890, at 111, 116.

156. Steinel, supra note 44, at 202.

157. See 2 Wiel, supra note 39, at 1238–39.

158. *The Ownership of Water,* Irrigation Age, July 1894, at 3, 5.

159. 6 Twelfth Census of the United States, Crops and Irrigation 814 (1902).

160. Joseph Nimmo, Jr., Uncle Sam's Farm: The Reclamation of the Arid Region of the United States by Means of Irrigation 30 (1890).

161. 2 Wiel, supra note 39, at 1149–50; see id. at 1237 n.8 (in which the earliest authorities cited in support of the public ownership theory are all cases from Colorado: *Wheeler, Southworth, Combs,* and *Wyatt,* discussed earlier in this chapter).

162. Id. at 1224, 1235.

163. Richard J. Hinton, *Water Laws, Past and Future,* Irrigation Age, Nov. 1, 1891, p. 269.

Chapter 5: Beneficial Use and Limits on Transfer

1. Colo. Const. art. 16, § 6.

2. On the inefficiency of the beneficial use rule, see Terry L. Anderson & P. J. Hill, *The Race for Property Rights,* 33 J. L. & Econ. 177 (1990); Dean Lueck, *First Possession,* in 2 New Palgrave Dictionary of Economics and the Law 132, 133–36 (1998); Timothy D. Tregarthen, *Water in Colorado: Fear and Loathing of the Marketplace,* in Water Rights: Scarce Resource Allocation, Bureaucracy, and the Environment 119, 123–24, 132–33 (Terry L. Anderson ed. 1983); Stephen F. Williams, *The Requirement of Beneficial Use as a Cause of Waste in Water Resource Development,* 23 Nat. Resources J. 7 (1983).

For the conservation view, see, for example, Eric T. Freyfogle, *Water Rights and the Common Wealth,* 26 Envtl. L. 27 (1996); Janet C. Neuman, *Beneficial Use, Waste and Forfeiture: The Inefficient Search for Efficiency in Western Water Use,* 28 Envtl. L. 919 (1998); Mark W. Tader, *Reallocating Western Water: Beneficial Use, Property and Politics,* 1986 U. Ill. L. Rev. 277.

On its supposed origin outside of the pure appropriation rule, see, for example, Mohamed T. El-Ashry & Diana C. Gibbons, *The West in Profile,* in Water and Arid Lands of the Western United States 1, 4 (Mohamed T. El-Ashry & Diana C. Gibbons eds. 1988); Sarah F. Bates et al., Searching Out the Headwaters: Change and Rediscovery in Western Water Policy 140 (1993); Terry L. Anderson & Pamela Snyder, Water Markets: Priming the Invisible Pump 34, 79 (1997).

3. Daphna Lewinsohn-Zamir, *More Is Not Always Better Than Less: An Exploration in Property Law,* 92 Minn. L. Rev. 634, 680–95 (2008), has recently made a valiant attempt to supply an efficiency-oriented rationale for the use requirement, arguing that it moves water from low-value to high-value users while avoiding the transaction costs of negotiating transfers. Unfortunately, the rule does not function in quite this way, since the value to the user of even a low-value use is typically higher than the cost of maintaining the use. Compare Richard A. Epstein, *Why Restrain Alienation?,* 85 Colum. L. Rev. 970, 981 (1985), discussing a similar phenomenon with regard to riparian rights.

4. Investigations by Colorado irrigation engineers determined that about one-third to two-thirds of diverted water returned to the stream (Elwood Mead, Irrigation Institutions 341 (New York: Macmillan, 1903); R. L. Parhsall, *The Importance of Return Flow to Colorado Irrigators,* in A Hundred Years of Irrigation in Colorado 57 (1952)), but court rulings seem to have assumed a higher percentage. For example, petitions by the city of Denver to transfer 396.80 c.f.s. of flow resulted in only 77.39 c.f.s. approved, reflecting an estimated consumptive use of 19 percent; see D. A. Seastone & L. M. Hartman, *Alternative Institutions for Water Transfers: The Experience in Colorado and New Mexico,* 39 Land Econ. 31, 35 (1963).

For the difficulty in measuring or estimating return flow, see George A. Gould, *Water Rights Transfers and Third-Party Effects,* 23 Land & Water L. Rev. 1, 20–21 (1988).

5. N.M. Const., art. 16, §3. For a quote, see, for example, Wells A. Hutchins, Policies Governing the Ownership of Return Waters from Irrigation 29 (U.S.D.A. Tech. Bull. No. 439, 1934). "This incantation is an accepted catechism in western water law," Neuman, supra note 2, at 920.

6. See, for example, Southeastern Colo. Water Conservancy Dist. v. Shelton Farms, Inc., 529 P.2d 1321 (Colo. 1974) (salvaged waters subject to prior appropriations). For explanations of how water conservation can actually increase overall depletions, see, for example, Chris Perry, *Efficient Irrigation; Inefficient Communication; Flawed Recommendations,* 56 Irrigation & Drainage 367 (2007); Frank A. Ward & Manuel Pulido-Velazquez, *Water Conservation in Irrigation Can Increase Water Use,* 105 Proceedings of the Nat'l Academy of Sciences 18215 (2008). For criticism of waste in western law, see, for example, Steven J. Shupe, *Waste in Western Water Law: A Blueprint for Change,* 61 Or. L. Rev. 483 (1982); Henry E. Smith, *Governing Water: The Semicommons of Fluid Property Rights,* 51 Ariz. L. Rev. 445, 453 (2007).

7. It places no restrictions on transfers to new owners who use the water for the same use at the same location.

8. See George A. Gould, *Water Law in 1986: Selected Issues,* in Water Resources Law 2, 3–4 (1986); Seastone & Hartman, supra note 4, at 32; Charles W. Howe, *Water Markets in Colorado: Past Performance and Needed Changes,* in Markets for Water: Potential and Performance 65, 67 (K. William Easter et al. eds. 1998); Charles J. Meyers & Richard A. Posner, Market Transfers of Water Rights: Toward an Improved Market in Water Resources 12–14 (1971); Barton H. Thompson, *Institutional Perspectives on Water Policy and Markets,* 81 Cal. L. Rev. 671 (1993).

9. A. Watson McHendrie, *The Evolution of the Doctrine of Priority of Water Rights,* 33 Rep. Colo. Bar Assn. 123, 137 (1930).

10. Willis H. Ellis, *Water Transfer Problems: Law,* in Water Research 233, 243. For transfers as the preferred allocative mechanism, see id. at 234; Jonathan H. Adler, *Warming Up to Water Markets,* 31 Regulation 14 (2008); Terry L. Anderson, *Introduction: The Water Crisis and the New Resource Economics,* in Water Rights: Scarce Resource Allocation, Bureaucracy, and the Environment 1, 4–5 (Terry L. Anderson ed. 1983); Jack Hirshleifer et al., Water Supply 38–39 (rev. ed. 1969); Meyers & Posner, supra note 8, at 3–4; Bonnie Colby Saliba & David B. Bush, Water Markets in Theory and Practice 23 (1987); Seastone & Hartman, supra note 4. For the negative effect of beneficial use on the efficiency of the market, see also Richard Moss Alston, Commercial Irrigation Enterprise, the Fear of Water Monopoly, and the Genesis of Market Distortion in the Nineteenth Century American West 149 (1978); Bonnie G. Colby, *Economic Impacts of Water Law: State Law and Water Market Development in the Southwest,* 28 Nat. Resources J. 721 (1988); Hirshleifer et al., supra, at 233, 240; Mary Leigh Livingston, *Institutional Requisites for Efficient Water Markets,* in Easter et al., supra note 8, at 67.

11. See Jedidiah Brewer et al., *Water Markets in the West: Prices, Trading, and Contractual Forms,* 46 Econ. Inquiry 91, 92 (2008).

12. See Stephen N. Bretsen & Peter J. Hill, *Water Markets as a Tragedy of the Anticommons,* 33 Wm. & Mary Envtl. L. & Pol'y Rev. 723 (2009). Ellis, supra note 10, at 244–45,

demonstrates that in some situations the no-injury rule will prohibit any transfer at all, though he argues that such situations will be relatively rare. See also Gary D. Libecap, *The Problem of Water,* available at www.u.arizona.edu/~libecapg/downloads/TheProblemOfWater.pdf (2005). For the anticommons in general, see Michael Heller, *The Tragedy of the Anticommons: Property in Transition from Marx to Markets,* 111 Harv. L. Rev. 621 (1998).

13. See Meyers & Posner, supra note 8; Timothy D. Tregarthen, *The Market for Property Rights in Water,* in Water Needs for the Future 139, 147–48 (Ved P. Nanda ed. 1977). Such a system has been instituted in the Northern Colorado Water Conservancy District for water from the Colorado-Big Thompson Project, and the results were as predicted by theory: a robust and efficient market for water rights. See Karin E. Kemper & Larry D. Simpson, *The Water Market in the Northern Colorado Water Conservancy District: Institutional Implications,* in Institutional Frameworks in Successful Water Markets: Brazil, Spain, and Colorado, USA 21 (Manuel Mariño & Karin E. Kemper eds. 1999).

14. Note that the argument that quantifying rights to return flows would be prohibitively costly (Ronald N. Johnson et al., *The Definition of a Surface Water Right and Transferability,* 24 J. L. & Econ. 273, 280 (1981); Smith, supra note 6, at 469) is valid only if third parties are granted rights to return flow. Granting the upstream senior appropriator a right to the entire amount he diverted, as advocated by the sources cited in the preceding note, would obviate the need for such measurement.

15. William E. Smythe, *The Struggle for Water in the West,* 86 Atlantic Monthly 646, 651 (1900).

16. H.B. 22 § 39, A Bill for An Act Entitled An Act Concerning Irrigation, Colorado State Archives (1879). See also id. § 13–14 ("it shall not be lawful for the owner of any ditch to take out of such stream more water than is actually needed for domestic purposes and for irrigating the land in cultivation under such ditch and then needing irrigation"); John E. Field, Irrigation from Big Thompson River 71 (U.S.D.A. Office of Experiment Stations Bulletin No. 188, 1902), at 65. For the background of the bill, see infra text at note 50. See below at notes 31–40 for court rulings in this vein.

17. See, for example, N. C. Meeker, in Report of the Public Lands Commission 294, H. Ex. Doc. No. 46, 46th Cong. 2nd Sess. (1880) (mentioning this as possible position); Field, supra note 16, at 26, 65.

18. See, for example, Field, id., at 56; Mead, supra note 4, at 146.

19. See, for example, Elwood Mead, *The Growth of Property Rights in Water,* 6 Intl. Q. 1, 6 (1902). The ranking (in terms of generosity to the appropriator) of these possible interpretations is not, logically speaking, necessarily as presented here; for example, a canal's capacity could theoretically be greater than the amount necessary to water all the lands under ditch. Nonetheless, that would typically not be the case, especially in the larger projects. For example, an 1892 investigation reported that less than 10 percent of the land under some large ditches was cultivated, Richard J. Hinton, A Report on Irrigation and the Cultivation of the Soil Thereby 155–56 (Washington, D.C.: G.P.O., 1892). In most

cases, then, the water needed for all lands under ditch would be the greatest measure, followed by the full capacity of the canal, followed by the amount actually diverted, followed by the amount actually used, with the amount strictly necessary for the actual use typically the smallest possible standard.

20. *Irrigation and Herding Laws*, Rocky Mtn. News, Dec. 28, 1871, p. 2.

21. S. W. Carpenter, The Law of Water for Irrigation in Colorado 27–28 (Denver: W. H. Lawrence & Co., 1886) (emphasis in original).

22. See Mead, supra note 4, at 87; F. H. Newell, Report on Agriculture by Irrigation in the Western Part of the United States at the Eleventh Census: 1890, 103 (Washington, D.C.: G.P.O., 1894).

23. *A People's Voice*, Rocky Mtn. News, Mar. 8, 1887, p. 6.

24. J. Warner Mills, Mills' Irrigation Manual 89–90 (1907).

25. 6 Colo. 530 (1883).

26. Plaintiff in Error's Br., 5–6, Thomas v. Guiraud (No. 861) (Colorado State Archives) (1882).

27. *Thomas*, 6 Colo. at 531–532.

28. *Sieber*, 2 P. 901, 904 (Colo. 1883).

29. In addition to the cases discussed in the following pages, see also Burnham v. Freeman, 19 P. 761 (Colo. 1888); Medano Ditch Co. v. Adams, 68 P. 431, 435 (Colo. 1902); and a decision of the state Court of Appeals, Taughenbaugh v. Clark, 40 P. 153, 156 (Colo. App. 1895).

30. 21 P. 711 (Colo. 1889), discussed in Chapter 4, "Special Charters."

31. 28 P. 966 (Colo. 1892), discussed in Chapter 4, "Stock Ownership as a Condition of Receiving Water."

32. 28 P. at 968.

33. Church v. Stilwell, 54 P. 395, 397 (Colo. App. 1898).

34. 34 P. 278 (Colo. 1893).

35. See, for example, New Mercer Ditch Co. v. Armstrong, 40 P. 989, 992 (Colo. 1895) (appropriator may not "divert more than he needs for the purpose of which the diversion was made"); Colo. Milling & Elevator Co. v. Larimer & Weld Irrigation Co., 56 P. 185, 186 (Colo. 1899) ("The appropriation of water for a specific purpose qualifies such appropriation by limiting the volume to the quantity necessary for that purpose"). The supreme court departed from this rule in Cache La Poudre Reservoir Co. v. Larimer & Weld Reservoir Co., 53 P. 318 (Colo. 1898), holding that applying water to increased acreage was permitted as long as it was not accompanied by an increase in the volume used, but this decision was overruled in Enlarged Southside Irrigation Ditch Co. v. John's Flood Ditch Co., 183 P.2d 552, 555 (Colo. 1947).

36. 1 Samuel C. Wiel, Water Rights in the Western States 506 (3d ed. 1911).

37. B. S. LaGrange, *Irrigation*, in E. S. Nettleton, Report of the State Engineer to the Governor of Colorado for the Years 1883 and 1884, App. 122, at 125 (Denver: The Times Company, 1885).

38. For contemporary discussions of excessive decrees and their causes, see David Boyd, A History: Greeley and the Union Colony of Colorado 125–26 (Greeley, Colo.: Greeley Tribune Press, 1890); L. G. Carpenter, *Irrigation Statistics and Progress in Colorado for 1890*, in 1 Richard J. Hinton, Irrigation in the United States: Progress Report for 1890, at 181, 185, Sen. Exec. Doc. No. 53, 51st Cong., 2nd Sess. (1891); Field, supra note 16, at 73; J. S. Greene, Acquirement of Water Rights in the Arkansas Valley in Colorado 14–15 (U.S.D.A. Office of Experiment Stations Bulletin No. 140, 1903); Clarence T. Johnston, *Discussion on State and National Water Laws*, 76 Trans. Am. Soc. Civ. Engrs. 677, 683 (1913); J. P. Maxwell, Fifth Biennial Report of the State Engineer to the Governor of Colorado, pt. I, 59 (1891); Mead, supra note 19, at 8–10; Elwood Mead, *The Law of Water Rights*, Irrigation Age, June 15, 1891, p. 79, 80; Elwood Mead, *Report*, in E. S. Nettleton, Third Biennial Report of the State Engineer of the State of Colorado 9, 13 (1887); Elwood Mead, Water Rights on the Missouri River and Its Tributaries 31 (U.S.D.A. Office of Experiment Stations, Bulletin No. 58, 1899); Newell, supra note 22, at 94, 103.

39. G. G. Anderson, *Some Aspects of Irrigation*, 1 Trans. Denver Soc'y Civ. Engrs & Architects 52, 54–55 (1890). See, for example, New Mercer Ditch Co. v. Armstrong, 40 P. 989 (Colo. 1895), discussed infra at notes 67–70; Wright v. Platte Valley Irrigation Co., 61 P. 603 (Colo. 1900) (attempt to apply water right of 1.44 c.f.s., originally used on 40 acres, to 120 acres of land). See also Maxwell, supra note 38, at 582.

40. See Charles E. Gast, *The Colorado Doctrine of Riparian Rights, and Some Unsettled Questions*, 8 Yale L. J. 71, 81 (1898). It should be noted that the *Wright* case, 61 P. 603, upholding a company's right to impose a condition limiting use of a customer's water right to the original intended acreage, seemed to imply that no such limitation would apply to an individual appropriator taking water directly from a stream: "[O]ne who diverts the water through his own channel directly from the stream, having made an appropriation of a given volume without any such limitations imposed, is at liberty to divert that volume when such diversion does not interfere with the prior rights of others, and apply it to the use for which it was originally intended, or on an acreage exceeding that for which the diversion was originally made." Id. at 606. But this must be an incorrect understanding of the case, as the statute quoted by the court in support of its restriction to original acreage, An Act To prevent the Waste of Water during the Irrigating Season § 2, 1876 Colo. Sess. Laws 78 (discussed in Chapter 3, "Territorial Legislation"), certainly applies to individual appropriators as well as consumers from a corporate ditch. The language quoted above can probably best be understood as giving a right to the individual appropriator to increase his irrigated acreage only if his extension would not interfere with appropriations made subsequent to his original appropriation but prior to his extension. In other words, the individual appropriator's extension of his decreed right to additional acreage would be considered, in effect, a new appropriation, and so subject to the prior rights of appropriations made in the interim.

41. An Act To regulate the use of Water for Irrigation and providing for settling the Priority of Right thereto, etc., 1879 Colo. Sess. Laws 94 [hereinafter 1879 Irrigation Act];

An Act to Make Further Provision for Settling the Priority of Rights to the Use of Water for Irrigation, 1881 Colo. Sess. Laws 142 [hereinafter 1881 Irrigation Act]. The two statutes are usually grouped together in the literature, as the 1881 law essentially was passed to remedy defects in the earlier law, particularly the lack of personal service on interested parties. See Union Colony of Colo. v. Elliott, 5 Colo. 371 (1880); Robert G. Dunbar, *The Origins of the Colorado System of Water-Right Control*, 27 Colo. Mag. 241, 256, 259 (1950).

42. Frank J. Annis, *The Limitations and Qualifications of Statutory and Equitable Water Right Decrees*, 18 Rep. Colo. Bar Assn. 94, 98 n. 11 (1915); Boyd, supra note 38, at 123; Dunbar, supra note 41. On Bromwell, see Chapter 3, "Public Property."

43. See Chapter 3, "Priority"; *The Farmers' Congress*, Rocky Mtn. News, Dec. 8, 1878, p. 1; *Meeting of the Colorado Agriculturists*, Rocky Mtn. News, Nov. 21, 1873, p. 4; Wayne E. Fuller, A History of the Grange in Colorado 115 (unpublished M.A. thesis, U. Denver 1949); Wayne E. Fuller, *The Grange in Colorado*, 36 Colo. Mag. 254, 259 (1959).

44. Central City Water Co. v. Kimber, 1 Colo. 475 (1872); Gregory J. Hobbs, *Colorado's 1969 Adjudication and Administration Act: Settling In*, 3 U. Denv. Water L. Rev. 1, 5 (1999).

45. See supra sources cited in note 38.

46. Victor A. Elliott, quoted in Mead, supra note 38, at 29.

47. Cf. Letter from Exec. Comm. Farmers' Protective Association, Rocky Mtn. News, Mar. 3, 1887, p. 6 ("it is. .. beyond the power of nine hundred and ninety-nine farmers out of a thousand, to ever enter the courts against [the corporations]. If they should combine and compel obedience still there is no penalty attached and the farmers come out of such a contest impoverished"); Charles Harvey, *The Way of Ditches*, Colo. Farmer, Mar. 29, 1888, p. 12, (difficulty of litigating and enforcing rights against ditch companies); Leonard Peter Fox, Origins and Early Development of Populism in Colorado, chap. 3, pp. 9, 14–15 (unpublished Ph.D. thesis, U. Penn. 1916) (farmers' support in 1890s for increased state involvement in measurement and distribution of water).

48. Richard J. Hinton, *Water Laws, Past and Future*, Irrigation Age, Nov. 1, 1891, at 269.

49. 1879 Irrigation Act §§ 5–35, 1879 Colo. Sess. Laws 97–106; see *Meeting of the Colorado Agriculturists*, Rocky Mtn. News, Nov. 21, 1873, p. 4.

50. H.B. 22 § 39, A Bill for An Act Entitled An Act Concerning Irrigation, Colorado State Archives (1879) (emphasis added). As noted by Robert Dunbar, the text of the bill contradicts the account given some years later by David Boyd, one of its drafters, according to which it called for tying water rights to diversions by ditches, rather than to actual use by irrigators. See Boyd, supra note 38, at 122; Dunbar, supra note 41, at 251–53.

51. 1879 Irrigation Act § 30, 1879 Colo. Sess. Laws 104. Elwood Mead explained the legislature's decision in favor of registering rights by ditches in terms of administrative feasibility, while Dunbar hinted at the influence of Benjamin Eaton, representative of the English Company. Mead, supra note 19, at 6; Dunbar, supra note 41, at 253.

52. For the modern proposal, see supra note 8 and accompanying text.

53. Elwood Mead, The Ownership of Water 6 (Denver: Times Print Works, 1887); see also id., 2–3, 6–7. See Paul K. Conkin, *The Vision of Elwood Mead*, 34 Agr. Hist. 88 (1960);

James R. Kluger, Turning on Water With a Shovel 14–19 (1992); Dunbar, supra note 41, at 253.

54. 17 P. 487 (Colo. 1888).

55. 21 P. 1028 (Colo. 1889), discussed in Chapter 4, "Priority, Prorating, and Overselling."

56. 1879 Irrigation Act § 30, 1879 Colo. Sess. Laws at 104.

57. See, for example, Fox, supra note 47, chap. 2, pp. 5, 25.

58. William Russell Thomas, unpublished manuscript (1904), in Alvin T. Steinel, History of Agriculture in Colorado 221 (1926). The "two controlling cases, decided in 1888 and 1889," were *Wheeler* and *Southworth*.

59. 26 P. 770 (Colo. 1891).

60. *Wheeler*, 17 P. 487 (Colo. 1888); *Southworth*, 21 P. 1028 (Colo. 1889); *Sieber*, 2 P. 901 (Colo. 1883), discussed supra in text accompanying note 28; *Platte Water Co.*, 21 P. 711 (Colo. 1889), discussed supra in text accompanying note 30. See also Chapter 4, "The Law of Water Corporations."

61. 30 P. 1032 (Colo. 1892).

62. 30 P. at 1033.

63. 30 P. at 1033, citing 21 P. 1028 (Colo. 1889), discussed in Chapter 4.

64. 30 P. at 1033.

65. Boyd, supra note 38, at 126.

66. 26 P. 770 (Colo. 1891), discussed supra in text accompanying notes 59–60.

67. 40 P. 989 (Colo. 1895).

68. Irrigation Act 1881 §§ 26, 35, 1881 Colo. Sess. Laws 156, 160. See Nichols v. McIntosh, 34 P. 278, 280–81 (Colo. 1893).

69. 40 P. at 990, 992.

70. 40 P. at 991.

71. The June 1, 1860, priority of Yeager quantified in the 1882 decree as 24.8 c.f.s. (Fig. 15, Priority 1), is indeed listed in a later map of the water district as consisting of a mere 3.50 c.f.s. (see Fig. 14, p.111, at Fort Collins City P.L.), and this list has no record of his 1863 appropriation (Fig. 15, Priority 8), indicating that it was completely erased by the judicial decision in *New Mercer*.

72. See Mead, supra note 38, at 70; J. C. Ulrich, Irrigation in the Rocky Mountain States 46 (U.S.D.A. Office of Experiment Stations Bulletin No. 73, 1899); Gould, supra note 4, at 21–22.

73. See Greene, supra note 38, at 13–15; Michael V. McIntire, *The Disparity Between State Water Rights Records and Actual Water Use Patterns: "I Wonder Where the Water Went?,"* 5 Land & Water L. Rev. 23 (1970); Richard A. Posner, Economic Analysis of the Law 58 (2nd ed. 1977); Seastone & Hartman, supra note 4, at 36. It should be noted that even had records been completely reliable, the prospective buyer or appropriator would still have had to invest in determining the available supply to determine the value of his right, Ray Palmer Teele, Irrigation in the United States 167–72, 178–80 (1915)—but estimating available

supplies would still have been less onerous than quantifying both supply and the consumptive use of upstream appropriators.

74. See Ellis, supra note 10, at 237–38; Seastone & Hartman, supra note 4, at 36.

75. Field, supra note 16, at 71.

76. See, for example, Thomas v. Guiraud, 6 Colo. 530 (Colo. 1883), discussed supra at notes 25–27; Sieber v. Frink, 2 P. 901 (Colo. 1883), discussed supra in text accompanying note 28; New Mercer Ditch Co. v. Armstrong, 40 P. 989 (Colo. 1895), discussed supra at notes 67–70.

77. See Gregory S. Alexander, Commodity & Propriety passim, especially at 34–36 (1997).

78. See Paul K. Conkin, Prophets of Prosperity 245–46 (1980); Nathan Fine, Labor and Farm Parties in the United States, 1828–1928, 21 (1961); Paul W. Gates, *From Individualism to Collectivism in American Land Policy,* in The Jeffersonian Dream 97, 101–02 (1996).

79. See Alexander, supra note 77, at 56, 84, 338; Francis Bowen, Principles of Political Economy 506 (Boston: Little, Brown, & Co. 1863); John Taylor, An Inquiry in to the Principles and Policy of the Government of the United States 131–35 (1814) (1950); Sen. Walker, Cong. Globe, 31st Cong., 1st Sess., 1573 (1850); Mary E. Young, *Congress Looks West: Liberal Ideology and Public Land Policy in the Nineteenth Century,* in The Frontier in American Development 74, 108 (David M. Ellis ed. 1969).

80. For a negative appraisal of this lack of restriction on alienation, see Gates, supra note 78, at 108, 118.

81. John Wesley Powell, Report on the Lands of the Arid Region of the United States 44–45 (Wallace Stegner ed. 1962) (1878); Mead, supra note 19, at 6, 12; Mead, supra note 4, at 365; Elwood Mead, *The Plight of the Arid West,* 51 Century Mag. 634, 634–35 (1896); Levi Booth, in 3 Report of the Special Committee of the U.S. Senate on the Irrigation and Reclamation of Arid Lands 348, Sen. Rep. 928, 51st Cong., 1st Sess. (1890); *Farmers in Session,* Rocky Mtn. News, Jan. 7, 1887, p. 6; *Alliance Demands,* Rocky Mtn. News, Nov. 27, 1890, p. 2; Proceedings of Colorado State Grange, Seventeenth Annual Session 48 (Golden: Globe Print, 1891). See also *Litigation Multiplying,* Irrigation Age, Dec. 1896, p. 161.

82. Defendant in Error's Br. 8–9, Larimer & Weld Reservoir Co. v. Cache La Poudre Irrigating Co. (Ct. App. No. 1028), in file of Cache La Poudre Irrigating Co. v. Larimer & Weld Reservoir Co. (Sup. Ct. No. 3971) (Colorado State Archives) (1895). See also Slosser v. Salt River Valley Canal Co., 65 P. 332 (Ariz. 1901).

83. J. S. Greene, *Concerning Rights in the Water of the Natural Streams of Colorado,* 1892 Annual Am. Soc'y Irrigation Eng'rs 137, 142, using essentially the same language adopted in a resolution by the Colorado Grange, Proceedings of Colorado State Grange, supra note 81, at 48. See also, for example, E. H. Benton, *Irrigation Law,* Irrigation Age, Sep. 1, 1891, p. 161; John E. Field, *Water Laws of Colorado,* in Mead, supra note 38, at 39, 46–47; 1 Report of the Special Committee, supra note 81, at 77. To antebellum reformers, the sale of water was literally inconceivable; see Walker, supra note 79, at 1572 ("man cannot

produce land, nor can he increase its quantity any more than he can produce or increase the quantity of air or water; yet he is permitted to speculate and traffic in land").

84. See Henry C. Taylor, *Economic Problems in Agriculture by Irrigation*, 15 J. Pol. Econ. 209, 226–27 (1907); see infra at notes 90–95.

85. See 2 Wiel, supra note 36, at 1151.

86. Strickler v. Colorado Springs, 26 P. 313, 316 (Colo. 1891).

87. Id., Syllabus of the Court, 26 P. at 314, cited in Combs v. Agric. Ditch Co., 28 P 966, 968 (Colo. 1892).

88. *Combs*, 28 P. at 968.

89. *Strickler*, 26 P. at 316, 317.

90. 40 P. 989 (Colo. 1895), discussed supra at notes 67–70.

91. See Johnston, supra note 38, at 683–84.

92. See Hirshleifer et al., supra note 10, at 239–40 (criticizing this justification for restrictions).

93. Mead, supra note 4, at 174.

94. Field, supra note 83, at 46.

95. 40 P. at 992.

96. Frank J. Annis, *The Limitations and Qualifications of Statutory and Equitable Water Right Decrees*, 18 Rep. Colo. Bar Assn. 94, 103 (1915).

97. An Act in Relation to Irrigation, 1899 Colo. Sess. Laws 235.

98. See Mead, supra note 4, at 174.

99. See Gould, supra note 4, at 23.

100. See C. W. Beach & P. J. Preston, Irrigation in Colorado 24 (U.S.D.A. Office of Experiment Stations Bulletin No. 218, 1910).

101. See 3 Henry Philip Farnham, The Law of Waters and Water Rights 2077 (1904) ("It thus being settled that the entire policy of the law is against anything that may result in a monopoly of the water, the question arises whether or not this policy will preclude any storage in reservoirs."). See also Johnston, supra note 38, at 683–84.

102. An Act To regulate the use of Water for Irrigation and providing for settling the Priority of Right thereto, etc. § 38, 1879 Colo. Sess. Laws 106–07 [hereinafter 1879 Irrigation Act].

103. Combs v. Agricultural Ditch Co., 28 P. 966, 967 (Colo. 1892).

104. Letter from J.S.M., Ft. Collins, Rocky Mtn. News, Feb. 23, 1882, p. 3.

105. *The Water War*, Rocky Mtn. News, Feb. 24, 1882, p. 7. See also *A Meeting of Farmers at Fort Collins*, Rocky Mtn. News, Feb. 17, 1882, p. 3.

106. Abstract of Record, Larimer Cty. Reservoir Co. v. People *ex rel* Luthe (No. 1481) (Colorado State Archives) (1885).

107. Larimer County Reservoir Co. v. People *ex rel* Luthe, 9 P. 794, 796 (Colo. 1885).

108. Johnston, supra note 38, at 681–82.

109. 51 P. 505, 507 (Colo. 1897). For the practice of subordinating storage rights to later rights for direct use, see R. A. Southworth (Deputy State Engineer) to R. Q. Tenney

(Water Commissioner, District No. 3), March 7, 1894, R. Q. Tenney Papers, Colorado State University Archives.

110. An Act in Relation to Irrigation § 4, 1901 Colo. Sess. Laws 193, 194. For later developments in the law of storage, see Annis, supra note 42, at 109–11; A. Watson McHendrie, *The Evolution of the Doctrine of Priority of Water Rights*, 33 Rep. Colo. Bar Assn. 123, 137–40 (1930).

111. See, for example, Tregarthen, supra note 13, at 145.

112. For recent judicial recognition of the anti-speculation function of beneficial use, see High Plains A & M LLC v. Southeastern Colo. Water Conservancy Dist., 120 P.3d 710 (Colo. 2005); Pagosa Area Water & Sanitation Dist. v. Trout Unlimited, 170 P.3d 307 (Colo. 2007).

113. Appellant's Br. 10–11, Cache La Poudre Reservoir Co. v. Water Supply & Storage Co. (No. 3638) (Colorado State Archives) (1896). The brief was written by Victor Elliott and H. N. Haynes; for their careers, see Chapter 3, under "Public Property," in notes.

114. Field, supra note 16, at 59–60. "Duty" here refers to the ratio of land irrigated to water consumed. See also R. P. Teele, *The Organization of Irrigation Companies*, 12 J. Pol. Econ. 161, 171–72 (1904).

115. Mead, supra note 4, at 174, quoted supra at note 93. For the place of efficiency in the conservation movement, see the classic Samuel P. Hays, Conservation and the Gospel of Efficiency: The Progressive Conservation Movement, 1890–1920 (1959).

116. Smith, supra note 6, at 469. In contrast, Lee Anne Fennell, *Adjusting Alienability*, 122 Harv. L. Rev. 1403, 1429–34 (2009), has noted the utility of restrictions on alienability for combating overuse of a resource. For instream uses, see, for example, David M. Gillilan & Thomas C. Brown, Instream Flow Protection: Seeking a Balance in Western Water Use (1997). For a positive role for the anticommons in general, see Abraham Bell & Gideon Parchomovsky, *Of Property and Antiproperty*, 120 Mich. L. Rev. 1 (2003); Heller, supra note 12, at 674–75.

117. Alexander, supra note 77; Paul W. Gates, The Jeffersonian Dream 97 ff. (1996).

118. Compare Garret Hardin, *The Tragedy of the Commons*, 162 Science 1243 (1968); Carol Rose, *The Comedy of the Commons: Custom, Commerce, and Inherently Public Property*, 53 U. Chi. L. Rev. 711 (1986).

119. Susan Rose-Ackerman, *Inalienability and the Theory of Property Rights*, 85 Colum. L. Rev. 931, 960 (1985); Epstein, supra note 3, at 988–89.

Chapter 6: Conclusion

1. See, for example, James N. Corbridge, Jr., *Historical Water Use and the Protection of Vested Rights: A Challenge for Colorado Water Law*, 69 U. Colo. L. Rev. 503, 505 (1998); Joseph W. Dellapenna, *Adapting Riparian Rights to the Twenty-First Century*, 106 W. Va. L. Rev. 539, 566 (2004); Chennat Gopalakrishnan, *The Doctrine of Prior Appropriation and Its Impact on Water Development: A Critical Survey*, 32 Am. J. Econ. & Soc. 61, 63 (1973); A. Dan Tarlock, *Prior Appropriation: Rule, Principle, or Rhetoric?*, 76 N. Dak. L. Rev. 881, 881 (2000); Michael D.

White, *Legal Restraints and Responses to the Allocation and Distribution of Water*, in Water Needs for the Future 117 (Ved P. Nanda ed. 1977).

2. As a historical account. Whether the narrow view of appropriation law accurately represents modern law, on the books or in action, is a separate issue, beyond the scope of this study.

3. See, for example, Hanoch Dagan, *Takings and Distributive Justice*, 85 Va. L. Rev. 741 (1999). More generally, the imperative of improving the lot of the least well-off is associated with John Rawls, A Theory of Justice (1971).

4. Gregory S. Alexander et al., *A Statement of Progressive Property*, 94 Cornell L. Rev. 743, 744 (2009).

5. Joseph William Singer, Entitlement: The Paradoxes of Property 167–71 (2000).

6. See Louis Kaplow & Steven Shavell, *Why the Legal System Is Less Efficient Than the Income Tax in Redistributing Income*, 23 J. Legal Stud. 667 (1994).

7. Richard A. Posner, Economic Analysis of the Law 249–52 (6th ed. 2003); Paul H. Rubin, *Common Law and Statute Law*, 11 J. Leg. Stud. 205 (1982).

8. See Gordon Tullock, The Economics of Special Privilege and Rent Seeking 23 (1989). But see Richard O. Zerbe Jr. & Leigh Anderson, *Culture and Fairness in the Development of Institutions in the California Gold Fields*, 61 J. Econ. Hist. 114, 115 n. 7 (2001) (need to take into account language of fairness by contemporaries).

9. Mason Gaffney, *Economic Aspects of Water Resource Policy*, 28 Am. J. Econ. & Sociology 131, 139–40 (1969); Richard A. Posner, Economic Analysis of the Law 34 (2nd ed. 1977); Stephen F. Williams, *The Requirement of Beneficial Use as a Cause of Waste in Water Resource Development*, 23 Natural Resources J. 7, 8–11 (1983). Cf. Terry L. Anderson & Peter J. Hill, *The Race for Property Rights*, 33 J. L. & Econ. 177 (1990).

10. Jack Hirshleifer et al., Water Supply 240 (rev. ed. 1969); Posner, supra note 9, at 34; Timothy D. Tregarthen, *Water in Colorado: Fear and Loathing of the Marketplace*, in Water Rights: Scarce Resource Allocation, Bureaucracy, and the Environment 119, 132–33 (Terry L. Anderson ed. 1983); Williams, supra note 9, at 13.

11. For justification of the rules, see, for example, Alfred G. Cuzán, *Appropriators Versus Expropriators: The Political Economy of Water in the West*, in Water Rights, supra note 10, at 13, 16–18. For criticism of this argument, see Willis H. Ellis, *Water Transfer Problems: Law*, in Water Research 233, 241 (Allen V. Kneese & Stephen C. Smith eds. 1965); Hirshleifer et al., supra note 10, at 237.

12. See Chapter 5, "Water Decrees"; Elwood Mead, Water Rights on the Missouri River and Its Tributaries 70 (U.S.D.A. Office of Experiment Stations, Bulletin No. 58, 1899); J. C. Ulrich, Irrigation in the Rocky Mountain States 46 (U.S.D.A. Office of Experiment Stations Bulletin No. 73, 1899).

13. See Mark T. Kanazawa, *Efficiency in Western Water Law: The Development of the California Doctrine, 1850–1911*, 27 J. Leg. Stud. 159, 173 (1998).

14. See Church v. Stilwell, 54 P. 395, 397 (Colo. App. 1898), discussed supra in Chapter 5.

15. See Kanazawa, supra note 13, at 173.

16. The unequal ability of the small farmer and the large corporation to legally enforce their rights would have led to further inefficiencies in turn, with water rights held by small farmers being enforced at a less-than-optimal level. My thanks to Ariel Porat for this point.

17. Terry L. Anderson & Pamela Snyder, Water Markets: Priming the Invisible Pump 80 (1997).

18. An Act To regulate the use of Water for Irrigation and providing for settling the Priority of Right thereto, etc., 1879 Colo. Sess. Laws 94. See supra Chapter 5, especially "Water Decrees."

19. See Ellis, supra note 11, at 239.

20. See, for example, Louis Kaplow & Steven Shavell, Fairness Versus Welfare 28–31 (2002).

21. Including Kaplow & Shavell, id., passim.

22. Zerbe & Anderson, supra note 8, at 128–31. On fairness and efficiency, see also Elizabeth Hoffman & Matthew L. Spitzer, *Entitlements, Rights, and Fairness: An Experimental Examination of Subjects' Concepts of Distributive Justice*, 14 J. Leg. Stud. 259 (1985). On focal points and conventions, see Robert Sugden, *Spontaneous Order*, 3:4 J. Econ. Perspectives 85 (1989).

23. See R. H. Coase, *The Problem of Social Cost*, 3 J. L. & Econ. 1 (1960).

24. See Steven N. S. Cheung, *The Transaction Costs Paradigm*, 36 Econ. Inquiry 514 (1998).

25. See especially Gary D. Libecap, Contracting for Property Rights (1989).

26. Stuart Banner, *Transitions Between Property Regimes*, 31 J. Leg. Stud. S359 (2002), citing Saul Levmore, *Two Stories about the Evolution of Property Rights*, 31 J. Leg. Stud. S421 (2002).

27. Mancur Olson, The Logic of Collective Action 28–29, 35 (1965). See also Banner, supra note 26, at S369; Gary S. Becker, *Public Policies, Pressure Groups, and Dead Weight Costs*, 28 J. Pub. Econ. 329, 342 (1985); Libecap, supra note 25, at 32.

28. Olson, supra note 27, at 49–51. It should be noted that the agrarian forces may have overcome their collective-action disadvantage at least somewhat by organizing through groups that provided services to members other than lobbying, see id., 132–35, for instance the social, educational and professional activities organized by the Grange. However, it is unlikely that this factor would have been sufficient to overcome the vastly greater costs of organization faced by the farmers compared with those of the highly concentrated canal industry, in which, as we have seen, two companies could own most of the large canals in the state, supra Chapter 4, "Background."

29. Cf. Libecap, supra note 25, at 6, 32.

30. Id., at 30–31, 33.

31. Henry E. Smith, *Governing Water: The Semicommons of Fluid Property Rights*, 51 Ariz. L. Rev. 445, 446–47 (2007).

32. Cf. Libecap, supra note 25, at 17, n.5, and at 24, 27 (noting that entrepreneurial politicians may bear costs of organization in expectation of political returns), and at 34

(arguing that "widespread distribution of federal land ... offered important political benefits to members of Congress who could use land policy to fashion supportive constituents among groups of voters").

33. Cf. Gerald Berk, Alternative Tracks 17–18 (1994) (battle over railroad regulation better understood as one over world view than economic interest narrowly conceived).

34. See, for example, Libecap, supra note 25, at 4, n.2 ("Successful institutional change is defined as changes in governance structures that promote economic growth").

35. See, for example, Robert B. Elekund, Jr. & Robert D. Tollison, *The Interest-Group Theory of Government*, in The Elgar Companion to Public Choice 357, 371 (William F. Shughart II & Laura Razzolini eds. 2001) ("a public choice analysis ... would be seriously challenged if critics could show that the policies enacted by political representatives consistently increased the general welfare at the expense of narrow special interests"); Tullock, supra note 8, at vii (rent seeking defined as "the use of resources in actually lowering total product although benefiting some minority").

36. See, for example, Elekund & Tollison, supra note 35, at 370–72.

37. Douglass Cecil North, Institutions, Institutional Change, and Economic Performance 136–37 (1990). See also id., 23, 111; Thomas W. Merrill, *Introduction: The Demsetz Thesis and the Evolution of Property Rights*, 31 J. Leg. Stud. S331, S337 (2002); Sugden, supra note 22; Zerbe & Anderson, supra note 8.

38. Douglass C. North, Structure and Change in Economic History 56 (1981).

39. Id. See also Avinash Dixit & John Londregan, *Ideology, Tactics, and Efficiency in Redistributive Politics*, 113 Q. J. Econ. 497 (1998).

40. See Libecap, supra note 25, at 17, 116 (importance of prevailing distributional norms and precedents for institutional change). Cf. id., 33, 34 (influence of distributional norms on nineteenth-century land and mineral policy); id., 66–68 (distributional norms prevented change in favor of ranching and timber interests). For the influence of ideology on legislators, see also William R. Dougan & Michael C. Munger, *The Rationality of Ideology*, 32 J. L. & Econ. 119 (1989); Joseph P. Kalt & Mark A. Zupan, *Capture and Ideology in the Economic Theory of Politics*, 74 Am. Econ. Rev. 279 (1984). See also Hanoch Dagan, *Just Compensation, Incentives, and Social Meanings*, 99 Mich. L. Rev. 134, 141–43 (2000).

41. Joshua Getzler, A History of Water Rights at Common Law 3, 7 (2004). See also Joshua Getzler, *Theories of Property and Economic Development*, 26 J. Interdisciplinary Hist. 639, 669 (1996) (arguing for internalist understanding of legal evolution in general).

42. Getzler, History, supra note 41, at 6–7, 328, 342 and passim. But see id., 328–29 (admitting that philosophical ideas about property did play some role, though filtered through the vocabulary of the law).

43. See, for example, Maude Barlow, Blue Covenant: The Global Water Crisis and the Coming Battle for the Right to Water (2007); William Finnegan, *Leasing the Rain*, New Yorker, Apr. 8, 2002, at 43; Jennifer Naegele, *What Is Wrong with Full-Fledged Water Privatization?*, 6 J. L. & Soc. Challenges 99 (2004); Public Citizen, Waves of Regret (2005), http://www.citizen.org/documents/Waves.pdf; Erik Swyngedouw, *Dispossessing H_2O: The*

Contested Terrain of Water Privatization, 16 Capitalism Nature Socialism 81 (2005). For support of the privatization trend, see, for example, Fredrik Segerfeldt, Water for Sale: How Business and the Market Can Resolve the World's Water Crisis (2005).

44. Peter H. Gleick et al., The New Economy of Water 22 (2002).

45. See, for example, Erik B. Bluemel, *The Implications of Formulating a Human Right to Water*, 31 Ecology L. Q. 957 (2004).

46. For arguments of this type, see Public Citizen, Water Privatization Fiascos (2003), http://www.citizen.org/documents/privatizationfiascos.pdf.

47. Though the way forward for judicial recognition of public rights was facilitated in Colorado by relatively clear constitutional provisions, similar doctrines might be developed even in their absence. Cf., for example, Ill. Cent. R.R. Co. v. Illinois, 146 U.S. 387 (1892) (explaining the development of the public-trust doctrine in the common law); Joseph L. Sax, *The Public Trust Doctrine in Natural Resource Law: Effective Judicial Intervention*, 68 Mich. L. Rev. 471 (1970). It should also be kept in mind that the pro-consumer decisions of the Colorado courts were based on a self-consciously expansive view of what was mandated by the state constitution. See, for example, Wheeler v. N. Colo. Irrigation Co., 17 P. 487, 492 (Colo. 1888) (referring to the "beneficent purpose" of the constitutional provisions).

48. See Isabelle Fauconnier, *The Privatization of Residential Water Supply and Sanitation Services: Social Equity Issues in the California and International Contexts*, 13 Berkeley Planning J. 37, 48–49, 57 (1999); Gleick et al., supra note 44, at 30–31; Naegele, supra note 43, at 113, 115, 125, 127; Tim Reiterman, *Small Towns Tell a Cautionary Tale About the Control of Private Water*, Los Angeles Times, May 29, 2006.

49. See Finnegan, supra note 43 (foreign-controlled water company in Cochabamba, Bolivia, was given control of all area water, including cooperative wells previously dug by locals).

50. Cf. id. (reacting to perceived abuses by foreign water corporation, law passed recognizing traditional uses and customs).

51. See supra at notes 26–35.

52. Two recent works which do devote some attention to these issues are Zerbe & Anderson, supra note 8, and Andrea G. McDowell, *From Commons to Claims: Property Rights in the California Gold Rush*, 14 Yale J. L. & Human. 1 (2002).

53. Harold Demsetz, *Toward a Theory of Property Rights*, 57 Am. Econ. Rev. (papers & proc.) 347 (1967) (analyzing property rights in fur-bearing animals among aboriginal North American peoples).

54. See Robert Nozick, Anarchy, State and Utopia 149–231 (1974), especially at 177 (assuming little contemporary opportunity for initial acquisition of property).

55. John Locke, The Second Treatise of Government § 49, at 29 (Thomas P. Peardon ed. 1952) (1690).

56. See Haripriya Rangan & Mary Gilmartin, *Gender, Traditional Authority, and the Politics of Rural Reform in South Africa*, 33 Development & Change 633 (2002); Philip Woodhouse,

Water Rights in South Africa: Insights from Legislative Reform 8 (Brooks World Poverty Institute Working Paper 36, April 2008).

57. See, for example, Adam Rose & Brandt Stevens, *A Dynamic Analysis of Fairness in Global Warming Policy: Kyoto, Buenos Aires and Beyond,* 1 J. Applied Econ. 329 (1998); Benito Mueller, *Varieties of Distributive Justice in Climate Change,* 48 Climatic Change 273 (2001); Alice Kaswan, *Reconciling Justice and Efficiency: Integrating Environmental Justice into Domestic Cap-and-Trade Programs for Controlling Greenhouse Gases,* in The Ethics of Global Climate Change 232 (Denis G. Arnold ed. 2011).

58. See Art. 3, Kyoto Protocol to the United Nations Framework Convention on Climate Change, Dec. 10, 1997, UN Doc. FCCC/CP/1997/7/Add.2.

59. See the proposal of the Global Commons Institute, *Contraction and Convergence,* (www.gci.org.uk/contconv/cc.html).

60. It is also possible that the "underutilization" created by the anticommons might actually be efficient, if the benefits of reduced emissions outweighed the foregone production.

61. See, for example, Lawrence Lessig, *Re-crafting a Public Domain,* 18 Yale J. L. & Human. 56 (2006).

62. For ways in which this might be true in regard to copyright law, see Molly Shaffer Van Houweling, *Distributive Values in Copyright,* 83 Texas L. Rev. 1535, 1539–46 (2005).

63. See Anupam Chander & Madhavi Sunder, *The Romance of the Public Domain,* 92 Cal. L. Rev. 1331 (2004).

64. Carol M. Rose, *Romans, Roads, and Romantic Creators: Traditions of Public Property in the Information Age,* 66 Law & Contemp. Probs. 89, 107 (Winter/Spring 2003).

65. Cf. Patricia J. Williams, Alchemy of Race and Rights (1991) (arguing that legal rights are crucial for advancing minorities' causes).

66. See Thomas Streeter, Selling the Air 84–100 (1996).

67. Moves in favor of broader access have been made at various points since, but have been mostly marginal; see Streeter, id., at 193–95.

68. See, for example, Elia Werczberger, *Privatization of Public Housing: A Solution for What?,* 57 Social Security 82, 86 (2000) (Hebrew).

69. See, for example, explanatory note to Israel Public Housing Bill, 5758–1998, Hatzaot Hok 306 (Hebrew).

70. Contra, for example, Joseph W. Dellapenna, *The Importance of Getting Names Right: The Myth of Markets for Water,* 2000 Wm. & Mary Envtl. L. & Pol'y Rev. 317, 336–42; Posner, supra note 7, at 35.

71. Platt Rodgers, in 1 Report of the Special Comm. of the U.S. Senate on the Irrigation and Reclamation of Arid Lands, Sen. Rep. 928, 51st Cong., 1st Sess. 76–77 (1890). See also Frederick Haynes Newell, Irrigation in the United States 288 (New York: Crowell & Co., 1902); supra Chapter 4, "Private, Public, and Corporate Property."

72. Charles E. Gast, *The Colorado Doctrine of Riparian Rights, and Some Unsettled Questions,* 8 Yale L. J. 71, 71 (1898); see also id., 72. See also John Norton Pomeroy, *Riparian Rights—The*

West Coast Doctrine (part 16), 2 W. Coast Rep. 593, 594 (1884); S. W. Carpenter, The Law of Water for Irrigation in Colorado 8 (Denver: W. H. Lawrence 1886); Harvey Huston, The Right of Appropriation and the Colorado System of Laws in Regard to Irrigation 34 (Denver: Chain & Hardy 1893); 3 Henry Philip Farnham, The Law of Waters and Water Rights 2076 (1904) ("The doctrine was originated for the purpose of avoiding the narrow and exclusive use which it was thought would result from the adoption of the doctrine of riparian rights"); Samuel C. Wiel, *Public Policy in Western Water Decisions*, 1 Cal. L. Rev. 11, 21–22 (1912).

73. See, for example, Tom I. Romero, II, *Uncertain Waters and Contested Lands: Excavating the Layers of Colorado's Legal Past*, 73 U. Colo. L. Rev. 521, 538 (2002); Mark W. Tader, *Note: Reallocating Western Water: Beneficial Use, Property, and Politics*, 1986 U. Ill. L. Rev. 277, 284 (Coffin "recognized property rights in water that surpassed any interest protected at common law").

74. See, for example, Carpenter, supra note 72, at 11; George W. Haight, *Riparian Rights*, 5 Overland Monthly 561, 569 (1885); Ralph H. Hess, *An Illustration of Legal Development: The Passing of the Doctrine of Riparian Rights*, 2 Am. Pol. Sci. Rev. 15, 25 (1907); John Norton Pomeroy, Treatise on the Law of Water Rights 221–22 (St. Paul, Minn.: West Pub. Co., Henry Campbell Black ed. 1893); 1 Samuel C. Wiel, Water Rights in the Western States 202–05, 212–13, 227 (3rd ed. 1911). It seems, however, that the element of priority may have come to the fore by the early twentieth century; see C. W. Beach & P. J. Preston, Irrigation in Colorado 35 (U.S.D.A. Office of Experiment Stations Bull. No. 218, 1910) (describing Colorado water law with focus on priority).

75. 1 Clesson S. Kinney, A Treatise on the Law of Irrigation § 588, at 1011–12 (2nd ed. 1912). See also Pomeroy, supra note 74, at 31.

76. Joseph R. Long, Treatise on the Law of Irrigation 143 (2nd ed. 1916); see, for example, Clark v. Cambridge & Arapahoe Irrigation & Improvement Co., 64 N.W. 239 (Neb. 1895). See also Thorp v. Freed, 1 Mont. 651, 687 (1872) (Wade, C. J., concurring) (arguing that acceptance of the prior appropriation doctrine would impair the vested rights of railroads in their land grants).

77. See, for example, Robert C. Ellickson, *Property in Land*, 102 Yale L. J. 1315 (1993); Carol Rose, *The Comedy of the Commons: Custom, Commerce, and Inherently Public Property*, 53 U. Chi. L. Rev. 711 (1986).

78. For riparian law as a common-property regime, see Carol Rose, *Energy and Efficiency in the Realignment of Common-Law Water Rights*, in Property and Persuasion 163 (1994).

79. Cf. Margaret Jane Radin, *Property and Personhood*, 34 Stan. L. Rev. 957 (1982) (suggesting greater protection for property related to "personhood" than for other, "fungible," types).

INDEX

radical Lockeanism, 25–31; in Colorado
Constitution, 39–40; and corporations,
88, 97, 100; and property, 49, 80, 97,
135–36, 141, 143–45, 152, 161. *See also*
Locke, John
Ralph, Julian, 100, 197*n*60
Raz, Joseph, 16
reasonable use rule: in Colorado law, 36,
58–59; in riparian rights doctrine, 1–2,
22, 45, 48, 58, 185*n*60, 187*n*79
recordation of rights, 20, 106–7, 122, 126,
144–45
redistribution, 4, 149, 157, 175*n*38
regulation. *See* mining district laws; price
of water: controls on; regulation,
environmental; water corporations:
regulation of; water rights
regulation, environmental, 157–58
relation back, rule of, 93, 201*n*130
rentals of water. *See* water rentals
rents, economic, 38, 77, 79, 87, 88, 136,
150, 155
repose, 125–26
reservoirs, 43, 74, 98, 110, 111, 120, 132–34
res judicata, 126
res nullius, 22, 41. *See also* public domain
return flows, 17, 36, 106–12, 129–31, 136,
171*n*14, 204*n*4; rights to, 107–12, 121,
129–31, 136. 144
rights of way. *See* easements
riparian rights, 15, 37–38, 61; as common
property, 5–6, 142; criticism of, 46–48,
160–62, 169*n*27; doctrine of, 1–2, 51–52,
57–59, 89, 149, 173*n*20, 204*n*3; in mining
districts, 17, 22–24; as private property,
40–41, 60; rejection of, in Colorado law,
33–38, 40–44, 48, 52, 53–54, 99, 160–62
(see also *Coffin v. Left Hand Ditch Co.*);
rejection of, in mining districts, 23–24;
rejection of, in western U.S., 2–3, 5–6,
142. *See also* reasonable use rule: in

riparian rights doctrine
Rocky Mountain News, 73, 75, 79–81, 114
Rocky Mountains, 5, 132, 153, 155
Rose, Carol, 4, 138, 173*n*24, 184*n*49
rotation, 35, 171*n*14
royalties, 87, 89, 91, 122; controversy over,
73, 78–87

*San Luis Land, Canal & Improvement Co. v.
Kenilworth Canal Co.*, 203*n*152
S. Boulder & Rock Creek Ditch Co. v. Marfell,
200*n*101
Schilling v. Rominger, 57, 188*n*82, 190*n*101
Schneider v. People, 199*n*83
serfdom, rhetoric of, 30, 70–71, 79, 101,
194*n*20. *See also* aristocracy, fear of;
feudalism, fear of
settlers, 51, 61–62, 150, 175*n*39; and water
corporations, 38, 66–68, 72, 78–79, 100,
115, 133 (*see also* cooperative ditches);
conflicts between, 43–44, 49, 92;
protection of actual, 25–30, 99, 127–28
shortages, 114; liability for, 71, 93. *See also*
prorating
sic utero tuo ut alienum non loedas, 58
Sieber v. Frink, 116–17, 123, 201*n*130, 211*n*76
Sierra Nevada Mountains, 7, 28
Singer, Joseph, 141
slavery, rhetoric of. *See* serfdom, rhetoric of
Slosser v. Salt River Valley Canal Co., 211*n*82
Smith, Henry, 137, 150
Smythe, William, 47–48, 68–69, 70, 79. 113,
194*n*18. See also *Irrigation Age*
Snyder v. Warford, 190*n*103
socialism, 27, 57
South Platte River, 58, 60, 97–98, 133
*Southeastern Colo. Water Conservancy Dist. v.
Shelton Farms, Inc.*, 205*n*6
Southworth, R. A., 91–92, 201*n*119
Spanish law. *See* Hispanic law
Sparrow v. Strong, 179*n*59

water right (sold by irrigation companies),
71–72, 86, 90, 197*n*59, 198*n*64, 202*n*140;
conditioned on stock ownership, 87–89,
117; tied to land ownership, 38, 76–77.
See also contracts, water; price of water;
prorating; royalties
water rights
—broad distribution of, 63, 75, 80, 97, 140,
142, 146–53, 188*n*82; and corporate
regulation, 38, 73, 84, 87, 89; and
easements, 53, 56–57; in mining district
laws, 15; through private property, 154,
162; and transfers, 127, 132, 138; and
beneficial use requirement, 44, 113, 115,
135, 145
—in eastern states and England (*see*
riparian rights: doctrine of)
—size of, 114, 121–26, 144, 145, 148, 206
n19 (*see also* beneficial use rule: as limit
on water right)
—sold up to canal capacity, 72, 89, 93, 95
—for stored water (*see* storage rights)
—transfers of (*see* transfers of water
rights)
—tying to land, 121–22, 127–29 (*see also*
alienability; transfers of water rights)
—in western jurisdictions (*see*
appropriation doctrine)
*Water Supply & Storage Co. v. Larimer & Weld
Irrigation Co.,* 183*n*34
Water Supply & Storage Co. v. Tenney, 134
Webb, Walter Prescott, 167*n*23,
180*n*66
welfare, social, 3, 4, 6, 105, 142, 146,
149, 159

Wells, Ebenezer, 56–57
West Publishing Company, 73
Weston v. Alden, 186*n*70
Wheeler, Byron, 82, 85, 91
Wheeler v. N. Colo. Irrigation Co., 82–86, 87,
122, 183*n*36, 210*n*58, 217*n*47; quotes
from, 65, 74, 83, 84–85; relied on, 88,
92, 99, 123, 202*n*136, 203*n*161
wide distribution. *See* property: broad
distribution of; water rights: broad
distribution of
Wiel, Samuel, 57, 102
work, 23, 27
work requirements, 14, 19–22, 28–30, 77.
See also beneficial use rule; radical
Lockeanism
Wright v. Platte Valley Irrigation Co., 197*n*59,
208*n*39, 208*n*40
Wyatt v. Larimer & Weld Irrigation Co., 93–96,
192*n*3, 201*n*132, 203*n*161
Wyoming, 102, 122

xenophobia, 71. *See also* Act Preventing
Non-Resident Aliens from
Acquiring Real Estate in Colorado;
Anglophobia

Yeager, Joshua, 125–26, 129–30
yeoman ideal, 26, 69, 73, 127. *See also*
Jacksonian ideology; Jeffersonian
ideology
Yunker v. Nichols, 55–57, 99, 189*n*93, 190*n*110,
203*n*149

Zerbe, Richard 147–48, 217*n*52